WITHDRAWN
No longer the property of the
Boston Public Library.
Sale of this material benefits the Library

BOSTON
PUBLIC
LIBRARY

MARVELL, NABOKOV

MARVELL, NABOKOV

*Childhood
and Arcadia*

MICHAEL LONG

CLARENDON PRESS · OXFORD
1984

Oxford University Press, Walton Street, Oxford OX2 6DP

London Glasgow New York Toronto
Delhi Bombay Calcutta Madras Karachi
Kuala Lumpur Singapore Hong Kong Tokyo
Nairobi Dar es Salaam Cape Town
Melbourne Auckland

and associated companies in
Beirut Berlin Ibadan Mexico City Nicosia

Oxford is a trade mark of Oxford University Press

Published in the United States
by Oxford University Press, New York

© Michael Long 1984

All rights reserved. No part of this publication may be reproduced,
stored in a retrieval system, or transmitted, in any form or by any means,
electronic, mechanical, photocopying, recording, or otherwise, without
the prior permission of Oxford University Press

British Library Cataloguing in Publication Data
Long, Michael
Marvell, Nabokov: childhood and arcadia.
1. Marvell, Andrew, 1621-1678—Criticism
and interpretations   2. Nabokov, Vladimir
—Criticism and interpretations
I. Title
821'.4 PR354
ISBN 0-19-812815-0

Library of Congress Cataloguing in Publication Data
Long, Michael.
Marvell, Nabokov : childhood and Arcadia.
Bibliography: p.
Includes index.
1. Marvell, Andrew, 1621-1678—Criticism and inter-
pretation. 2. Nabokov, Vladimir Vladimirovich,
1899-1977—Criticism and interpretation. 3. Literature,
Comparative. I. Title. II. Title: Childhood and
Arcadia.
PR3546.L58 1984 821'.4 83-13505
ISBN 0-19-812815-0

Typeset by DMB (Typesetting), Oxford
and printed in Great Britain
at the University Press, Oxford

To my son,
GIDEON,
and to the memory of
FERNAND LAGARDE

PREFACE

The two authors whose works are discussed in this book are not the most obvious candidates for sustained comparative study. Nabokov, it is true, admired Marvell. He studied him while working on his edition of Pushkin's *Eugene Onegin* and made several references to him in his commentary on that work. Subsequently he gave him a place in his fictional writing. In *Pale Fire* Marvell is translated into French by Sybil Shade and into Zemblan by Charles Kinbote; in *Ada* he is translated into French again and evoked as a background presence in the book's imagery of an Arcadian, childhood garden. A determined reader may additionally come to feel that he has been translated still further in *Look at the Harlequins!*, emerging as 'the middle-aged bachelor Al Garden' who, in a Formosan version of what began life as *Lolita*, carries off a 'nymph' to the distress of her 'inconsolable parents'.

Such reference is intriguing; but Nabokov is so copious with reference to the work of earlier writers that it would take a very partisan mind to see here an avowal of influence or even a declaration of particular kinship. This book is not concerned with influence nor with any kinship with Marvell which the later writer has overtly declared.

None the less it cannot be denied that this book does set out to run the two writers steadily together. In some ways indeed it entangles the one with the other even more than is usual in comparative studies of two authors. The alternating chapters on each writer, taking themes, tones, and images from one and juxtaposing them with similar things in the other, make my association of the two writers very close. Even where no comparative thesis is pressed very hard, the alternating structure of the chapters will see to it that neither can escape the other's presence for very long.

But my aim has not quite been to compare. The intention is not to bind them up together in some fixed relation. I have juxtaposed them, even superimposed one upon the other; but only so that one may help us to see the other, not so that the pair of them should be packaged up in a thesis. No two authors, in fact, could better teach a critic the vanity of all efforts to bind and contain imaginative life within the strictures of exegesis and comparative theory. The open, complex, and playful wit of seventeenth-century poetry shares with the structural and tonal openness of Modernist narrative a resistance to systematic meaning. They resist interpretive assaults with equal dexterity. They have what Joyce called 'tenacity of heterodox resistance'. They have the Joycean lesson to teach that intelligence and sensitivity reside all with the open and never with the closed. In Marvell's great prose-work *The Rehearsal Transpros'd* it is the tyrannous Samuel Parker who seeks to herd complexity and variety into the narrow enclosures of religious conformity. In Nabokov's world it is Philistinism, in politics, business, education, and intellectual life, which seeks to reduce people of independent mind and imagination to the simple imperatives of systematic meaning. I trust I have learned enough from these two writers not to have written a book which might seem to come from the worlds of Marvell's Parker or Nabokov's Paduk.

So I have tried to leave my comparisons loose and provisional, with plenty of free play in the articulations of them, setting one writer beside another not in order to assimilate them to some denominator which might have the convenience of being low and common but with something of that unforced, unforeclosing air which, in seventeenth-century wit as in Modernist narration, leaves a reader free to do his or her own thinking, taking the offered conjunctions of things as an invitation to imaginative liberty, not as pressure to conform.

These are writers who invite a reader's freedom: that at least they have in common. They present, they offer, they invite, they allow. They are self-effacing, and when necessary self-rebuking, when it comes to giving commentaries or verdicts upon the images and fictions which they have made. Neither can long remain what Marvell called an *'easie Philosopher'*. Neither has written works which an easy philosopher may, in a comparative study, decode and interpret. There is an air of provisionality, experiment, and non-definitiveness about all that they do. They introduce gaps, silences, and deliberate fractures into their writings, shrinking from the steady linear march of argument, preferring the higher expressive modes of fiction and imagery to the lower modes of explanation and exegesis. Not only do they themselves behave thus. So do the great literatures within which they stand. Marvell is a late, rather private, idiosyncratic inheritor of a literary tradition to which Shakespeare, Donne, and Jonson had been the major contributors. Nabokov is a late, private, idiosyncratic inheritor of a tradition to which Flaubert and Joyce were the most influential contributors. It may not after all be so surprising to find the seventeenth-century and the Modernist author having things in common, since they stand in a similar relationship to traditions which themselves have points of contact.

Marvell was a signal part of Modernism's rediscovery of the seventeenth century. He was virtually an unreadable poet from his own time down to the early years of our century. Then, with Modernism, came his rediscovery; and where Modernism led everyone has followed. The nearly unreadable poet, in changed conditions of reading and writing, became, with extraordinary swiftness and ease, a normal part of every reader's literary world. The Modernism which formed Nabokov made us all read in a new way. It increased in readers a kind of aural patience. It increased our tolerance of doubt, ambiguity, and discontinuity in the written text. It increased our regard for the unbounded life of image and fiction as compared with the more bounded validity of judgemental or exegetical statement. It liberated the discourses of fiction and image from the discourse of ideas. And as soon as it did so Modernism gave Marvell, as a perfectly readable poet, to the readers of Nabokov's time.

So there are good background reasons for being less than completely surprised by the association of a seventeenth-century and a Modernist author. But what I see joining these two writers is in the end more individual than that. What makes each of them help me to read the other is something particular to them, beyond what is shared by their traditions as a whole. It is a matter of shared temperament and shared vision, shared tones and shared images. They have a personal world in common, a personal mythology shaping their minds in similar ways.

They both communicate a sense of the importance of memory and nostalgia. They are both full of feelings of exile and deracination, of severance from a once-perfect world which I have come to call Arcadia. They associate that Arcadian world with childhood and, more widely, with naïve, unsophisticated innocence. They figure it with images of sun, flowers, and unharmed animal life. Above all they figure it with images of water and greenery. It is a world at once free and secure, full of play, without labour. It is the source of all riches of the imagination and of mental composure. But it is also vulnerable, doomed to destruction; and older, wearied men who are torn from it hunger for it in memory and try to keep their exiled, adult imaginations in touch with its delights. Such keeping in touch with Arcadian origins is a kind of keeping faith. Without it adults are starved, impoverished, and ugly.

When I began to write about Marvell and Nabokov, planning two quite separate studies, it was this childhood Arcadia which drew my imagination in both cases and persuaded me that my two studies were in fact one. This Arcadia, and the experience of losing it, provides both authors with what I call their 'first subject'. The first three parts of this book, my first fourteen chapters, trace their dealings with this first subject in a variety of poems and novels in which lament, nostalgia, hunger, and a compassionate regard for exile and deracination are the keynotes. This strain in the two writers comes to its climax in the tragic masterpieces of Marvell's Mower poems and 'An Horatian Ode', and in two of Nabokov's greatest novels, *Pnin* and *Transparent Things*.

But the two authors are masters not only of nostalgia and lament for a lost innocence, but of wit, humour, and irony too, mistrusting, kindly and unaggressively, such treasured emotions. Each has another tone and with it comes a second subject. The second subject concerns adulthood, not childhood, and worldliness, not innocence. The second subject draws both authors, with their wit, their disbelief, their mercurial intelligence, and their wonderful humour, into a mistrustful confrontation with the Arcadian dreamer, creating all kinds of contest and dialogue between the hungry, other-worldly imagination and the undeceived worldliness of the adult mind. The first subject is not displaced, for the two authors do not betray their imaginative origins to an all-pervading irony and their humour is beautifully gentle. Innocence remains revered; but it is also confronted, smiled at, disbelieved, and even taunted at times. The last three sections of my book watch the progress of these confrontations. First there are the ironic works discussed in Part Four where the first subject is to some degree rebuked, then the more boisterous comedies of Part Five, where in a way he has his revenge upon his worldly rebuker. Finally, in Part Six, *Pale Fire* and 'Upon Appleton House' offer the whole of the writers' shared world to our contemplation. Kinbote and Shade in the novel, Marvell and Fairfax in the poem, trace the lines of dialectic between first and second subjects, bringing each writer's personal mythology to its fullest expression.

No doubt my book is idiosyncratic. Perhaps there are dangers involved, possibilities of appropriation. But at least I have tried to stay close to the human matter of the writers' worlds and in that I am sure I have the emphasis right. One rather depressing thing which Marvell and Nabokov have in common is that they have fallen victim to allegorists for whom the plastic particulars of image and story do not exist and for whom 'human matter' would seem to be a vulgarity. Marvell becomes thereby an intellectually disengaged allegorist of religion, Nabokov a detached and rather dandyish allegorist of art. There is a great deal of such criticism, though mercifully there have been protests against it and I fancy it may be on the decline. I have refrained from speaking in abstract and allegorical terms. I have tried to avoid the terminology of forensic moral debate when talking about stories. I do not think Nabokov's books are books about books or Marvell's poems 'ultimately about themselves' (as the tiresome saying is apt to go). My view is that they both have some important human concerns about which to write, so I have tried to say what I think they are.

ACKNOWLEDGEMENTS

I owe many debts to Robert Hodge (on Marvell) and to Anthony Sharpe (on Nabokov). Robert Hodge, now of the University of Murdoch, Western Australia, wrote a Cambridge thesis on Marvell some years ago. I had the benefit of many conversations with him over a long period and would not know how to disentangle his ideas from my own in some areas of this study. Anthony Sharpe, now of the University of Lancaster, wrote a Cambridge thesis on Wallace Stevens under my supervision. Our discussions often wandered to Nabokov. Later he read a messy typescript of the bulk of this book and got me past a crisis in its development with the most judicious insights.

Otherwise I have benefited from being in the same Faculty as Christopher Ricks and Wilbur Sanders who have had splendid things to say about Marvell and bracingly unconvinced things to say about Nabokov. I also profited from conversations on Marvell with John Wallace and was warmly encouraged by George Steiner when my ideas about Marvell first began to emerge in a form very different from what is given here. Adrian Poole, Stephen Watts, and Stephen Xerri all helped me by reading early drafts of a good deal of the work.

I am not sure that anyone has helped me with the idea that the two authors share things. This is no doubt unsurprising. People were kind when the project was outlined to them but you could see the panic in their eyes. Gabriel Josipovici was kind enough to say he saw the point; and an American graduate student I met in Paris unnerved me by saying he thought it all sounded 'obvious enough'. Otherwise I have been on my own and will have to take complete responsibility for what has been produced.

John Bell and Kim Scott Walwyn at OUP have been very kind, looking with favour and encouragement on a project that might easily have inspired disbelief.

My greatest debt is to my wife. She twice kept her belief in the work when I was discouraged. She had help and suggestions at every turn. She reads both authors better than many who have published on them. She regards this book as an extended commentary on Marvell's great poem 'The Mower to the Glo-Worms', which I think is probably right.

Cambridge,
May 1982

CONTENTS

PART ONE

Childhood

1

SPEAK, MEMORY

Nabokov's autobiography is a book written by a man in late middle age.[1] It sets out ostensibly to deal with the first forty years of his life, but it is in fact overwhelmingly devoted to his childhood and adolescence. An adult looks back over a chasm to another world irretrievably lost, long unreachable, but unforgettable. His mind is dominated by the image and memory of his childhood.

Even in the later chapters, where he turns at last to his adult life, the child's world is ever-present, for the author is now married and has a child of his own. The author's own childhood was a fortunate one, where parkland seemed to cover the whole world and where great estates and woods, provinces and entire continents were traversed by magnificent trains. His child is in his turn fortunate, but less easily so. The child is sheltered and loved, seen always in the settings of parks and gardens. But these parks are smaller. They are located in the cities of exile and adulthood and they have railings round them. But peace, security, and enchantment may well survive there none the less. If they survive anywhere it is there.

His own childhood world was one of space and delight. It was geographically huge in reality and is now larger still in memory. It was in reality, or has become in memory, a world so limitless that the middle-aged man can now say that probing back into childhood is 'the next best thing to probing one's eternity'. It was free from the curses of limit, labour, and frustrated desire which dominate the world of adults. It was 'a veritable Eden', 'harmonious', not yet ruined by the catastrophe which, in his late teens, cut him off from it forever. Now, after the catastrophe, it so governs his imagination as to make him feel that the memory of childhood is a more real and 'robust' presence in the adult mind than the mere 'ghost' of the actual world which has supplanted it. To harbour that memory is to keep alive in the adult mind the dream of an Arcadia where

Everything is as it should be, nothing will ever change, nobody will ever die. (Ch. 3, section 7)

A remembered Arcadia is the most potent and cherished of all images for the adult Nabokov on the other side of the chasm. It was the first world of a pacific and imaginative creature called *'homo poeticus'*, a creature both superior and anterior to his *sapiens* relative. The Arcadia of *homo poeticus* is a man's childhood; but it is also the world's childhood, the world's beginning; for Nabokov believes that 'the world was made on a Sunday', contrary to the labour-oriented falsehoods which may be found in 'old books'. Man's greatest spiritual pleasures are a matter of 'outtugging and outrunning gravity'. It is in the child's world that such pleasures are first learnt. It is in the memory of that world that they find perpetual renewal. In the world of a fortunate child everything is *poeticus*, it is always Sunday, and gravity, in both senses, is always being bested by tugging creatures who get free and running creatures who stay free.

The Arcadian world of 'a perfect childhood' is simultaneously free and secure. In memory it is always a world of 'summer warmth'. It is, without work, limitlessly wealthy. It is magical, full of fairy stories and romances of knights and damsels and of games of 'intricate enchantment and deception'. Its meadows are 'like a grassy wonderland'. At first it is full of pre-pubescent dreams of sexual delight. Later, in a summer pine-grove, the dreams give way to sex itself without pain or difficulty:

everything fell into place, I parted the fabric of fancy, I tasted reality. (Ch. 12, section 1)

In Arcadia such momentous transitions are as simple and as instantly delightful as that.

The catastrophic event which cut him off from this world had nothing to do with sex. It came from the adult world of politics, war, revolution, and violence:

Lenin took over, the Bolsheviks immediately subordinated everything to the retention of power, and a regime of bloodshed, concentration

camps, and hostages entered upon its stupendous career.
(Ch. 12, section 3)

This is the intrusion which cuts him off from Arcadia; and exile is then the chasm across which the middle-aged man looks back with a longing to reconnect, to make good the break. Looking back he laments and mourns:

Tamara, Russia, the wildwood grading into old gardens, my northern birches and firs, the sight of my mother getting down on her hands and knees to kiss the earth every time we came back to the country from town for the summer, *et la montagne et le grand chêne*—these are things that fate one day bundled up pell-mell and tossed into the sea, completely severing me from my boyhood.[2]

That severance and the long ache of the wish to heal it are the dominating images of his life and work.[3]

So in *Mary*, his first novel, Ganin lingers in a Berlin boarding-house hungry for the childhood and wildwood world he has lost. So too, in rented rooms, does Fyodor, in *The Gift*. So does Martin in *Glory*, until he finds himself driven back from Berlin to Russia in a futile and fatal effort to recover it. Pnin once lived there, and even in the years of his maturity and in the relative good fortune of an American exile he frequently longs to make good the break, drifting into reverie in a park or trying to knit his life to that of the young boy, Victor, whom he longs to treat as his own son. Krug, in *Bend Sinister*, knows that his son David still lives there and he tries to protect the boy from the brutal intrusions of the adult, political world. Luzhin, in *The Defence*, lived there fleetingly, if at all, and is impoverished all his life in consequence. Franz, in *King, Queen, Knave*, may have lived there, but if he did he has forgotten it and in such feckless neglect of 'an abolished boyhood'[4] his mawkishness and spiritual ugliness are born. Ada and Van try to stay there for ever. So too in his way does mad Kinbote in *Pale Fire*, unable ever to forget his wonderful childhood in distant Zembla. So too does Humbert in *Lolita*, whose love for a child involves him in a desperate attempt to outtug and outrun all the real world's efforts to prevent him.

2

FORTUNATE AND UNFORTUNATE CHILDREN

Nabokov has recorded his childhood and laid bare the roots of his fictional images in his own life. Of Marvell's childhood, by contrast, we know nothing. One would like to know, biographical curiosity being the insatiable thing it is, whether the woods and waters of the rural East Riding of Yorkshire were to his youth what Vyra and the Oredezh river of north-western Russia were to Nabokov. But speculation is idle, if tempting. The materials must come from the poems alone.

Here however children, childhood, youth, and Arcadia are not hard to find. There are numerous children in Marvell. They are apt to have Arcadian connections with gardens, flowers and woods. They are apt to live precariously in an innocent world which is vulnerable to later intrusion and destruction. Children's lives stand hauntingly juxtaposed with a more cruel and more sophisticated world where desire is often frustrated, sexuality painful, innocence and wildwood cut down. The image of childhood carries all sorts of hopes and fears. Here too it grades into further images of innocence and woodland.[1]

In 'The Picture of little *T. C.* in a Prospect of Flowers'[2] the young child lives in Arcadia and is watched by an older figure who is exiled from that world. He is absorbed in a kind of celebration of her, perhaps enviously, perhaps nostalgically. He is also fearful of the child's own imminent exile from the world of flowers and greenery and fearful of her future participation in a world more savage. The 'young beauty of the Woods', courted by Nature 'with fruits and flow'rs', is the centre of a dream of Arcadian non-violence, treasured and hungered after the more for its fleeting insubstantiality. The dream is the more poignant for the manifest opposition to it both of time and of the violent warfare of the adult world whence come the poem's menacing images of wounding, conquest, triumph, parley, and surrender.

Even the 'Darling of the Gods' herself, though clearly a very fortunate child, is not safe from such intrusions. Marvell has hopes that are centred in the image of a fortunate childhood; but he has his fears too. An angry Nature may well

Nip in the blossome all our hopes and Thee;
(40)

and in doing so, robbing the human world of a child, she will be protecting her own children, for flower-buds are 'Infants in their prime'. Powerful emotions, protective and vengeful, seem to gather to the image of a child, human or non-human.

The child of 'Young Love'[3] is likewise a dweller in an innocent world, 'free' and 'unsuspected'. Here too, however, there is an element of the precarious, for Fate is a 'doubtful' thing and

time may take
Thee before thy time away.
(17-18)

Here too there is hope as well as fear, hunger mixed with a sense of the fleeting, celebration beginning to shade into lament. It is a mysterious poem, tonally difficult, obscured, and recessed in some thoughtful and anxious corner of Marvell's mind where the core images of childhood, Arcadia, greenness, and blossom draw his imagination into hardly expressible realms.[4]

'The Nymph complaining for the death of her Faun'[5] presents another young girl whose world of innocence has now already been invaded by violence and death. As with T. C. the image of childhood extends and grows from the central figure, there to the infant buds, here to the young animal which the girl keeps as a pet and memento. The poem presents a life disrupted and ruined, first by the false love of Sylvio and then by the war and casual violence of the 'wanton Troopers'. It is another difficult and mysterious poem, with its strong, hungry sentiment and also with its reserve or distance, which is very hard to gauge. The core image is of a childhood Arcadia suddenly and irretrievably lost. The speaker of the poem has many Nabokovian relatives, exiled from Arcadia and left with nothing but bewilderment and sentiment dominating their imaginations ever afterwards.

Maria Fairfax,[6] another child in another garden, may be a creature fortunate enough to escape or survive catastrophe. Even more hope, parental and authorial, is invested in her than in T. C. She may even redeem the world's post-Arcadian catastrophe, if her soldier-father's withdrawal from the world of war to the world of gardens and waters can establish there the promise of a life in which severance will not necessarily be the norm. With Maria Fairfax the contemplation of childhood in an Arcadian setting becomes one of the central concerns of Marvell's longest and most complex poem.

Exploratory and searching, the poem drives ever further out from the world of adult labour, mentality, and houses, out into a garden, out further into meadows, out beyond that into the green depths of the wildwood where, in 'Natures Cradle', in the 'Nursery of all things green',[7] the hatching thrush looks out at the world from its nest with a 'shining Eye' in which there is no fear and the '*Hewels young*' are nourished with ease by the probing, 'tinkling' beak of their parent.

In Marvell the Renaissance tropes of innocence, pastoral, and paradise take on a peculiar idiosyncratic force and psychological urgency. They are no longer the standard vocabulary of a shared, social fiction. In a curiously personal way they evoke realities felt once to have existed in the world of children and in the childhood of the world and now conjured in memory and imagination by hungry or anxious adults. That is why 'Upon Appleton House', his most comprehensive survey of the validity of such tropes, concludes so fittingly with the contemplation of a fortunate child in an Arcadian garden. It is also why the life of the fortunate Maria is contrasted in the poem with the life of a less fortunate child, Isabella Thwaites, abducted by nuns who made away with her

> Like Gipsies that a Child hath stoln.
>
> (268)

Other pastoral, childlike figures in the poems have their stories told and their voices recorded with a fine attentiveness to the sense of human loss and need carried by the imagery of Arcadia. Some are given very poignantly, like Thyrsis and Dorinda[8] who seek the release of paradise in a suicide pact. Others are given merrily, like Ametas and Thestylis[9] who will find paradise by kissing in the hay. Poignantly or merrily a common need or desire is recorded. It is the need or desire to be done with the limit, work, complexity, fear, bewilderment, or solitude of the post-Arcadian world.

Marvell's Mowers[10] bring these concerns alive to a quite extraordinary degree. These childlike men, untypical of ordinary pastoral, have voices and beings which echo and reach back into the world's primeval green. The marvellous poems of forlorn love spoken by the Mower are haunting evocations of a life ruined and a world destroyed by the intrusion of violence and bewildering sophistication. The complaint of 'Damon the Mower' might be spoken for all his exiled Nabokovian relatives. The opening lament of 'The Mower's Song' might stand as epigraph for all Nabokov's stories of loss and severance:

> My Mind was once the true survey
> Of all these Medows fresh and gay;
> And in the greenness of the Grass
> Did see its Hopes as in a Glass.
>
> (1-4)

But the 'true survey' and that magically faithful mirror have now been lost, and the Mower's word for what that loss feels like is extremely painful. In 'The Mower to the Glo-Worms' he says his mind is now 'displac'd'.

Such displacement from the childlike is the centre of adult pain. The childhood or childlike state is the centre of all hope. The death of a child, anticipated by the complaining Nymph or feared by Marvell in the cases of T. C. and the child of 'Young Love', represents perhaps the absolute of violation. Even the deaths of non-human children, like the fawn of 'The Nymph complaining' and the rail of 'Upon Appleton House', are key images of loss. They leave behind the helpless Nymph with her long lament and the 'Orphan Parents'[11] of the rail with the muted 'Death-Trumpets' of their mourning.

Even when a child has grown to adulthood such catastrophe may still intrude. Cromwell, in the poem on his death, is said to have died in shock and grief after the death of his daughter Elizabeth. She was an adult, a married woman. But the poem looks through Cromwell's parental eyes and has no difficulty in seeing the shock as enough to kill him.

3

A DOMESTICK HEAVEN

In *Bend Sinister*[1] the death of Krug's son, still in childhood, is also more than a father can bear. Cromwell died as a 'Parent-Tree' may die when an 'untimely knife' too drastically prunes a side-growth. Krug in his turn loses his child. He doesn't die but his mind simply disintegrates in the face of the unendurable, the unthinkable.

The two authors share images, share a pervading vision. *Bend Sinister*, giving those images and that vision very directly, may not be Nabokov's finest book. More deflected or mediated treatments of vision and image may, in their succinctness, make for finer fictional life. *Bend Sinister* has something of the quality of a personal testament, perhaps over-personal, for its matter may well be too cloyingly near to the author for the book to break free of his personal preoccupations and obsessions. But such testaments have the merit of drawing outlines very clearly. Even if in the end we prefer books more shadowed and mediated we should take the testament for what it is and respect it as such.

Bend Sinister is a book about the political violence and philistinism of the totalitarian state. Its author was hesitant about the obvious comparisons but he wanted one to think of Kafka rather than of Orwell, of 'the great German writer' rather than of 'the mediocre English one'.[2] This clear, direct and very specific book does not haunt one like Kafka, does not ramify like Kafka, does not reach so disturbingly into the recesses of the mind. But it has a subtler fictional life than *Nineteen Eighty Four*.

Not the least of the reasons for that is that Nabokov has a far surer sense than the Orwell of *Nineteen Eighty Four* of what it is that violence violates. The sense of a living consciousness as a unique but vulnerable treasure is beautifully given in some of Orwell's non-fictional writing. But what is there in 'A Hanging'[3] for example, or in the writing from the war in Spain, is sadly missing from *Nineteen Eighty Four*. *Bend Sinister* by contrast is

centred in a fine sense of just what it is that is vulnerable to violation, just what it is that stands at risk. The key image of that is of
a child and

it is for the sake of the pages about David and his father that the book
was written and should be read.[4]

The violation of all violations is the political kidnap and political
murder of a child. The ultimate invasion is the invasion of what
Marvell, at Nun Appleton, called 'a *Domestick Heaven*'.[5] The invaders closely resemble the soldiers who kill his Nymph's fawn.
  The book is a celebration, a lament, and a gesture of contempt.
It celebrates the intimacy of a '*Domestick Heaven*' and of a wider
heaven of the peaceful and the peaceable where parent and child
might live undisturbed in their 'creamy house in the sunshine'. It
laments their vulnerability before the world's violent intrusions.
Its gesture of contempt, with contempt's classic mixture of
anger, laughter, and hurt, is directed at the intruding world of
'civic ardour', 'civic nonsense', and 'civic maturity' which
trample such heavens with gross boots. *Homo civis* is an even
more brute beast than *homo sapiens*.
  The world that is celebrated and whose loss is lamented always
has a child at its centre, immovably implanted at the centre of his
father's mind and love. The father's mind is always fixed upon
the life of his child where all value seems to lie and the book in its
turn fixes upon that life with rapt attention. Both author and
hero are rapt by the child's 'powdery-white, blue-veined feet',
the child's easily lifted and vulnerable body, the child as a tiny
mammal sharing 'the perfection of nonhuman creatures', the
child who in his turn delights in stories of 'small humanized
animals', the child whose whole being is overwhelmingly evoked
to his father by the sight of any of his possessions (his ball, his
coat, his toy car, his enamel ring), the child whose apparent
disappearance sends his father rushing into a nightmare of
terror:

searching an intricate dungeon where, somewhere, a shrieking child
was being tortured by experienced hands; hugging the boots of a
uniformed brute; strangling this brute amid a chaos of overturned furniture; finding a small skeleton in a dark cellar; (Ch. 6)

then in the end the child whose actual seizure by uniformed brutes will be beyond the powers of his father's mind to endure. The first intrusion into the Domestick Heaven was when Krug's wife died. She was ill: the intruder was nature, not politics. Her death already left Krug an exile in the 'November wind', in fog, in a 'labyrinth'. If left him a heavy and fumbling man without the strength to lift a pencil to write, without the will 'to rebuild the world which had crashed when she died'. But now there are further extremities of outrage and intrusion peculiar to the political world and centred not on the dead wife but on the surviving child. The abduction of a screaming and kicking child, the brute, idiot killing of a child, the apologetic, kitschy laying-out of the child's body dressed in crimson, gold, and mauve: these are ransackings of the Domestick Heaven too outrageous for consciousness to endure. Krug screams: 'They have torn my little one in two', 'I want my own child'. When all is lost he simply goes insane.

Krug was a man who did not feel himself seriously upbraided when told that he was 'romantic and childish'. He had his creator's complicity when a capacity for 'talking intelligently to a child' was seen as one of the touchstones of human excellence. A mind with that kind of orientation has its sanity rooted in a living instance of the Arcadian. The sudden, intruding severance displaces such a mind completely and irrecoverably, just as Damon's mind was 'displac'd' by Juliana.

There are others whose minds do not have that orientation and their lives are made gross and ugly by its absence. Philistinism is the prime Nabokovian enemy of Arcadia. It may be defined as the condition of the human mind when the Arcadian dimension is missing from it. Philistinism is the mode of the non-Arcadian world, the ransacker of Arcadia, the enemy against which the book's gesture of contempt is directed. It turns homes into 'lists of addresses'; it strikes people down with its 'pig-iron paw'; it loves man-replacing institutions and man-replacing machines like the padograph which simulates handwriting; it is served by 'guardian soldiers, all leather and cartridges'; contemplating Shakespeare's *Hamlet* it finds itself praising Fortinbras as 'a blooming young knight, beautiful and sound to the core'; it upholds the virtues of plain language, 'intelligible to man and beast alike'; its metaphors are all 'mongrels'; it protrudes its comfortable elbows from the windows of usurped cars.

It is also capable of the diabolical cunning of the 'lever of love', the perfected manipulation of humane sensibility, blackmailing a father with threats to his kidnapped child, 'tying a rebel to his wretched country by his own twisted heartstrings'.[6] *Bend Sinister*, in its hurt and anger, directs all Nabokov's powers of contempt at this the most hated of his targets.

Philistinism, the enemy of Arcadia, is found everywhere in Nabokov. Sometimes it evokes the powerful sarcasm of his contempt, sometimes the lighter laughter of his ridicule. It is the main topic of his two Berlin books, *King, Queen, Knave* and *Laughter in the Dark*. It is always the enemy of childhood. In *Pnin* it offers crass pedagogical instruction to the young. In *Lolita* it offers even more crass pedagogical instruction to the even younger. In *The Defence* and *The Real Life of Sebastian Knight* it entrepreneurially manipulates the genius and quiddity of young individual lives.

Bend Sinister is perhaps not Nabokov's finest book. There is more cloying sentiment, more narrow exclusiveness here than elsewhere.[7] Though it contains much of the elegance, wit, and silvery fluency of his prose at its best, it pays for its clarity with a slightly embarrassing certitude or simplicity of conviction. It does set forth however, with the directness of personal testament, the basic images of his world. The body of his fiction as a whole transmutes, mediates and plays with those images with wonderful variety and facility. Even at the farthest reaches of his fancy, indeed perhaps especially there, the basic images are still to be found supporting the great edifice of anti-Philistine artistry which his books as a whole set up.

Krug holds back from the child the shattering news of his mother's death. He wants to leave him in Arcadia for as long as possible. But the shattering is inevitable, survival is a very precarious business indeed. The whole treasured miracle of a new individual consciousness can be annihilated at any moment, either by the inexorable forces of nature or by the political world of men with pig-iron paws.

'This child was still a happy child', thinks Krug, withholding the news for as long as he can. But the word 'still' already portends the catastrophe. It is a word with a chasm just beyond it.

4

THE ORPHAN OF THE HURRICANE

For Marvell the word 'still' also portends chasms. So does the word 'yet'. Both words hold precariously to the last moments of a security about to be lost. They come with just this sense at the opening of 'The unfortunate Lover'.[1]

> Alas, how pleasant are their dayes
> With whom the Infant Love yet playes!
> Sorted by pairs, they still are seen
> By Fountains cool, and Shadows green.
> But soon . . .
>
> (1-5)

The Infant Love 'yet' plays and is 'still' in Arcadia. But then the chasm opens and we are reading the most terrible poem Marvell ever wrote, full of desperate anger and lament for the laceration of mind and body in a non-Arcadian landscape of storm, wind, salt-water, rock, war, and predation.

It is his most sustainedly powerful picture of the world's ransackings. The Unfortunate Lover is also an unfortunate child, with an unfortunate birth, an unfortunate upbringing in the 'cruel Care' of his cormorant guardians and an unfortunate end in 'Storms and Warrs'. The whole picture of outrage and violence is one of childhood and youth savaged. Its saddest and angriest image is of childhood shattered as soon as commenced, making the poem's hero 'The Orphan of the *Hurricane*'.

One need have no sense here, as one had with *Bend Sinister*, of a work for which apology or hesitation is required. 'The unfortunate Lover' is a very great poem indeed. That it has not been widely recognized as such is probably due to the excessive concern of Marvell critics with those qualities in his work which were powerfully set forth by T. S. Eliot.[2] He has his wit, his ambiguity and urbanity; but there are other kinds of fine writing in Marvell to which Eliot's critical vocabulary itself, let alone its lesser, diluted derivatives, can do little justice. 'The unfortunate Lover' is not witty or ambiguous or urbane. It is mordant, angry, compassionate in hurt, pained in indignation, and almost vatic in the intensity and directness of its manner. It tells a human tale of wounding and violation so great that neither wit nor urbanity could properly have anything to do with it. It is great writing of a kind for which Marvell has not been famous, but which none the less we shall encounter in him again.

The landscape of Arcadian peace, of 'Fountains' and 'Shadows' where 'the Infant Love' plays and where suffering, loneliness, and severance are unknown, either in childhood or in early sexuality (for the boy Cupid evokes both), passes swiftly in four lines. Thereafter all is desolation. The misfortune of being born

> when the Seas
> Rul'd, and the Winds did what they please
> (9-10)

is complete. Two stanzas tell of the Lover's birth, two of his upbringing, two of his career in love and war. Then the life of 'my poor Lover' is done: the last stanza is his bitter epitaph. The whole is worthy of Blake in its fierce diagnosis of the misfortunes of youth; and indeed Blake's poem 'The Mental Traveller',[3] a tale of the cruel vexations of youth, is very close to 'The unfortunate Lover' in theme, in tone and in the hurrying urgency of its octosyllabics.

In the initial mischance of the Lover's birth all is virtually lost at once. His helpless 'floting' body, 'cast away' from the very outset of its life, born amidst the violence that 'drave' his mother against a rock and 'split' her there in Caesarian section, is malevolently deprived of Arcadian days amid 'Fountains' and 'Shadows'. His sighs and tears are perpetual, as caught in that small, wailing word 'alwaies'. They are the perpetual manifestation in him of an outer world of wind and water which simply goes roaring through his being. 'No Day he saw', only a scene of unrelieved tumult whose 'ratling Thunder' belongs to a hostile nature, and to war. War is the great Marvellian political theme. It is his greatest anti-Arcadian image, just as Philistinism is Nabokov's.

'While Nature to his Birth presents' nothing but violence, so nurture will continue the attack. The 'cruel Care' of his cormorant guardians is like the 'dismal care' of repressive parental and priestly figures in Blake.[4] Their 'insulting' presence is very like that of the dreadful old woman of 'The Mental Traveller' who exults over the pains of her child victim. Marvell's victim is made 'abject' by their attentions. Words like 'entertain' and 'bill', the first normally suggestive of kind hospitality,[5] the second of pastoral love, are here charged with an indignation for which Blake again might be our touchstone.

Born thus and brought up thus, to what kind of manhood can the Unfortunate Lover look forward?

> See how he nak'd and fierce does stand,
> Cuffing the Thunder with one hand;
> While with the other he does lock,
> And grapple, with the Stubborn Rock:
> From which he with each Wave rebounds,
> Torn into Flames, and ragg'd with Wounds.
>
> (49-54)

There is an heroic defiance in the figure which has, perhaps, its own kind of magnificence. But at what price? With what laceration of that tormented mind and wounding of that naked body? Such fruitless wrestling is involved with the intractable stubbornness of the world's rocks and the even more intractable malevolence of a Heaven which, enjoying a 'spectacle of Blood', will set the poor Lover to fight before it against impossible odds. He 'braves' the Tempest with a kind of greatness, but in the end he is much more like a victim than a hero, physically bloodied and psychologically humiliated at the behest of a strange and cruel 'Heaven'[6] whose purpose can only be guessed at but whose power seems too complete to allow human heroism to have any meaning.

This is the world without Arcadia, and the savagery of which it is capable. The Unfortunate Lover is the emblematic hero of that world, its true Banneret, the knight created on its fields of battle. His heraldry is

> In a field *Sable* a Lover *Gules.*
>
> (64)

We may glamourize his life with heraldry, or with 'Perfume' and 'Musick' to sweeten memory. But the truth is otherwise. Sable is dark. Gules is red. The heraldic field becomes a battlefield, dark in the aftermath of the fight. The soldier hero lies on it 'drest/In his own Blood'.[7]

We would do better with Marvell if we had ears not only for his wit and urbanity but also for that impassioned and compassionate sense of violation and loss which underlies a great deal of his verse. Nothing is more characteristic of him than lament, as he records the hapless voices of severance in the knowledge of our exile from Arcadia and of our continued yearning for it.

Nowhere else does Marvell write, in Blake's phrase, such an 'indignant page'[8] as this. But the tone of it will be heard occasionally elsewhere and there are other Orphans of the Hurricane in his work. The great lament for a lost garden of Eden in 'Upon Appleton House':

> What luckless Apple did we tast,
> To make us Mortal, and The Wast?[9]

is born of very similar feelings. The Cromwell of 'An Horatian Ode' suffers a destiny as violent as that of the Unfortunate Lover. One is 'the Orphan of the *Hurricane*'; the other is 'the Wars and Fortunes Son'. The two phrases resonate interestingly together.[10]

PART TWO

The Voices of Loss

5

THE COLOURS OF ARCADIA

Not all the Orphans of the Hurricane are drawn on this epic scale. Recording the loss of Arcadia, Marvell's normal manner is much more subdued. So is Nabokov's. *Mary*,[1] his first novel, begins a long and quiet line of enquiry into severance and hunger. The herione of the book never appears in the textual present. Only her name is there, from first to last. We gather her life almost entirely from the memories and fantasies of Ganin. She is recalled in the thoughts of others. She is awaited. But the book ends with Ganin turning away from the expected meeting with her and she is again left to fade back into the mystery and insubstantiality that surround her throughout.

She was, in memory or in fantasy, Ganin's first love. As such she was the culmination of his childhood and his partner in the first blissful step into the adult world. Her history, before that, is obscure, and afterwards she slips gradually into obscurity again, leaving her life to be pieced together from fragments of letters, rumours, surmises, and snippets of information revealed by her exiled husband. Ganin remembers her, or creates her, from the surviving fragments.

As his creation she is lifted briefly out of obscurity into brilliant-coloured life before sinking back into the distance of exile's oblivion and the remoteness of rural Russia. Her voice is heard in snatches, ever quieter and more receding:

I've been in Poltava for a whole week now, hellishly boring . . . Today it's so boring, boring . . . the days go by so pointlessly and stupidly . . . where has it all gone, all that distant, bright, endearing . . . (Ch.13)

Life in the present for Ganin is post-Arcadian, life after the severance, lived in what he calls 'dispersion of the will'. So too for the other Russian exiles whose memories are all dominated by the image of a Russia 'before time began'. The Berlin boarding-house in which live 'seven Russian lost shades' is like a cruel parody of a Domestick Heaven, where pieces of furniture that once composed the living body of a home lie scattered about the various rented rooms with 'the inept, dejected look of a dismembered skeleton's bones'. The tenants' party is a sad-grotesque attempt to recreate life and colour where all is drabness. It is a pathetic failure, garish rather than colourful. All gestures of delight are reduced to mawkishness.

Ganin's half-hearted affairs share this sad-grotesque and garish quality. Klara's clichés of romantic passion ('I think about him literally all day ...') echo with the spirit's mawkish attempts to breathe life back into a dead world. Lyudmila's clichés of voluptuousness ('her factitious charms, her modishly yellow hair ...') are full of similar echoes of the body's hunger for magic. Klara's starved imagination limps after romance, Lyudmila's wretched body toils after voluptuousness. Ganin moves among this desolation in the mood in which we first see him at the novel's opening, 'annoyed', 'irritable,' 'with a grimace of impatience', ludicrously trapped in a broken lift and beating its walls with his fist in the gestures of imprisonment.

Mary gives Nabokov's first version of Arcadia, lost and remembered by Ganin, and the brillant colour of an Arcadian transfiguration in which the life of Mary is briefly lifted out of rural obscurity into delight. There was a house, a home. Beyond them, gardens and parkland. Beyond them again, wilder woodland and waters. There was sunlight and summer. All the contours of Marvell's meditations at Nun Appleton are given here in the Arcadian moment of the lives of Ganin and Mary. The world, in memory, is suddenly full of colour after the gloom of the Berlin boarding-house. A child's coloured silk ball rolls across a sunlit floor of 'amber-yellow parquet'. Life is a 'kaleidoscope', the memory of it a 'bright labyrinth'. Adolescent twilights are blue. The women sit in a 'hot yellow glare' at the barn concert wearing 'crimson and silvery headscarves'. Sunsets are of 'red fire'; in the park pavilion where the lovers first meet the light pours in through glass panes of many colours.[2] Everywhere there is the perpetual green and liquid light of the Arcadian landscape, before the autumn of fallen leaves and the winter white-out of blanketing snow. Nabokov, like Marvell, is a brilliant colourist. Both writers paint their dreams, memories, and visions of Arcadia with the brilliant, liquid colours of flowers, grass and water.

The public park where Ganin and Mary later meet is a sad remnant of this spacious woodland, bleak and railed where the woodland was open and full of light. Thereafter we go back to the boarding-house with Ganin while Mary settles into the boredom of what is now mere dull unenchanted countryside. The book's vision and power is all in those brilliant, lyric, and liquid images of a lost world where childhood graded into adolescence and innocence into sexual pleasure without pain or severance. The glittering colours are like those of Fairfax's garden at Nun Appleton, or of the kingfisher's feathers, or the thrush's 'shining Eye' in the wildwood beyond it.[3] Such colours are briefly a waking presence in the lives of growing children. Later they create a place of dream-refuge and dream-longing in adult memory.

This kaleidoscope world is a world for play, made on a Sunday, where *homo poeticus* is at home with himself and with all the green trees and bright creatures that surround his delight. Its labyrinths are bright, not tormenting, just as for Marvell the curls and coils of the forest, the windings of river and caterpillar, are images of pleasure, relaxation, and ease. Play is the keynote, word-play and sex-play and room for both to unwind their slow labyrinths. All acts of the body, all verbal descriptions, are full of revelling sensuality:

He arranged to take them boating all next day; but she appeared without her companions. At the rickety jetty he unwound the clanking chain of the rowboat, a big heavy affair of mahogany, removed the tarpaulin, screwed in the rowlocks, pulled the oars out of a long box, inserted the rudder pintle into its steel socket.

From some distance came the steady roar of the sluice gates at the water mill; one could distinguish the foamy folds of the falling water and the russet-gold sheen of pine logs that floated near.[4]

Such a place for the body's pleasure and thus for the soul's undispersed content haunts the worlds of Nabokov and Marvell. Fortunate children are born in it. Fortunate children have their first sexual experiences there. Fortunate adults may still be capable of contact with it if the threads of their lives are unsevered, or if they can reknit them, if the patterns of imagination and recollection can be folded into a whole.[5]

Both authors pursue these labyrinths of colour in memory and imagination as the deepest growing-points of the soul. But in the works of both authors, the people who speak, or whose stories are told, have been denied such places, or have lost them, or have been wrenched from them. They thus feel 'displac'd', like Damon, 'irritated' like Ganin; or, on a vaster scale, 'restless' like Cromwell.[6]

6

SHORT DELIGHTS

As Ganin abandoned Mary so Daphnis abandons Chloe.[1] Before
their affair, if such their tale of missed opportunity may be
called, she was almost imperceptible, pent in silence:

> Till Love in her Language breath'd
> Words she never spake before.
> (25-6)

After it we hear no more of her. The affair itself, her only
emergence into the public world of the poem and the adult world
of love, is all barriers, deceptions and misunderstandings. In
Arcadia love is an easy passage through the labyrinths of colour.
Here it is lost, before it is found, in a tangle of mistrust.

Mary was a slight enough book. 'Daphnis and Chloe' is probably an even slighter work. Marvell is playful about the tale,
dismissing it all at the end as an amusing story of deception and
folly. But none the less it does touch, howsoever lightly, some
quietly disturbing notes.[2]

Before Daphnis' game is given away in the poem's last two
stanzas we have listened to the love story of an inept and hide-
bound pair, obstructed at every turn by barriers to their pleasure.
Even if Daphnis turns out after all to be an untroubled
philanderer who, leaving Chloe, passes on to the pleasures of
Phlogis or Dorinda, there is still the wretched Chloe herself to
trouble the poem with darker thoughts:

> Nature, her own Sexes foe,
> Long had taught her to be coy:
> But she neither knew t'enjoy,
> Not yet let her Lover go.[3]

Perhaps it is all trivial enough; but it has a way of seeming fitfully to evoke real dilemma, a real sense of painful tangledness.

Even Daphnis quickens and deepens one's interest at times.
Philanderer or no, he has been obliged to spend 'Labour' and

'Art' on his proposed conquest and, expert in the maintenance of seiges, he seems clumsily to lack the quicker, defter powers that instigate or rouse. Taken up by his factitious, theatrical grief he has 'not so much Sense'[4] as to respond to her yielding when it comes. His distraction, hair-tearing and eye-rolling may be fake, but they are barriers to communication none the less, just as surely as if they had been real. His feigned talk of cruelty and wounds and of the 'short Delight' of a condemned man given a drink before his execution seems suddenly not to be entirely feigned. It goes on a little too long and a little too frenziedly. Like the clichés of Klara and Lyudmila, such spurious gestures of passion have their own unfortunateness. They mimic the real just a shade too well for pure amusement.

So too does the imagery of his peroration:

> Gentler times for Love are ment:
> Who for parting pleasure strain
> Gather Roses in the rain,
> Wet themselves and spoil their Scent.
>
> Farewel therefore all the fruit
> Which I could from Love receive:
> Joy will not with Sorrow weave,
> Nor will I this Grief pollute.
>
> (85-92)

No doubt he is just a practised rogue, handled lightly by this nimble poem. But there is a note of something genuinely distraught, for all the posing, in that sense of lost perfume, lost fruit, spoiling, and disappointment. These factitious gestures are after all not very far remote from the profoundly serious language of spoliation, disappointment, and fruitlessness to be found in 'The Coronet':

> Through every Garden, every Mead,
> I gather flow'rs (my fruits are only flow'rs)
> Dismantling all the fragrant Towers
> That once adorned my Sheperdesses head.[5]

The philandering Daphnis is acting; but has he not after all found himself acting some very real griefs?

And what of Chloe, who is not acting? What do we make of her coyness, her ignorance, her clinging to him, her last-minute change of mind in an effort to hold on to him? Whence such extreme bewilderment? Whence such an inability to follow 'the Lawes' which would see love satisfied? Why such inhibition, and such unhappiness with inhibition? It is all cavalier enough, pleasantly light and brisk, not to be over-read; but it tends to leave behind a surprisingly strong after-image. The pair have nothing like the haunting presence of some of Marvell's other bewildered lovers, lost in the tangles of complexity. But there is some reality here none the less as Chloe emerges from her silence to the first words of love only to hear its language of quails, manna, roses, and fruit in a desert of mischance.

Marvell's masterpiece in this vein is 'The Nymph complaining'. There the richness of romantic language is made to feel curiously forlorn since the speaker of the language is only its speaker, not its possessor. She is isolated, unrequited and thus deprived of the very richness which her own language seems to promise. But even the light 'Daphnis and Chloe' gives oddly strong hints of such matters. Here already the language of flowers, fruit, and nourishment echoes to Chloe in the void left by her first lover's departure.

7

A MAN WITHOUT A NAME

Luzhin's love story in *The Defence*[1] is weightier. He is one of the most unfortunate lovers of Nabokov's world and his hapless sterility can be traced back to his never having had a childhood. Here the key figure of the father enters Nabokov's fiction for the first time. The first version of it is baleful. Luzhin's parents are quite unable to relate to a child's mind. His father's books for children are full of dead stereotypes. The father's desire that his son should show distinction is a mere cliché, relating not at all to what real distinction (and its tribulations) might actually come to look like. When his son's distinction begins to show itself, in the sad, parody-art of chess, the father again produces clichés and stereotypes when trying to write the story of his son's life.

All Luzhin's early life is a scene of emotional incompetence and mawkishness. His childhood is frittered away without joy or fruition. He is asked to become a man, assuming the dread patronymic,[2] before he has ever filled out his own personal name in childhood. The assumption of the patronymic is a symbolic closing of the door upon an Arcadia that he has missed. The personal name that never came to life in that vacant world is not revealed until the book's last sentences. By then the man is dead. The child never existed. 'There was no Aleksandr Ivanovich'.[3]

His childhood is a kind of prison. His body is cramped within irritating, enclosing cloaks and mufflers. His body is injected for anaemia and the effect is to make him smell unpleasantly. His body is put into a sailor-suit for the special occasion when other boys, of his father's choice, are invited, sailor-suited and pomaded in their turn, to come and play with him. Conjurors (who are pseudo-artists)[4] and puppets (who are pseudo-people) make their dismal contributions to this prison world. His father's crass books stand ominously provided for him in his 'nice bright room'. His teeth are grotesquely clamped behind a scaffolding of platinum wire.

His adult memory of this world is of a sunlight which, however, he has always somehow missed. In his childhood itself he sought the absent magic of colour and labyrinth first in jigsaws, then in mathematics, and finally in chess. His chess-set, 'a fascinating and mysterious toy', is the centre of all his hunger and of all his impoverishment, hidden away in his room by a boy who is starved of magic. All that has been sought and missed elsewhere is sought and found here, apparently; only later will he discover the hollowness of the surrogate.

Once he tries to flee the encroaching adult world. He escapes to the cool silence and dampness of tress and ferns in a dense wood beyond a fence and a wicket-gate,[5] but his father has him brought back by main force. In his school-yard he cowers with his collar turned up on a pile of sawn logs. Logs are the dead bodies of trees; so are wooden chessmen on a wooden board. Chess is a complex, labyrinthine game; but thirty-two pieces of wood on sixty-four black and white wooden squares are a stiff, colourless surrogate for the trees of the forest.

But the wooden men on the wooden board must do service for the missing Arcadian woodlands. Then they must do service for his growing teenage sexuality too. He has lived in the sexless ambiance of his parents' dull marriage and of his father's anodyne books. The awakening which comes with puberty is pathetically weak and is soon deflected or dissolved by chess. His copper-haired aunt is the only sexually-alive person in the whole book of his life. The growing boy seems to respond in his way to the sexuality and freedom of life that is in her. He sits close to her on the carpet watching her hand and her bracelet as she moves the chessmen. He kisses her hand. He seeks out her house. She comes from her bed to greet him wearing a bright kimono. Secret assignations begin. He cuts school in the afternoons, then for whole days, then for 'a rapturous intoxicating week'. But after all it is only chess that she is teaching him, not sex. His haste to arrive at her house for each new lesson mimics cruelly the excitement of sexual discovery.[6]

Arcadia flickers around him, near him, but always beyond him. Sunlight; flowers, woods, gardens, trees; river and water; imaginative adventure, sex and the exotic: Luzhin brushes by them all but is never drawn into them. On a garden terrace in the sun on the Adriatic coast he does nothing but play games of chess in his head. There is some sort of pathetic and childish freedom in this, for 'nobody could forbid him' to play chess in his head, but it is spurious and unsustaining. An adult identity cannot be founded on such sterile things, so he is driven back into the prison of his own head. Sun, garden, and water are merely the irrelevant, and ignored, background.

At this point we are fewer than fifty pages into the book. His next sixteen years of chess achievement and human nothingness pass in a single paragraph. In fewer than fifty infinitely sad and charitable pages Nabokov has given the condition of his childhod abandonment and adolescent longing. The rest of the book will now survey the life of a man made without benefit of Arcadia, a man who inherits a patronymic but who has no personal name, no private being brought to life by sun and water.

Chess has its own kind of magic. There is brilliance in it, genius, imaginative vibrancy, intellectual complexity, pattern. The fatal game with Turati has its music, its mystery, and its labyrinths. But these labyrinths are in the end not places of discovery or haven but places of endless exhaustion and labour. They take Luzhin's spirit and desire and give him back only fatigue. And while he is occupied in them the rest of his life, un-nurtured, falls into dereliction. His adult mind and body are places of vacancy and neglect.

He is overweight. He chews his nails. He smokes endlessly. All three are evident in his hands, which are splayed, ragged and nicotine-stained. He is gloomy and melancholy. He is easy prey to the Philistine and manipulative impresario Valentinov who manages his career and who is, in an awful phrase, his 'chess-father'. Luzhin sits hunched. His profile is heavy. In the hotel gardens of his chess-gatherings Arcadia stands grotesquely imitated in grottoes and earthenware gnomes. All the cities of Europe are alike to him, all equally places of such unlovely hotel gardens. Whatever 'celestial dimension' is still open to him belongs only in the inhuman and attenuated world of chess. Otherwise he seems a person whom 'life itself had overlooked'. People find him ridiculous. They think of him as an absurd, even an insulting presence in the world. The world in its turn is to him full of 'smelly human warmth' from which the abysses of his labyrinthine game are a retreat.

This is a Nabokovian Unfortunate Lover, who, like his great Marvellian counterpart, is the 'unfortunate and abject Heir'[7] to an absent childhood, permanently registered in his namelessness. He meets, and eventually marries, another unnamed person. She too has a void in her. If Luzhin never was a child, Luzhin's wife in many ways still is one. Unlike him she had a childhood, in which there was tenderness and delight. She remembers it with poignancy and it is the source of her adult gentleness, sentiment, and capacity for pity. But not for love or sex. The vital trans- figuration of Arcadian delight into adult sexuality has not occurred in her. Her being shows

something lacking . . . a promise of real beauty that at the last moment remained unfulfilled. (Ch. 6)

She has lived among the mawkish Russian bric-à-brac of her parents' home which mimics the world they have lost. But the bric-à-brac only testifies to the very severance which its collectors seek to heal. The real threads are broken: only these sham ones remain along which no life can pass. Her life has stopped at the moment of its potential flowering. She is kind to Luzhin as she used to be kind to animals. She caresses him as she would a child or a pet. Her love for him is pitying and compassionate, but com- pletely without sex.

Such love brings its awakening to Luzhin, but it is forlorn and partial. She nurses him. She protects him. She empties his mind of chess for a while and finds new objects for his delight. But what is awakened in him is rather the knowledge of his hunger than the means to satisfy it. She awakens in him a child's world which twenty years before would have fed him, but which is now incapable of giving sustenance. Like Marvell's Nymph toying with her fawn, Luzhin and his wife live on childish pleasures in their adult vacancy. The Russian bric-à-brac is for him a new set of toys. He makes drawings and pins them on the wall. He pores over a child's atlas. She naïvely hopes he will 'blossom out' at this late stage. She treats him like a boy, calls him a boy. He is delighted with this new world of affection. But adults cannot live long with such constant need for protection, distraction, and deception. The new haven is temporary. The mere fact of his manhood, howsoever weakly established, cannot help but make him grow troubled again in this artificial nursery world. Step by step he goes back to his chess.

He also begins to search back in memory for his pre-chess childhood. But the patterns will not connect. The lost years are too completely lost; the origins for which he is searching were too insubstantial. He is reaching back from the vacancy of adulthood through years of vacancy to look for his being in a time that was vacant itself. An empty childhood leaves an emptiness in the man and remains empty when the hungry man tries to reach back to it for nourishment. There is nothing there. After a brief and troubled effort, thinking his way back and rereading books that he read in childhood, he is defeated.

Vacant adulthood follows on from vacant childhood. Only by having a childhood and by holding to it in memory and imagination can adults retain the coloured, Arcadian *poeticus* quality that will redeem them from drabness. Unfortunate children are likely to be unfortunate lovers.[8]

The unfortunate Luzhin kills himself by jumping from a high window. He has difficulty since he is clumsy and fat and finds it hard to get on to the ledge and through. His friends come looking for him but by then he has jumped. It is only as they come upon the empty room that we hear his name for the first time: 'there was no Aleksandr Ivanovich'. There never had been. There was not enough substance in him to support a personal name or withstand the weight of the imposed patronymic.

8

A NYMPH WITHOUT A NAME

The young girl of 'The Nymph complaining'[1] is another creature famished and lost in the transition from child to adult. It is sadly appropriate that she too should have no name. She complains for the death of her fawn in a wistful, fleeting voice of bewilderment. Her voice is briefly and faintly heard in a world of abandonment and war.

If we reach back before the moment of her complaint the voice quickly recedes and vanishes. It has no history, little force of unique human presence to press it forward to be heard and to claim attention for itself. She emerges, momentarily and fatally, into the adult world of war as a consequence of the troopers 'riding by'. She recalls 'unconstant Sylvio' who came and went like Ganin in the life of Mary. Before that there was nothing. After that there is only the pitiful memorial to his passing that lived in the fawn. Then the troopers, the fawn casually killed, her complaint, and finally her resignation. She resigns herself to a life spent in perpetual mourning and weeping and to an early death figured in the stillness, coldness, and silence of tears in alabaster.

This scarcely embodied voice heard briefly in the great world of history, adult sex, and war is childlike in the extreme.[2] The Nymph is naïve, hurt, and solitary. Though destroyed as soon as she has set forth she declares that she wishes no ill to the murderers of her defenceless pet. She speaks briefly and movingly of the criminality of the intrusion, the uncleanliness of the act, the injustice of its grossness, the sanctity of the 'warm life blood' which has been spilt. Then the rest of her speech is recollection and resignation. The unaggressive, undefended world of her Arcadia has been broken into irreparably. She is dispossessed, and left with the shattered pieces of her life. Sylvio, with his inconstancy, began the dispossession, the troopers complete it. As a consequence of these two intrusions, a life is obliterated. The key word is perhaps 'wanton'. The final act of destruction is casual: the troopers, who live in the adult world of history and war, simply shoot as they ride by.

The Nymph's brief, muted complaint in the name of the fawn's 'warm life blood' comes straight from a Nabokov-like dream of Arcadia where the violence of adult human life has not yet intruded into the woodland harmonies of childhood. The moment of severance and shattering leaves the Nymph living, like Luzhin, a pitiful surrogate childhood in a world where the images of childhood delight and sexual delight are only the pathetic solaces of an irrecoverably wounded being. The fawn is a pet, a toy. It invites her to its game. She plays her solitary time away with it. She nurses it at her fingers. This might be life, delight, and nourishment in the nursery. But here, on the edge of adulthood, it is full of a sense of hopeless substitution, like Luzhin's drawings and his atlas.

Here again sexuality is twisted and thwarted. She kisses and fondles the pet animal. She takes delight in its feeding on her garden. She watches its upwelling tears. She resolves to mix them with her own in a golden phial to be kept in a shrine dedicated to the goddess of, alas, chastity. Sentiment piles up in her language as her emotions crave release, as they hunger for room enough to live. All the language of sexual pleasure is here in the poem, especially the great erotic imagery of the *Song of Songs* which is hinted at and alluded to again and again. But here that language is full of sadness, bathos, cloying sentiment, and the sense of surrogate. The language of the erotic is reduced to the garnering of precious things, to a rapt fascination with flowing liquid, to a languid preoccupation with the touchable surface of skin and stone and the coats of soft animals.[3] All the language of gold and silver, milk and sugar, gardens, roses and lilies, balsam and fankincense, eyes, lips and breasts pours out its lyric and romantic heritage in what is inert, fading, solitary, unrequited.

The greatness of the poem comes from Marvell's wonderful powers of attentiveness. He has the patient, self-effacing ability to let his characters talk, to listen to them and to refrain from commentary. He hears voices as if from within. He creates a silence around the words of monologue and dialogue, leaving the words suspended there to be heard and reheard with uncanny clarity.

No wonder, therefore, that he was so well heard by the creator of Prufrock. No wonder it was Modernism which discovered Marvell. His self-effacing attentiveness is a precursor of Modernist monologue and Modernist narration. Deference to other people's voices comes naturally to him. Authorial commentary is as minimal as may be. Speech hangs suspended in its own free space, and what cannot be known or understood is not presumed upon in judgemental commentary but left with every Modernist scruple in the silence that comes before and after words.

Some critics have hunted in the poem for allegory. But allegory is commentary, and Marvell, like Nabokov, is not a commentator. Instead of offering allegories and meanings, he tells stories, or lets the stories tell themselves.[4] 'The Nymph complaining' is a great and typical Marvellian story. It is one of the many tales of forlorn love and bewildered desire which his poems present. The Nymph is a hapless victim of severance. Like Mary she is a remote, rural casualty of the great world of love and war. Like Luzhin, she is famished. Her life, like his, hardly begins before it is shattered. Like him, she enters her adult life in a sad imitation of childhood and a lonely imitation of sex.

9

A MOMENT IN HISTORY

Nabokov's next figure in the wilderness is as mysterious as the Nymph. Where the narrative of Luzhin's life unfolded in clear and simple chronology, Martin, in *Glory*,[1] is much more shadowy. He is a man of impressions and half-revealed desires. His story is told in less visible sequence. His end is strange and obscure: 'Martin seemed to have dissolved in the air'. His is a semi-disembodied voice, retaining its mystery and privacy, which we overhear as he passes briefly and idiosyncratically through the public world of history. Then, like the Nymph, he disappears into obscurity again, half expecting death and no doubt finding it somewhere or other.

It is again a tale of severance, but now there is also an attempt to heal the severed self. Perhaps Martin is healed and remade in his Glory, his *podvig*, his 'inutile deed of renown'.[2] Or perhaps not. It may be just a matter of clutching at the ungraspable and trying to recover what is irredeemably transient. Martin is shadowy enough, and Nabokov hesitant enough, to leave one never quite knowing.

There was a time when the generations of Martin's family succeeded one another in secure and solid order and had their portraits preserved in a big leather album. Confident, nineteenth-century narratives tell the stories of such dynasties. But in Martin's immediate family the sequence and the order begin to break, and a new Modernist fragmented narrative will try to catch some of the broken pieces.

His parents' marriage is unsuccessful. As a child he already has reveries of escape into the woodland of the picture over his bed. The love between himself and his mother is intense, but shadowed everywhere with a faint sense of their clutching at it in hunger and solace. His relationship with his father hardly exists. The eventual break-up of the marriage and then his father's death continue this sense of something missed or something fading. His delight in stories read to him by his mother is partly Arcadian, feeding the growing imagination; it is also partly unreal, giving him tales and pictures of woodland rather than woodland itself. Both mother and child are troubled by the rupture with husband and father, the mother with a sense of shame, the child with a vaguer notion of pure absence.

The child's reveries about his father are set (as now begins to seem inevitable) in a Russian park with trees, shrubs, sunlight, and water. It is also to a park that he flees when his mother punishes him, violently, 'with a riding switch of tawny bullgut'. He gradually becomes ever more apt to retreat (or is it to expand?) into reverie and fantasy. The fantasy is always Arcadian, ever more child-centred yet at the same time ever more sexual. Childhood memories become clearer, more intense, more sustaining (or at least apparently so) the more he is removed from actual childhood in time and place.

He is a child on a train in France. He is a child in the huge Atlantic waves at Biarritz. He is a child in the pinewoods of the Charlottenburg. All seem at first to be easy extensions of his Russian childhood. But in his multi-lingual upbringing and in his exile he is not French or Basque, or German. Nor is he really Russian. Nor is he really Swiss, for all the Edelweiss side of his family, nor British, for all his early English education, later completed at Cambridge. His exile in the world of political fact, in Turkey, in Greece, and then in Western Europe, merely deepens and confirms a more basic condition of what may be fluidity and richness, or may simply be deracination.[3]

His childhood was Arcadian. There were woods, and there was water. But he can now find only fleeting and precarious belonging in Cambridge, with the trees and waters of the Cam, in Provence, with the vines and irrigation-waters of Molignac, in Switzerland, with the fir-forest and melt-waters of the Alps. All places eventually elude him, even Molignac, where his stay is longest, where his roots are put down deepest, and where the waters of fertility gush with wonderful power; but which eventually turns out to have been the wrong village anyway. Trees, light, and water, in a blend unique to each place, seem to offer the life of linking memory to his soul. But all eventually turn out to have the wrong tonality. In his Russian childhood there were other, different trees. Or was it only a nursery picture of them?

Around him there are others who know where they belong. Some, like Zilanov and Gruzinov, know just what they will make of their exile. Some are so clear about their belonging that they reply to the 'restless' queries of others 'but where would we live if not in the Crimea?' Edelweiss is at home in Switzerland. Martin's mother makes herself learn to be at home there too. Moon has his romantic dreams of Russia well under control and is perfectly at home in Cambridge. Darwin carries an easeful, Anglo-Saxon solidity with him wherever he is.[4]

For Martin they are sometimes enviable, sometimes pitiable. Sometimes they seem to have worked all the threads of their lives together. Sometimes they seem merely to have accepted the curtailment and containment of the endless imaginative possibility they once had. For Martin, Darwin's mature and employed life involves the death of the spirit. For Darwin, Martin's unemployed and immature life is mere 'drifting'. The same pattern is repeated with Gruzinov. Is the mature adjustment to life's realities an unbearable, shameful acceptance of limit, the cessation of imagination and dream? Or is keeping faith with dreams the mere immaturity of the restless and rootless? One man is hungry and restless and apt to find others banal; others are rooted and stable and apt to see in him a figure of precarious drifting. Is the dreaming and drifting man deracinated or is he free? Is he distinguished in imagination or merely feckless? Is he lucky or cursed? This classic Modernist book hovers on these lines of demarcation with beautifully tantalizing indecision.

Martin has three love affairs, which between them trace the contours of his restless life. Lida belongs to his childhood and to Russia. Alla belongs to the start of his exile and his teenage awakening. Sonia belongs to the years of his continued exile and unachieving manhood.

Lida is his pre-sexual desire, an exciting but undisturbing presence in his still intact youth. Martin thinks of her legs, as Humbert will of Lolita's, as 'evenly coated with a laquer-smooth reddish-gold tan'.[5] But Martin, unlike Humbert, is at this stage still a child himself. No agonies are involved. There is no pain of

distance when her body remains withdrawn from him, hidden
with propriety behind some rocks while his boyish body is swimming naked in the waters of the Black Sea. His companions are
another boy and a fox-terrier.

Alla is the moment of his sexuality's awakening, a moment
when dream and reality are wonderfully united. In two brief
chapters of magnificent presto rhythm and playful comedy her
fully adult world (she is twenty-five and married) meets the
world of the growing boy in the satisfying delights of impermanence.

Alla is a precursor of the mature Nabokovian comedies of flamboyance. She writes battered and kitschy erotic poems:

> On purple silks, beneath an empire pall,
> You vampirized me and caressed me all,
> And we tomorrow die, burned to the end;
> Our lovely bodies with the sand will blend.
>
> (Ch. 8)

She casts herself into romantic poses:

sometimes she said that her life was but the light smoke of an amber-
perfumed Régie cigarette. (Ch. 8)

She dupes her husband, delighting in the dupe for its own sake as
well as in the sexual pleasure thereby attained. She glories in a
romantic grandeur whose falsity is no barrier to its excellence:

I shall remain for you a glamorous dream . . . I am insanely voluptuous
. . . you will never forget me . . . (Ch. 9)

She dreams, or claims to dream, of priests in ancient Greece. She
calls Martin 'a wild boy, goodness, what a wild boy'. She says sex
is 'a peek into paradise'. Her freely-offered body and sexuality
conform perfectly to all his pre-adolescent fantasies of anticipation. The Mediterranean breeze in her skirt makes him think of
the breeze in the sails of Ulysses.

The pages on Alla are purest delight. For the first time in
Nabokov, the clichés of glamour are treated indulgently, indeed
with enthusiasm. Alla lives out her glamorous clichés with such
verve that cliché escapes from itself and takes on new force.
Humbert and Kinbote will later display the same verve. All three

characters have a genius which makes highly-coloured kitsch seem to keep some kind of bizarre imaginative faith with our genuine expectations of paradise. But in Martin's life this is a brief passage. His exile is ever-deepening, his fantasies ever less able to keep up with and make contact with the facts of his life. Alla no doubt will hold to her outrageous career, as Humbert and Kinbote hold to theirs. But Martin does not have their kind of imaginative daring, or madness, or verve, or genius. He goes into the quiet and deepening troubles of his exile saner than they are, but weaker. Martin is of the world of the hapless and bewildered. Alla prefigures the later heroes of Nabokovian comedy. But she is left behind after two brief chapters, arm in arm with her unsuspecting husband on the pier at Piraeus, 'smiling and waving a mimosa branch' at Martin's departing ship. The drifting hero has no such aplomb.

Sonia is the unachieved mistress of his unachieving manhood. She is apparently an adult woman, apparently sexually alive, yet hopelessly linked to his childhood, and provoking his fantasy-desire for the girls of his childhood rather than his sexual desire for adult women. The two kinds of desire, once briefly united when he was with Alla, grow ever more separate as his exile goes on. In the halting episodes of his vague affair with Sonia, his ungrowing spirit is caught and held between childhood and adulthood. To abandon his hopeless and not very strong longing for her is, in some obscure way, to abandon the hope of being reunited with his lost past. To stay with her is, equally obscurely, to abandon the hope of an adult future. The two of them relate, fitfully and episodically, in largely childlike ways. As adults they exasperate each other.

There Martin stays locked, with only his final gesture of an 'inutile deed of renown' to bring him the Glory of his self-making. Nabokov said that his story and his final quest engaged with 'the glory of this earth and its patchy paradise'.[6] He thought of Martin's story as one of 'the glory of personal pluck; the glory of a radiant martyr'. Maybe; but it is doubtful whether Nabokov really felt so unambiguously fulsome about his hero at the time of writing the book. This later acclaim, coming nearly forty years after the book itself, smacks of an attractive but deceiving love for the creature who is so clearly 'a distant cousin' of his creator 'with whom I share certain childhood memories'. The story itself is much more mysterious, shadowy and strange, quieter and sadder in its record of life's fitful dealings with paradise and radiance. No very resonant notion of Glory or martyrdom can be derived from it.

Nor, however, should one think of irony or judgemental reserve. Martin is given with more respect, more open-endedness than that. Quietly elusive, discontinuous, fading and vanishing, his voice and his story have much in common with those of Marvell's Nymph. Nabokov shares with Marvell the respectful and attentive patience, inimical to summarizing authorial comment, which can listen to such a voice. Here, as there, the earth's paradises are distinctly patchy, and very easily invaded. Here, as there, the imagery of romantic lyricism and transfiguring magic lives unsustainingly in a lonely life with little history, little specificity, and an obscure, death-bound future. Alla had her peek into paradise and lived no doubt to peek again. But the imagery of paradise evoked by Martin's less assured being is full of the unreal, hungry frailty of the Nymph's devotion to her fawn.

Other people walk the earth more confidently. At the book's close, the Anglo-Saxon Darwin goes to see Martin's mother in Switzerland to report his friend's disappearance. The images of woodland and water return. He walks through the fir-forest and hears the gurgle of water running under the snow. He pauses to listen, then walks on. The windings of the path and the shapes of the branches are 'mysterious' to him; but the word is untroublesome, quickly and easily joined to the word 'picturesque'. This solid and striding man, employed and about to be married, has in any case only cut through the wet forest because it is 'the shortest way', avoiding the hairpin bends.

10

TRANSPARENT THINGS

The three couples who speak in Marvell's pastoral dialogues, 'Thyrsis and Dorinda', 'Clorinda and Damon', and 'Ametas and Thestylis',[1] are bound for different versions of paradise. Each of these versions is presented without authorial comment, without irony.[2] The different voices are attended to with patience and, even in the slightest of the poems, with an extraordinary ability to find real life and longing in the simplest statements of desire. Martin's story was one in which he attempted to unify his rather solitary life in consonance with his memories of Arcadia. Here a hunger for paradisal unity is shared between lovers.

Pierre Legouis, considering the strange and disturbing dialogue 'Thyrsis and Dorinda', wondered whether, in the complicated religious life of the mid seventeenth century, Marvell had come upon a nonconformist sect whose hunger for paradise led them to practice suicide pacts.[3] Perhaps he had, for there is reality enough behind the two voices he records. They are the voices of two curiously naïve and yearning people, desirous of the ease, security, sweetness, and harmony of the paradisal. Thyrsis offers its imagery to the woman's imagination. Dorinda conjures it in her thought and in her 'silent thinking'. Thyrsis, prompted further by her heeding him, pictures paradise for them in full sensuous proximity as the realization of all dreams of concord and rest. The pair resolve to take the straightest way to it by means of a potion mixed from poppies and wine:

> So shall we smoothly pass away in sleep.
>
> (48)

Whether this resolve is to be called folly, or delusion, or sin, or faith, or courage, or martyrdom is not revealed by Marvell. What is revealed, without further comment, is the spiritual longing that goes into it. No more, no less.

This tale of the fatal quest for a Glory in which all division will be brought back to unity is handled with no contempt or distaste. We listen, overhear, and are sympathetically taken into the couple's longings and dreams, shadowy and semi-comprehensible though they may remain. Two more voices without a history emerge fleetingly into the public world where religious commitments are made and where poems are written and read. In the end what stands out is a transparent candour, a genuine radiance, and a good deal of love.

The two lovers are anxious that their 'divided Lids' (divided in wakefulness, divided in separateness) should close in unity when 'thou and I' die.[4] Singular pronouns call back and forth to each other in restless protest against individual solitude. The call from one to come 'with mee' gets the response from the other of 'I cannot live without thee'. In the paradise they seek both the importance and the equality of all people, of both sexes, will be established and recognized. The patchy paradise of the earth will be extended and made secure. Sheep, grass, birdsong, garlands, wind, water, and sun, the sources of life's comfort and delight, will no longer be threatened. Wolf, fox, and bear will present no menace. The shepherd's dog will not be needed. There will be an end to all labour and all danger.

Fear and hesitation are gradually overcome. The anxious voice of 'but how can I ...?' is stilled. Momentary miracles of the Arcadian earth, such as the flight of birds and the flickering of flames, are taken into the realm of the human, closed with and made miraculously permanent. Animal life, plant life, and the elements themselves are linked with the human in easy and constant pleasure. The real and the imagined are one. Mind and body are one. What seemed in advance 'a sure but rugged way' is in fact a welcome flood of release, washing over them in sleep.

Clorinda and Damon, a second pair of pastoral lovers beset with thoughts of religion and pleasure, seek a different version of union and a different version of paradise. Pan, who is probably a pastoral image of Christ, wins the couple's devotion in what is therefore a more conventional idea of Christian resolution. The final chorus resolves all in what is probably a stoutly uncomplicated Christianity. But with Marvell one cannot be sure. Pan may be Christ or he may not.[5] And even if he is, there is still that idiosyncratic resonance. The process of arrival at even so foregone a conclusion is not by way of the most well-trodden paths. Here again there is transparency giving on to unusual depths.

In Clorinda's invitations to sexual pleasure, in sun and flowers or in the coolness of a cave, there is some of the same ache to be feasted and rested as went into Thyrsis' and Dorinda's ache for paradise.[6] In Damon's counter-talk of heaven's watching eye and of his meeting with the almost frightening figure of Pan there is a very real sense of dilemma and anxiety. One of Damon's questions, seeking reassurance, gives these depths perhaps more clearly than anything else:

> Might a Soul bath there and be clean,
> Or slake its Drought?
>
> (15-16)

He is troubled by the arresting demands of Pan, yet still drawn by Clorinda's talk of Flora's pride and the hidden 'cool bosome' of the 'unfrequented Cave' where the gaze of God will not be upon them. His question makes one feel his thirst and his fear to satisfy it. One feels him drawn, and then one feels his sudden fear with the addition of 'and be clean'. Then 'slake' and 'Drought', following on full of longing, are immense words to come upon in a poem apparently so conventional.

These lines from Damon haunted Malcolm Lowry's Consul.[7] He recognized in them a figure answering to his own gigantic thirst, fear, and guilt. It is a curious tribute to the power of this little poem that so great a figure of human craving, severance, and bewilderment as the Consul of *Under the Volcano* should have been able, without disproportion, to recognize himself and his desperate condition in Damon's lines.

The third pair of pastoral lovers propose to themselves yet another kind of union, yet another version of paradise. Ametas concludes to a compliant Thestylis:

> Then let's both lay by our Rope.
> And go kiss within the Hay.
>
> (15-16)

It is an even simpler, even more straightforward tale than the last, with the uncomplicated sexual pleasures of libertine pastoral at its end. But even here there is transparency. A sense of real need, and then of release from need, is caught in the poem and its happy resolution. It is release from work, from the ever-winding complexity of those hay-ropes, from strife and threat, from any kind of captivity more consticting than the casual, opportunist, 'looser' bond of love. Even here something real is briefly touched. Both Ametas' opening threat to 'disband' and his warning to Thestylis that 'your selve' is at stake in such matters strike a deeper note than the simple one of pastoral licence. Even here there is an after-image, stronger and longer-lasting than one would expect.

All three couples are given with equal authorial courtesy, equal non-intrusion, equal lack of explanatory context and history. In each case there is simply the readiness to listen. As in the dramatic monologue of the Nymph, so in the dramatic dialogues of these lovers, Marvell is content to dramatize, to record the unique voice and to refrain from commentary.

All are stories of the desire for union, release, and paradisal resolution. It would be a very confident critic who, tracing lines of irony or wit in the poems, could arrange them in such a way as to suggest some system of relative evaluation distinguishing the three kinds of union. But criticism should not attempt such a thing. The different trajectories of different human needs are given as the various modes of a common dilemma. The poems are triumphs of a very Nabokovian artistic scruple and tenderness, like that which tracked the elusive shape of Martin's life and which will later do the same, in perfect miniature, for the life of Hugh Person in *Transparent Things*.[8]

It is the transparency of human things that Marvell has caught in these poems. He seems to know, as Nabokov knows, what elusive depths of imagination and experience may lie beneath the minute fraction of a life which is all that reaches the surface in words and deeds. In these poems the surface clears for the brief duration of a dialogue. Unexpected depth is thereby given to three simple statements of the desire for paradise.

PART THREE

The Tragedy of the Displaced

11

THE WATER FATHER

From the voices of loss in Marvell's love stories one may pass straight on to the great tragic monologues of Damon the Mower. With Nabokov, one could likewise pass directly from the 'lost shades'[1] of his early Russian novels to their descendants in the English-language books, *Pnin* and *Transparent Things*. But while there is continuity there is also change and deepening.

The love poems of Damon are, like the stories of Pnin and Hugh Person, still brief miniature things. But both authors are now[2] masters of suggestive economy and brevity. There are new, even more haunting depths of pain and hungry sentiment to be found in the plight of people severed from an Arcadia for which they still yearn. The new depth becomes a genuinely tragic depth. *Pnin* is often at the brink of tragedy, *Transparent Things* is stretched over an awful void, Damon's voice echoes endlessly in its helpless appeals and confessions. Then finally there is the great tragic figure of Cromwell, 'the Wars and Fortunes Son' of 'An Horatian Ode'.

In Nabokov, the deepening is first a sharing. *Pnin* is a much less exclusive book than *Mary*, *The Defence*, or *Glory*. Pnin himself is much less exclusively its hero and his plight is a much more commonplace one. He is exiled, marginal, and abandoned in country, work, love and marriage. He is a precarious and injured survivor. He has all the uncommonplace distinctions of Ganin and Martin and all the ache to re-find his childhood which they shared with Luzhin. All the images of loss centre in Pnin and all the images of imagination and memory. But now there are others who share in such things. There are many exiles in *Pnin* and many children. There are also many parents, together with people who, like Pnin himself, long to become parents or long to remain parents by holding on to their children.

The vision still centres on Arcadia, childhood, and loss; but there are now countless instances of ordinary loss, ordinary yearning, and ordinary memory. Pnin, the unfortunate hero, must share his book with other people apparently more fortunate, but not necessarily so. He is, as hero, the representative of his fellows rather than their opposite.[3]

This deepening and sharing took time. There is a distinct pause in Nabokov's career as a novelist. The Russian phase lasted a little over a decade during which nine novels followed one another with prolific fluency from 1926 to 1938. There then followed seventeen years which saw the publication only of *The Real Life of Sebastian Knight* in 1941 and *Bend Sinister* in 1947 before the second prolific flowering began with *Lolita* in 1955.

Even the two intervening novels mark a kind of pause for they refer back closely in theme to the last two Russian books. *The Real Life of Sebastian Knight* replays many of the themes of *The Gift*,[4] *Bend Sinister* replays much of *Invitation to a Beheading*.[5] Only with *Lolita* does the new start really come and after it everything is transformed. The new depth of *Pnin*, which immediately followed *Lolita*, is part of this transformation. So is the taut and poignantly muted tragedy of *Transparent Things*.

But there is not only *Lolita* to stand between the Russian 'lost shades' and later forlorn lovers like Timofey Pnin and Hugh Person. The change of language, the Second World War, Nabokov's second exile, a new academic career in the United States: any of these would be sufficient in itself to make for a long pause and a crucial change. This period also saw the first versions of his critical work on Gogol, and of his autobiography, so that Nabokov was still extremely busy, energetic, and creative. But in the novels themselves there is none the less a pause and the transformation is one which stems not only from the world in which Nabokov lived but also from the inner logic of his imagination.

It was an inner imaginative logic which demanded the creation of a father for these sons, exiles and orphans. Luzhin and Martin had their fathers, but the figure stayed firmly in its background place. The father initiated the life of a son and set going the son's story of loss. But it was the son's story that mattered exclusively. The father was a simple, known, categorical figure in the initiating background of a son's life. The son was allowed to determine the space into which the father fitted and from which he did not move. The father was circumscribed as a fact of interest only within the trajectory of the son's life.

Then, at the end of the Russian phase, *The Gift* began to change things.[6] The son's version of the father tried to be categorical, but it was no longer reliable. What the son said about his father was no longer the sole relevant truth, perhaps hardly the truth at all. The father's life was seen to have occupied a space at least the equal of his son's. The father was interesting in his own right. He had a career of his own. He had a wife as well as a son. He was a son in his turn. He too bore a patronymic. What his son saw of him was by no means the whole story.

Nor was any one father necessarily a typical Father. Fyodor's father was the great Count Godunov-Cherdyntsev, but Yasha's father was an ordinary, humble, Russian exile, Chernyschevski's father was a country priest, and Chernyshevski himself was the harassed and fretful father of children he hardly knew. In the cases of Yasha's father and of Chernyshevski it is the 'lost' sons who are seen through the fathers' eyes rather than the reverse; and in both cases it is the father, not the son, whom we see in the sufferings of exile. Matters complicate and deepen. Mystery, distinction, and human depths are no longer the sole prerogatives of sons, nor of any special and exclusive kind of person.

The Real Life of Sebastian Knight[7] carries on from here, investing the father with depths and shadows by giving him two very different sons, each with utterly different experiences of the family. One of them, V, is, like Fyodor in *The Gift*, a narrator who cannot be trusted. The other, Sebastian, can offer his different testimony only through the distorting glass of his half-brother's mind. Everything is thus cast into doubt, including the father, who thus becomes interestingly unknown in his own right.

Then comes *Bend Sinister*, which is Krug's book as much as David's, the father's as much as the son's; then, at last, *Lolita* where, in hopeless comic entanglement, father and child meet as hapless lovers and co-orphans in the long journeys and precarious domiciles of displaced persons. *The Gift*, *The Real*

Life of Sebastian Knight and *Bend Sinister* have brooded over the image of a father. All are very personal. The first two are careful, ironic novels with a sustained autobiographical interest in exiled writers. The third is a political novel which reads like a personal testament. Then comes *Lolita*,[8] a new freedom and a new beginning.

All the old themes and images continue but now they move, change, and develop more freely, transposing material from autobiography to fiction in freshly inventive ways. The old imagery is freed from the inhibitions of the personal, stories open and turn away from exclusivity. *Pnin* and *Transparent Things*, separated from the earlier Russian books by the renewing presence of *Lolita*, carry on the work of the Russian books but, in addition, benefit from the renewal. There is thus continuity but also a radical new depth.

When *Lolita* began the second phase of Nabokov's work his novels had found a new tone and a new form. The new tone is richly comic and the new form is comic romance. But with the turn to comic romance there is also a paradox; for while comic romance is a new form for Nabokov representing a new departure in his work it represents also a turning back towards the traditional core of the Modernist novel. The new start takes Nabokov nearer to his two greatest non-Russian masters in prose, Joyce and Flaubert. Both Joyce and Flaubert stand behind the later fiction. They are behind the comic-romance form of *Lolita* and *Pale Fire*,[9] behind the fictionally transposed autobiography of *Ada* and *Look at the Harlequins!*[10] and behind the delicate mixture of pathos and disbelief in *Pnin* and *Transparent Things*.[11] We are back with the mainstream of the Modernist novel which runs from Flaubert through Joyce to these later books, turning autobiography to fiction, finding indulgently comic romance in the small journeys of ordinary people and above all mingling tones, especially the tones of pathos and laughter, with incomparable expertise.

But *Pnin*,[12] none the less, is a beautiful, small, straightforward book whose appeal is immediate. It hardly requires this propaedeutic excursus into the typical forms of Modernism and the novels of Flaubert and Joyce. Even Joyce, who is the nearer of the two, can be set fairly well back in one's mind, for occasional recognition, as the book is read. Timofey Pnin and Hugh Person descend fairly directly from Martin, Luzhin, and the 'lost shades' of *Mary*. They are joined with them by their innocence, their sadness, their muted distinction of humane spirit, their status as precarious survivors in the world. They are like them in having rich but pained inner lives. They are like them in being able to make sadly little connection between those inner lives and their outer lives as they move hesitantly in the world. They are like them in their hauntedness; and like them they are looked upon with great tenderness by their creator. In all these things they have their Joycean and Flaubertian forebears, reaching back to Mr. Bloom, then back further to Bouvard and Pécuchet, then to Frédéric Moreau, then to Emma Bovary. These are also the things which link them to the speakers of Marvell's monologues and dialogues, including the tragic, 'displac'd' figure of Damon the Mower.

Nabokov thought *The Defence* was the most warm-toned of his Russian books.[13] *Pnin* must surely be the warmest-toned of all. The author, well-tried now (after *The Gift* and *The Real Life of Sebastian Knight*) in the arts of irony and detachment, can afford a more openly affectionate tone than was found in the earlier Russian books. And there is an ease of theme, as well as tone, for the old motif of parent and child recurs, but in a new, non-exclusive, way. Pnin, with his memories of beloved parents, with his childlessness, with his eager love for the boy Victor, is the centre of a book which is however saturated throughout with images of childhood and parenthood. The author is now able to consider loss and severance as part of a widespread, shared dilemma of love. The special dilemma of Pnin himself is an intensification of what is commonplace.

Pnin stays at the Clements' house as a lodger in a room which once belonged to their daughter. He Pninizes the room, erasing the traces of the child's presence, and giving it the imprint of his own. But the room resists him as well. He doesn't notice the child's scribble on the wall, and the child's measurements on the doorjamb, so the life of another child and family is allowed to remain written in what is not only his exclusive text. The same thing happens when the daughter comes back to reclaim her room. Pnin must move on yet again. It is another thread severed in his life. But for the Clements family, the move means quite different things. For them it means that a daughter has left home, is now returning, and will probably leave again. Once more, their stories survive in the text. There is space in the book to see beyond its hero, to look at others who are unlike him but also like him.

The real marvel of the book's non-exclusive spirit is the fifth chapter. It is one of the finest pieces of writing in all Nabokov, interweaving numerous stories of exile, loss, and attempted refinding. Pnin himself is eventually allowed to become the central figure in it, but only after many other voices have been heard.

All the Russian refugees of this chapter participate in the common dilemma. Bolotov reads *Anna Karenina*, and is taken back in memory to the time when he read it as a boy in Russia. Madame Shpolyanski remembers her childhood governess. Praskovia was a nurse to the two Kukolnikov boys in their exile in Harbin. Château was an orphan, deriving his name from a Russianized Frenchman who adopted him. These Russian parents now find themselves with American children who are distant and aloof, hovering in the margins of their parents' nostalgia, and unconcerned with it.

The house where they gather is a place of reunion and memory. Inevitably, it is in a forest; inevitably, there is a stream and a pool. But it is still a place of continuing exile as well. The house's owner is the former Alexandr Petrovich Kukolnikov, now a prosperous American, happily married to an American wife and amiably accepted by his new countrymen as Al Cook. But the theme of severance is still heard poignantly even in his fortunate life. His wife is unable to have children, and his guests are in many ways substitutes for them. Also, his father was tortured to death in a Soviet jail. The kindly American welcome extended to his name has the unintentionally cruel side-effect of re-murdering this dead father. By dropping the patronymic, Petrovich, the memory of Piotr is erased.

The Clements family and the Russian families at Al Petrovich Cook's house are the most important, or the most visible, participants in Pnin's theme. But echoes of it are everywhere. The ticket man at Whitchurch who leaves Pnin luggageless has left work to drive his wife to the maternity hospital. The Hagens have a daughter, glimpsed from time to time in the background of her parents' worries about her. The painter, Lake, dreams of having the talented Victor as his apprentice and surrogate son. Bill Sheppard dreams of the farm where he spent his childhood. Even at the extreme margins of the book, Pnin's images are given to the most minor characters. The college janitor has a gifted son away in the army. Children's books, team pennant, and basketball net remind us of earlier presences in Pnin's house. Pnin got the house only because these children's father had died.

None of this removes Pnin from the centre of the book. Much of it indeed intensifies the pathos of his loneliness and childlessness. None the less, he is obliged to share with his fellows the emotions which the book arouses. His painful solitude is only the most extreme instance of what all sorts of people experience.

Even when Pnin's dilemma is at its most moving, the book's openness to other people continues. His weekend with Victor brings out all Pnin's loneliness. It awakens memories of the cruellest episode in his marriage when his ex-wife Liza coldly deceived him into seeing himself in the role of father. She tricked him, for pragmatic reasons, on the Atlantic crossing to America and then blandly consoled him with the notion that he was 'water father' to the child since he had been its parent for the duration of the ocean crossing. Now the duped and abandoned 'water father' responds eagerly to the idea of a weekend with his surrogate son. The prose catches his anxious care, his fussing efforts to make things go smoothly, his dejection when things go wrong, his rallying to try again. But it still leaves room for Victor to remain separate from him, responding kindly but keeping his distance. Victor is another being with another life to lead. His most intense emotions about fatherhood have nothing to do with Pnin, nor for that matter with Edgar Wind, but with his dream-father, a Slovenian king.

(Pnin meanwhile has become 'water father' to a squirrel by giving it a drink at a public fountain. It is a lonely memorial scene. The squirrel, in its turn, is not effusively grateful.)

The paradox (if something so obvious merits the term) is that the central figure of Pnin becomes thereby more powerful, more poignant, and more singular. As a special case only in degree he is able to represent more than the Russian heroes did. He is a summarizing image of many separate and special lives. He has a transparency through which other lives are perceived. When his imagination goes on the characteristic meandering journey of remembrance, it takes more of us with it. When he recalls pursuing the Arcadian labyrinths of pattern in the wallpaper of his childhood room, more of the mind can follow him than could follow Martin in the same reverie. His memories of childhood amateur theatricals are more involving, less protected as unique, than those in *Mary*. His 'divestment' of the ego in 'communion' with parkland and Arcadian nature belongs to us more completely for being less specialized and less cherished as the only meaningful imaginative experience in the world. It also belongs to us the more for being resisted too, as something which the adult mind, beset with adult realities, cannot always afford to indulge.

Pnin's ordinary and extraordinary readiness to find delight in the bits and pieces of Arcadian colour and Arcadian labyrinth which survive in the post-Arcadian world also bring him closer to us. A thoroughly Joycean genius animates this descendant of Mr Bloom. Mr Bloom dreamt of Flowerville, the New Bloomusalem and the orange groves of the Middle East, but side by side with such exotics went the more mundane concerns of an inhabitant of Eccles Street. As in Bloom, so in Pnin, there is a beautiful dialectic between what is humanly rare and what is humanly commonplace.

In the ease of that dialectic there is play. Neither solemnity nor even seriousness could have given Pnin (or Bloom) with such exact and tender delight. Pnin's words and gestures are rejoiced in as openly as is the author's ability to notice them and recreate them in a language of Joycean, or Flaubertian, mimetic dexterity.[14] Pnin teaching, Pnin putting on a coat, Pnin driving, Pnin swimming, Pnin miming a football, Pnin filmed 'in a polo shirt, a Giaconda smile on his lips' as an illustration of the gestural genius of Russian speech: the book is full of the creator's pleasure in his creature's innumerable small movements. The writing is a festival of the limitless genius of gesture. Its greatest moment of celebration occurs, fittingly enough, with Pnin playing a game. At croquet the normally marginal and awkward Pnin is, for once, the expert:

> the man was transfigured. From his habitual, slow, ponderous, rather rigid self, he changed into a terrifically mobile, scampering, mute, sly-visaged hunchback. It seemed to be always his turn to play. Holding his mallet very low and daintily swinging it between his parted spindly legs (he had created a minor sensation by changing into Bermuda shorts expressly for the game), Pnin foreshadowed every stroke with nimble aim-taking oscillations of the mallet head, and then gave the ball an accurate tap, and forthwith, still hunched, and with the ball still rolling, walked rapidly to the spot where he had planned for it to stop. With geometrical gusto it ran through the hoops, evoking cries of admiration from the onlookers.[15]

The gestural art of play is matched by the mimetic art of narration. Nabokov's narrative games and tricks are beautifully tuned to the human matter of the book.[16] Pnin's forgotten birthday, for example, is timed to steal upon the reader in the form of a couple of poignant afterthoughts, whereby it slowly dawns that his two most painful uprootings take place, unbeknown to him, on the Gregorian equivalent of the Julian date upon which he was born. Nabokov's semi-concealment of the fact is a game, but it serves his human purpose exactly. The coincidence of dates would, if pushed more to the fore, make for sentimental distortion since what happens to Pnin on February 15th, 1953 and 1956, is that he loses his home twice, and finally his job. These are far more important matters than a lost birthday. The game, with the reserve of its concealment, judges the relative stresses to perfection.

There is the same perfect judgement of stress in the game of the squirrel. Nine times the squirrel appears in the novel, but always it remains an elegant pictorial ornament in the margins of the narrative.[17] Its importance, and unimportance, are those of decoration and intriguing coincidence. A succession of squirrels clamouring loudly for our attention would have ruined the book's poise.

The same applies to the game of the narrator. It too serves the human matter of the story. For six chapters we hear the delicate voice of narrative. Then, at the end, Vladimir Vladimirovich emerges from the shadows to take over. Nabokov the novelist, narrating the first six chapters, is a master of deference, play, tact, and sensitivity; the raconteur and memoirist of the last chapter is a ghastly blunderer. The inomniscient novelist gives way to the know-all, a crass intruder, strong in opinions and weak in sympathy. The gentle Pnin cannot possibly survive being molested by such a voice. So he fades from view, eluding his predatory pursuer at the end and leaving the intruder in possession of the well-lit foreground, strutting in the morning sun, cock-sure, with Jack Cockerel's cocker.

This change of voice gives a final heightening to our sense of the muted genius and human greatness of Pnin, whom no such voice could remotely capture. It also heightens our sense of the delicate genius of response necesary to create him. When Nabokov makes play with the idea that novelist and memoirist are the same person, such play suggests how fine may be the line between genuine sensitivity and mere elegance; and how vital an act of self-overcoming is involved in producing the humanity of an artist from within his lesser, opinionated, self.

It is much like the self-overcoming that turned Stephen Dedalus into James Joyce, or that turned Flaubert's bilious projects for a crushing book about human stupidity into the kindly and celebratory comedy of *Bouvard et Pécuchet*. Nabokov the man, with his Strong Opinions, disliked the paintings of Van Gogh. Nabokov the novelist, however, saw and respected the print of his characters' lives on all their belongings, including the reproduction of Van Gogh's 'La Berceuse' on Bill Sheppard's wall. No rousting is given to Sheppard for his poor taste; nor to the Clements, for all that 'Girl with a Cat' and 'The Belated Kid' hang in their daughter's bedroom; nor even to Gramineev who executes a painting called 'Three Old Friends', glossed by Nabokov as 'lad, nag, dog'. Excessive aesthetic punctilio has gone. The prose is kind to many tastes.

The delicate record of the life of Timofey Pnin is built on a transmutation of the basic Nabokovian image of Arcadia lost, yearned for, and perhaps fitfully found. All the basic details of the image are there, but tacit now and submerged, lying beneath the story rather than on its surface. Pnin had his 'fervid and receptive' youth and now he has his reverie in Whitchurch Park, the sense of 'expansion' involved in pursuing Arcadian labyrinths, the poignant dreams of Russian wildwood and racemosa, the partial recovery of it all at a country house, reached through a 'maze of forest roads', in a landscape of exile which is like and unlike its Russian original. He has his Arcadian imaginative integrity, preserved in Pninized form in his respose to the fitful delights of the post-Arcadian world. He keeps faith with Arcadian labyrinthine complexity in his enthusiasm for electricity, zip-fasteners, chess, croquet, the intricacy of a cunning lock on his filing cabinet and the whirling tangle of dolphin-clothes in the glass door of a washing machine.

Above all he is a man who keeps faith with Arcadian colour as it sunbursts from time to time to the receptive eye. Such colour survives precariously in the lilac light of his sun-lamp, in the pink and pearly deep-sea flora of his new false teeth in a glass, in the night-time lights of Waindelville suburb, in his crystal candlesticks refracting the morning sun, in his sybaritic smoking jacket of blue silk with tassels and satin lapels, and finally, triumphantly, in the aquamarine bowl, full of its own light and of the 'blazoned blur' and 'brilliant being' of its donor, which he lifts from the 'carnival storm' of its wrapping paper and lifts again, mercifully unbroken, from the shining suds of his washing-up basin.

12

THE WOUNDS OF DAMON

The greatest of Marvell's childlike, displaced people are his Mowers. It was their good fortune to live close to the simplicity and easy riches of Arcadia; but then it is their tragedy to be, like Pnin, Hugh Person, and their Russian predecessors, easy prey to invaders from a tougher world.

There are Mowers at Nun Appleton working and dancing in the meadows, half-way between the elaborate garden and the unworked wildwood. It is a Mower who speaks the poem of complaint against the elaborate gardens of 'luxurious man', accusing him of turning his back upon the 'wild and fragrant Innocence' of the Mower's simpler world.[1] But the poems of the Mower's wounding are the love-poems, 'Damon the Mower', 'The Mower to the Glo-Worms', and 'The Mower's Song'.[2] They are three marvellous poems in which the fatal Juliana has, as invader, wrought havoc with a peaceful, pre-pastoral world where Mowers (not shepherds or reapers, who are much less primitive beings) were once at home.

The Mower's voice in these three great poems is uncannily haunting. It comes from much further back than pastoral, further back in the mind and memory, back in a deep, primitive vision of a world violated and lost. Once caught, the Mower's tone will never be forgotten. His voice is hapless, defencelessly candid, normally muted in lament, though once he is driven to call out in desperation for revenge on his sophisticated tormentor. He is one of the most abiding presences in the works of either author, matching even Milton's fallen Adam as a great, tragic seventeenth-century image of man exiled from paradise.

Not even Pnin and Hugh Person have this stature. They are the greatest summarizing images of the lives of all Nabokov's 'lost shades', but even with them Nabokov dares not be quite as simple, direct, and tenderly unguarded as Marvell is in these three poems. The lovelorn Mower reaches back into all one's sense and memory of loss, privation, and bewilderment, back into all dreams of a simpler, less aggressive, less conscious world. His voice comes from somewhere naïve and primal, from 'Nature's Cradle' or from the 'Nursery of all things green'.[3]

He speaks of his present plight and deracination with awesome directness:

> My Mind was once the true survey
> Of all these Medows fresh and gay;
> And in the greenness of the Grass
> Did see its Hopes as in a Glass.[4]

That undistorting glass gave back a faithful reflection. Light passed in clear, unbroken, unrefracted lines from an undeceiving world to an undeceived mind. The 'true survey' recorded the unfalsified image, giving the Mower's mind the same authentic innocence as may be found at Fairfax's estate where Maria is brought up in a world which is said to be the *only Map* of paradise.[5] His 'survey', like that *'Map'*, can be trusted not to distort; so his hopes lie easily on the surface of things and the freshness of the meadows flows unimpeded into his receptive mind, as at Nun Appleton it flows from garden to child.

These four lines say everything about the bewildered lovers of Marvell's world and everything about the Nabokovian heroes whom we see reaching back along the twisted, distorted or fractured lines of their lives to a half-remembered time in childhood when the world was made of meadows and the mind 'was once' in easy contact with them. The Mower is a distillation of all one's sense of conscious and adult life as a kind of distortion, an outrage against the greenness of the grass. He is naïve and candid enough to say such things directly and without eloquence. His ineloquent brevity allows every word to hang clear in its envelope of silence.

In 'Damon the Mower' his simple gifts for Juliana are offered with pathetic candour and expectation. The gifts are rejected and the giver ignored. Stung by the rejection he is moved to stake a claim for recognition of the significance of his life and being. He presents himself as an uncomplicated man, warmed by the sun, refreshed by the dew and completing the pattern of his days by 'going home' in the sweetness of the evening. Does he not in his primitive agricultural work scythe more ground than is taken up by the whole flock of that sophisticated, affluent and leisured man, the shepherd? Is he not rich in hay even as the shepherd's sheep are rich in wool? Is it not a kind of fleece, indeed a 'golden fleece', that he shears when he mows the dry grass for hay? Is he not led in dances by 'deathless Fairyes'? Perhaps the Mower himself hears, as we certainly do, a note of futility in this rather desperate listing of his minor triumphs, though there is at the same time real gold in his fleece of autumn grass.

But the sense of troubledness grows as he makes these claims for himself. There is something plaintive in his insistence that he is not 'deform'd to sight' and in his anxiety about being outdone by shepherds and sheep. He seems to glimpse the comfortable, wealthy shepherd, ominously secure in the background of his fear. The Mower's woe and disturbance are audible even in the earnestness of his claims. They come to a stumbling climax when he cuts his own leg with his scythe. The stricken Mower blunders and falls in the scorching world of Juliana where only the glittering snake and the shepherd survive, the one crafty the other 'piping' in unconcern as he surveys his 'unnum'red Flock'. The wounded Mower is more like the 'hamstring'd frogs' who limp along in the summer heat of Juliana's influence.

The man used to 'going home' in the sweetness of the evening becomes, in 'The Mower to the Glo-Worms' a lost, nocturnal traveller in a world where 'I shall never find my home'. He recollects with tenderness and undefended straightforwardness the 'matchless' songs of the nightingale and the 'courteous' lights of the glow-worms. His gratitude to these sources of pleasure and security in his unsophisticated and intimately known world is full of his characteristic candour. So too is his modest sense of himself as a wanderer, a chaser after foolish fires, a man who cannot live without the regular assurances of his known and benign world. So too is his straightforward, utterly ineloquent confession of the devastation wrought by Juliana:

> She my Mind hath so displac'd
> That I shall never find my home.   (15-16)

That 'displac'd' mind was once the 'true survey' of its world.

Here, in the awesome quiet of these poems, are all the lost Arcadias, lost childhoods, uprootings, and exiles of Nabokov's world. The Mower is like a prime original for all the individual lives of Nabokov's heroes. Those heroes are like the fragments of the Mower's unitary being. They all carry with them the tormenting memory of the true survey. The Mower's troubled sense of being insignificant or deformed, audible in his very denial, seems to lurk everywhere in the precariousness of their lives and their occasional claims for themselves.

Nabokov has his Julianas too, the tormentors of his uprooted heroes. Sonia, Liza, and Armande are to Martin, Pnin and Hugh Person what Juliana is to the Mower.[6] They all have a glitter and hardness which makes them successful in a world through which their lovers, husbands, and ex-husbands limp with such discomfort.

Then there is the glittering snake saved by his craft, and the shepherd whom the Mower glimpses over his shoulder. Again they are everywhere in Nabokov, exasperating figures of comfort, success, or strength where Nabokovian Mowers are uncomfortable, failing, and weak. Both Pnin and Hugh Person are ominously overshadowed by acclaimed and successful authors, the one by the smooth-talking Vladimirovich, the other by 'R', the rich writer of suspect prose who lounges in his mountain villa while Hugh toils along in the world below. Another of Pnin's numerous displacers, Falternfels, who muscles in on Pnin's study as Wind and Vladimirovich had muscled in on his wife, strongly recalls that 'piping' shepherd as he sits at his gleaming desk, smiling all the time as he writes the academic articles that will soon secure his elevation above the likes of Pnin. Humbert too is pursued and tormented by such a figure in the person of the successful author Quilty, whose gleaming, expensive, high-octane, sexually symbolic sports car plants itself irremovably in poor Humbert's fleeing rear-view mirror.

The Mower speaks out of their collective dilemma. He is a great mythological image set up unforgettably in a handful of small poems. Once his pain is too much for him. In 'The Mowers's Song' there is a cry for revenge upon his tormentor and a desperate resolve to snatch back from the clutches of the intruder both himself and his world, by destroying both:

> But what you in compassion ought
> Shall now by my Revenge be wrought:
> And Flow'rs, and Grass, and I and all,
> Shall in one common Ruin fall.
>
> (19-22)

The fates of Luzhin, Hugh, and Humbert are written there. So are the repeated thoughts of defeat and hopelessness which Pnin has to shake from himself to renew once more the long effort of his precarious survival.

The vision of the three brief poems is powerful beyond all expectation. Marvell has caught to perfection the pace and rhythm of the Mower's voice, the tone of his singing and of his intimate speech. We hear the tramp of his primitive music in 'Damon the Mower':

> I am the Mower *Damon*, known
> Through all the Meadows I have mown.
>
> (41-2)

We hear the dignified measure of his speech in 'The Mower to the Glo-Worms'. We hear the collapse of words and music together in the extended, limping final line of the stanzas of 'The Mower's Song':

> For Juliana comes, and She
> What I do to the Grass, does to my Thoughts and Me.
>
> (29-30)

The poems are brief. 'The Mower to the Glo-Worms' consists of a single sentence. They achieve their intensity with astonishing speed and with no clamorous rhetoric. Their language is, even by Marvellian standards, extraordinarily rich. Marvell has the self-effacing tact of a great listener; and his language then has the complexity to remain undistortingly faithful to everything that he hears. A whole life thus seems to come, unimpeded and unglossed, through these transparent things. What Milton gave on an epic scale in the tremendous post-lapsarian speeches of Adam, Marvell has given, in miniature but with comparable power and depth, in these hapless speeches of Damon.

13

OUVRE TA ROBE, DÉJANIRE

The Arcadian colour of Pnin's aquamarine bowl and Ganin's 'bright labyrinth'[1] of memory bursts upon Hugh Person when he meets a woman in a train 'one dazzling afternoon'. Her hands are gloved in black, her suit is black, her eyes are dark, but there is a spot of colour in the 'flame-and-soot' paperback which she holds in her lap. The paperback is called *Figures in a Golden Window*, which brings more colour into the scene. But the colour that really matters is that of her 'honey-hued' skin. *Transparent Things*[2] traces Hugh's fatal obsession with it.

A good deal of that fascinating skin is visible to Hugh's enraptured eyes for 'her skirt was very short'. His memory of her that evening will be dominated by its colour, spreading from

adorable naked brown legs and golden sandals (to) toffee-cream neck with a tiny gold cross and a *grain de beauté*. (Ch. 9)

By then she has completely taken over his imagination. She is 'the new irresistible person'. She stirs thoughts of 'paradise' and 'translucence':

lovely girl, lovely wake of the sun through semi-transparent black fabric. (Ch. 9)

But, as with Juliana, the sun is fire as well as light, heat as well as brilliance. It is fire as well as light as, in the late afternoon, when the train is running by a lake, it ripples and reddens in the water; and, looking back, the 'flame-and-soot' cover of her book is much more suggestive of fire and burning than merely of colour. Hugh's reveries stir about the subject; but at a key point he switches to French and half conceals there (from himself perhaps, as well as from his readers) an ominous word and an ominous name:

Ouvre ta robe, Déjanire that I may mount *sur mon bûcher*. (Ch. 9)

If her dress opens what he will mount is a *bûcher*, a funeral pyre or flaming faggot. The woman who fascinates him is *Déjanire*, Deianira, the wife of Herakles with whom the centaur fell in love and who, in her hapless anxiety to hold on to her husband inadvertently caused his terrible burning death in the shirt of Nessus which the aggrieved centaur had poisoned.

Colour and brilliance are tokens of delight, of brimming desire and of 'irresistible' attraction. But the main colours of the book are the colours of flame, evoking the poisoned shirt of Nessus and the flame of Herakles' funeral pyre. *Transparent Things* looks back for motifs and inspiration to the great tragedy of domestic love and misfortune in Sophokles' *Women of Trachis*. Hugh is partly the centaur, a misshapen, rejected, Mower-like figure. He is also partly Herakles himself, the husband, a big man with strong hands who is fatally burnt. In both roles he suffers miserably.

This is the last of Nabokov's love-stories. It is sad and hapless and, in its miniature way, it has some of the tragic impassivity of the great Greek play. This very short novel presents the life of an Unfortunate Lover in the slenderest outline. But such now is Nabokov's sensitivity to this kind of fleeting, semi-visible, semi-audible life that he is able to give his hero a strong, abiding presence in our after-memory of the book. The narrative veers and circles about the chronology of a life, touching a salient detail here and there until he has caught his man as deftly as may be, live, unharmed by the weight of any heavier rhetoric.

Hugh Person has a name, an individuality. The name is completely his, for as the first non-Russian in this series of heroes he is the first man without a patronymic. But his surname is about as near to the anonymity of namelessness as a name could be; and he will recede further still when his Swiss wife mispronounces his Christian name and he becomes a mere You Person.

Person had a sad childhood, somewhat reminiscent of the nameless Luzhin's. His father was headmaster of the school where Person was a pupil. Person was the recipient of 'cruel remarks about his father' made by his school-fellows. Luzhin's father, the author of books for boys, was in a similarly expanded, all-embracing tutorial-parental role.

The father is elderly. Person is twenty-two when he dies. The son's life is in some ways prefigured by the life of his father, who suffered the 'lone grief' of a widower and who had 'clumsy hands' which fumbled with 'inept gropings'. Both lives engage painfully with

handwringing ... in the dark of remorse, in the dungeon of the irreparable. (Ch. 25)

The son of this father used to sleep-walk naked when a child. He 'begged to be locked up' at night, in fear and humiliation. In later life he is still subject to dreadful nightmares wherein the immense, submerged, inner life of his being renders the small, precarious outer life of a 'nervous male' defenceless. He is rather tangentially employed in a job which makes no demands on this inner being and his sex-life is said to be 'blundersome'. Both predicaments are caught in a sad and mischievous pun. Hugh is said to be 'a rather ordinary American with a not very solid job'.

The centaur part of him is probably given in his 'long, lean, doleful face' and slightly 'horsey' appearance. He is less attractive than Pnin, being 'a sulky person', 'sullen' in his work. Formerly he had been cruelly curt and impatient with his father's fumblings and blunderings. The prose Nabokov uses for him is much cooler in tone than the prose of *Pnin*. There is always something half-amused, half-mocking, blended in with its kindly sympathy for the plight of 'our poor friend', whereas the prose used for 'my poor Pnin' always smiled warmly and indulgently upon its recipient.

The waking world in which the surface of Hugh's being engages in the tangential blunderings of employment and sex concerns only a small part of him. The rest, the much greater part, where his 'real fancies and feelings are housed', is scarcely graspable. To probe far into it would involve matters 'too sad, too frightful, to face'. He is once thought of kindly as 'a young man of dark genius'. Once, with whimsical generosity, his inner being is surmised as possessing something called 'fantastic majesty', though whether the surmiser is a sympathetic Nabokov or a narcissistic Hugh is left beautifully and tantalizingly in doubt. There would seem to be inner labyrinth and colour in him but no sustaining memories linger from his sad childhood to draw the Arcadian element into connection with the adult present. Between the 'angular bulk' of the outer man and the 'fantastic majesty' (if such it is) of his 'dark genius' (if such it is) there is hardly any discourse. When his 'fantastic majesty' is alluded to, Hugh, a gangling and stooping person, is standing, as Ganin once did, in the narrow cage of a lift. His tale is simple but extraordinarily powerful. The miniaturist in Nabokov, the author of the fine, Chekhovian short stories, is helping the novelist to a supreme economy. The typical outlines of a Nabokov story are given with masterly brevity. The coloured, labyrinthine man breaks the surface of his drab, waking world when he falls in love with a women on a dazzling, sunlit train. He breaks it again when he kills her in a nightmare of flames. Then both men, inner and outer, are consumed in a final fire in a hotel.[3] That last fire is the shirt of Nessus and the funeral pyre of Herakles.

The first phase watches the birth of Hugh's love for the fascinating, coloured, translucent woman, 'the bare-thighed girl in the sun-shot train' whose vibrant reality in the mind makes the reality of the real mere 'sham and waxworks'.[4] Colour and lyricism grow richer as a 'gangling and gloomy' person's waking mind is overwhelmed by a brilliant dream. The sun and gold of her grow in his mind and the prose watches them grow with masterly tenderness and never quite silent amusement.

The prose of the second phase, when they are married and the exasperating, glittering coldness of Armande is established, again combines tenderness and mockery in its tone. Here the 'humming frost of her tidy mind' hums relentlessly. She is all coolness, unlovableness, self-centredness, bitchiness, and 'morbid *amour-propre*', but none of this can undo any of Hugh's love for her or his need to love her. The 'armor-smooth stockings' which she wears during their 'decently-clothed' love-making drive poor Hugh to the extremity of frustrated desire and the prose retains both its helpless sympathy and its quiet mockery. He interrupts his study

to walk into her room and advance toward her on his knees and elbows like an ecstatic, undescribed, unarboreal sloth, howling his adoration.
(Ch. 17)

He tries to break down the extremity of her resistance with the extremity of his words:

my princess, my sweetheart, my angel, my animal, my exquisite beast.
(Ch. 17)

Still the calm prose looks on in near silence.

Hugh is 'perplexed and distressed' by her sexual peculiarities. He is denied even the ordinary, daily affection and kindness of marriage. Her sexual exploits with 'only a dozen crack lovers' on three skiing trips are mercifully kept secret from him, at any rate from his waking mind.

Our Person's capacity to condone all this, to find reasonable explanations and so forth, endears him to us, but also provokes limpid mirth, alas, at times. (Ch. 17)

What relevant response could there be, other than this impassivity and calm, touched with 'limpid mirth, alas, at times'? What more commentary or explanation or token of authorial viewpoint could be given, or wanted? The prose can offer no more, so the half-bewildered chapter on the nature of love simply stops short in a kind of sudden, helpless vacancy: 'we must end now our discussion of love'.

The story goes inevitably on. The husband is at best allowed, on infrequent occasions,

to touch with reverent lips her temple and a strand of blond hair.
(Ch. 19)

Often she feigns 'a feminine ailment to keep him away'. But his love for her is 'ever growing, ever more tender'. It can hardly be explained, no more than can the love of Pnin for Liza, or of Martin for Sonia, or of Cincinnatus for Marthe, where the sad motif of the Mower and Juliana appears again and again. Here the Mower is again displaced and wounded, Juliana again a figure of fire. The inner Hugh, who probably knew of the existence of the twelve crack lovers and who may have guessed the nature of those feminine ailments and even suspected the presence of the marks of love hidden on her body by her refusal to undress, breaks out again amidst flames and lurid light. He kills this Juliana in his sleep while dreaming that the house is on fire, haunted by a flickering, violet electric sign outside their window.

At the end, after eight years of fruitless attempts to explain in the clumsy prose of psychoanalysis what cannot even be explained in the infinitely more subtle prose of this marvellous short novel, Hugh will mount his *bûcher* in the third phase of his life. The hotel burns in a mockery of a consummation and Hugh burns with it in some kind of distraught reunion with a woman who died in flames:

flames were mounting the stairs, in pairs, in trios, in redskin file, hand in hand, tongue after tongue, conversing and humming happily ... As he reached the window a long lavender-tipped flame danced up to stop him with a graceful gesture of its gloved hand. (Ch. 26)

At the last moment his mind goes back to his childhood:

rings of blurred colour circled round him, reminding him briefly of a childhood picture in a frightening book about triumphant vegetables whirling faster and faster around a nightshirted boy trying desperately to awake from the iridescent dizziness of dream life. (Ch. 26)

But these now are not the colours of Arcadian memory, linking dream to dream and weaving together the disparate elements of a life, but the nightmare shreds of their dissolution roaming free and fearful round a body that is all angles and torment.

Transparent Things is a great book about love recorded, as in *Pnin*, in the loss of it. It is a great book about sex, picking up themes that were there in Pnin's helplessly continuing passion for the unreciprocating (but to him still blazingly coloured) Liza.

Like *Pnin* it is also generous enough not to insist upon entire exclusivity for the dilemma of the central character. Where Hugh is blundersome others are sexually athletic. At any rate they say they are, or think they are, or are thought by him to be. But there is no special plea, no aggressive comparative dismissal, or even explanation, of Armande or Julia or R, whose apparent sexual prowess gives them something denied to fumbling Hugh. Nor is much comment ventured upon that bright trio of sexual alpinists, Jack, Jake, and Jacques, who glitter in the high snows in their coloured anoraks; nor on Madame Chamar, whose 'main bulk', now inserted with difficulty into a swim-suit and a deck-chair, would seem to have had its day; nor on the widowed romantic author Mrs Flankard (perfect name) who looks at Hugh in a way which suggests that she is considering having her day again. The book is far too kindly and unopinionatedly disposed towards the sexual dilemma of the human body, unreasonably asked to bring true all dreams, to give Hugh any false uniqueness. Instead it gives him the transparency of Pnin or the Mower. Through them all allied dilemmas can be seen a little more sympathetically.

Person's Arcadia blazes on fatal occasions. It will otherwise only haunt him with its unreachableness. He trudges through the forest, but gets rained on. Anyway, the forest in question is only 'a dismal group of old firs' with 'thickets of wet willow herb': the combination of greenery and water is not always Arcadian. His story is told with subdued compassion. The book doesn't have, or pretend to have, the warmth of *Pnin*. Its play is muted. Its narrative has its games, but they are quiet games of only fitful festivity, more elaborate in some ways than the narrative games of *Pnin* but much more reserved and austere in atmosphere. Its prose is clear, calm, utterly unclamorous, and with that trace of amusement attending all its dealings with the sad comedy of Person's blunders. Slight stylistic ripples on a calm surface do all the work of such prose. Single telling words, semi-puns, momentary flashes of lyricism or tiny gestural movements of syntax are enough to record the immense presence of that 'much greater portion' of a life which lies below.

So, surrounded by silence and given all the attentiveness of which Nabokov is now the master, Hugh's story is haunting out of all proportion to what one might expect of such brevity. It is uncannily like Marvell's Damon poems:

> Only for him no Cure is found
> Whom *Juliana's* Eyes do wound.
> 'Tis death alone that this must do.[5]

It also has something of the tragic impassivity of the great Greek play to which it alludes:

> You have seen a terrible death
> and agonies, many and strange, and there is
> nothing here which is not Zeus.[6]

14

THE WOUNDS OF CROMWELL

On the face of it the Cromwell of 'An Horatian Ode'[1] could hardly be less like Damon. Damon wandered and strayed, permanently benighted, permanently out of touch with his home, no longer guided back by the glow-worms' lights. Cromwell marches indefatigably on through the night, terrifying the nocturnal spirits not so much with the Christian cross of his sword's hilt as with the steel of its blade, held upright and ungirt.[2] His tread is weighty, his march straight, his force virtually irresistible. He has broken from the pack of his rivals and colleagues. He has brought down the King and the Irish. The Scots will be next, shrinking from him and hiding from his hunting dogs in the undergrowth. He seems lethal.

But for all that there is another side to him which recalls the Mower, and which takes the idea of severance and deracination to new levels of genuinely tragic intensity. This altogether more formidable inhabitant of the post-Arcadian world of politics and war was once a gardener, a planter of pear-trees. Now, in the chilly, bleaker world of his marches, he is arguably a lonely and certainly a wounded man. He is perhaps also an exhausted man, or a man braced against exhaustion only by his will and his relentlessness. He is a man who, as the falcon of war, is not allowed to rest for long from his labours on the 'green Bow'. He is a man who accepts his wounds as the ordinary price of our 'forward', 'restless', and 'adventurous' condition in the non-Arcadian world. Such acceptance is brave; but it also has a tragic side.

The 'Horatian Ode' is a notorious riddle of complicated tones. It is also one of the works in which the equally notorious riddle of Marvell's political allegiances in and around 1650 is centred. The classic and brilliant analysis of it by Cleanth Brooks[3] has, for thirty years, been the model for critical attempts to get at its tone and significance. The words with which Cromwell seems to be praised carry, as Brooks saw, a powerful counter-sense of violence, impulsion, and frightening single-mindedness into the portrait. How do the thrusts and counter-thrusts of irony weigh in the final balance of the poem? Is 'irony' the right word for such an extreme and urgent drama of tonal conflict?

There have been critics who, *pace* Brooks, see no riddle in the Ode itself. Brooks has sometimes been found perversely ingenious and the Ode's praise of Cromwell secure, despite reservations.[4] But it is hard to be convinced by such attempts to make Marvell behave less troublesomely. There has, on the other hand, been another way of getting rid of this trouble which has been more widespread. Brooks's point has been taken. The poem has been seen to be full of irony. Marvell, one may therefore conclude, is impartial, non-partisan, fair-minded. He praises Cromwell, but with reserve; and he is broad-minded enough to praise the dead King as well. Such is his poise, his balance, his urbanity. This way the irony is acknowledged, and then the problem resolved by the political idea of the man of the centre who is fair and who takes no sides.[5]

But this overtly political solution to the poem's problems takes away from it all its dramatic force, its passion and torment, the violent play of its contraries, its highly-charged and highly personal life.[6] The great poet who poured his anxiety, fear, anger, and sorrow into the poem is cut down by such language to the untroublesome figure of the fair-minded man of the centre. For Brooks, the ironies raised the temperature of the poem; but the ordinary idea of Marvell as non-partisan sees his ironies as lowering the temperature, establishing easy distance. The effect is to tame the poem. It may be that what we most need to learn from Brooks now is not so much his sense of the ironies themselves, as his sense of the human temperature of the poem in which they are brought to urgent and dramatic life.

Brooks argued against the notion of 'indifference' and 'Olympian detachment'. Nor was 'impartiality' a sufficient word:

To read it in this fashion is to miss what seems to me to be a passionate interest in the issues ... My own guess is that some young Cavaliers who shed their blood for the King thought and felt less deeply about the issues than does the speaker of this poem.[7]

This 'passion' and 'interest' are urgent and human. The compound attitude which they breed in the poem is felt as one which, however complex, 'could be held by a human being'. But at the high temperature of dramatic and personal engagement: it is not a matter of 'the cold and detached honest broker between the factions'.

Reading the poem at the right temperature, we find that there is a great deal of violence, carried by such words as 'burning', 'rent', 'ruine' and 'blast', in the poem's opening account of the Cromwellian drive. There is a great deal of sarcasm involved when the emergence of this drive is linked with the pushy court or metropolitan career of a 'forward Youth' who wants to 'appear'. There is a strong sense of outrage and violation in the declaration that just and rightful complaint against Cromwell is 'vain', and in the statement that his power makes all moral protest 'Madness'.

Whatever else it might also be, the Cromwellian spirit is a headlong, destructive force of violation and ruin driving all before it. It rides roughshod over protests in the name of traditional justice. It looks upon ordinary hesitation with a casual insensitivity which is sarcastically imitated in ''tis all one ... Emulous or Enemy'. It is bitterly satirized as capable of dismissing all the 'Arts of Peace' with the single contemptuous word 'inglorious'. Its 'Courage high' is made to seem heady and reckless. Its masculinity is full of a sense of rapine, as the 'comely Head' of the King is laid on the block 'as upon a Bed' at the moment when Cromwell's 'forced Pow'r' has its way with him before the deed is applauded by men of blood and armour.

The victim's mind is innocent, without meanness, commonness, or spite. Cromwell's mind, on the other hand, is not said to be capable of more than cruel cunning, 'twining subtile fears with hope'. It may further be hinted that even cunning is beyond him since the real story of the King's flight from Hampton to Carisbrooke was not so much a matter of Cromwell's 'wiser Art' as of his luck. He may simply be irresistible, and fated to win. If we therefore call him 'the Force of angry Heaven's flame' we may be making some grim acknowledgement of God and His ministering purges. Or we may simply be talking of mere thunder and lightning ('Heaven' is a tricky word) and glamourizing a phenomenon of brute force ('as men are strong or weak') with an untenable theological apology.

These strong and often highly sarcastic ironies from the poem's first half cannot simply be removed. The terrible work they do in diminishing Cromwell cannot be undone, nor could it be cancelled by some equal and opposite praise which would leave the whole poem poised and urbane in its political balance. If the poem did attempt to undo their force it would hardly be very admirable, for its duplicity could then only involve an attitude of studied indifference and mandarin externality. It would be politically safe, perhaps; even poised. But it would be a good deal less than human. It would involve a retreat from the pained and passionate anxiety which these ironies have brought to life and a reduction of the ironies to a kind of cleverness.[8]

What the poem does in fact add is not an equal and opposite praise. There is actually very little in the poem which can with any accuracy be called praise. 'Much to the Man is due' and 'So much one Man can do', which sound most like the rhetoric of praising, are riddled with disbelief, the praise taken away by sarcasm as soon as it is offered. What one can however find, neither in competition with the irony nor removed by it, is the language of a profound sorrow. There is pathos, sympathy, and a candidly recorded sense of helplessness in the face of an unresolvable dilemma. Such things prevent the sarcasm and irony from writing off their recipient. Instead they make the poem keep faith with Cromwell as a human being. They bind Marvell to Cromwell by making Cromwell seem as helpless and sorrowing in his driving career as Marvell is helpless and sorrowing in beholding it. The ironies still hold and work, uncancelled, but they are joined with an extraordinary weight of sorrow at the Cromwellian condition. Cromwell is, and remains, terrible; but he is also helpless, made by something not himself. In this way he is as unfortunate as the Unfortunate Lover and as forlorn as the wounded Mower.

> So restless *Cromwel* could not cease
> In the inglorious Arts of Peace.
>
> (9-10)

What force is it that has made Cromwell 'restless'? What is it that is born in this unquiet brain, propelling the man so that he 'could not', even if he chose, live with satisfaction in the 'Arts of Peace'? What misfortune is involved in having such an 'active Star', to which his own urging is eventually leagued but which puts the ultimate source of his career outside him and beyond his power to resist or control? What does it feel like for a human being to be possessed by the mere 'force' of an angry Heaven, or to have the tremendous energy of an active star and of 'Heavens flame' burning in him, whether the star and the heaven are theological or merely cosmological? What misfortune is there in being a creature who is 'nurst' not in a nursery but in the inhuman and unpropitious environment of lightning and thunder-clouds?

The birth of the Unfortunate Lover 'in a *Cesarian Section*' was a violent affair, prelude to a life of torment. The birth of the Cromwellian drive is just as terrible. He

> Did thorough his own Side
> His fiery way divide.
> (15-16)

The metaphor is very highly charged. There is a kind of meteoric magnificence in it. But it suggests too the mutilation of his own body and self in Cromwell's violent separation from his savage nursery and in his ruthless separation of himself from his own colleagues.

The imagery of restlessness and unquiet gives Cromwell as the suffering victim of powers beyond himself. Even when he lived in his 'private Gardens',

> As if his highest plot
> To plant the Bergamot,
> (31-2)

an outside force was at work within him. His life was 'private', 'austere', 'reserved', his mind preoccupied in quiet among his pear-trees. But a power external to himself was already stirring, already preparing, independently of Cromwell's consciousness, the ferocious transformation which turned the garden plot to a political plot. It seems to work independently of any 'wiser Art' of Cromwell's own.

Hence the tremendous sense of sadness and of Cromwell's suffering of a malign force within him in the reference to his 'industrious Valour' and the 'deepest Scars' which he receives on the battlefield. Brooks was right to be arrested by 'industrious

Valour', to find it 'a strange collocation'.[9] As the phrase sinks into the mind, 'industrious' comes to seem a more and more wretched word to apply to 'Valour'. The boldness of emotional and physical life suggested by the noun seems caricatured by the idea of extended labour in the attendant adjective. All the sorrow of Cromwell's condition is there in the aura of this unforgettable phrase.

So it is too in the image of his scars. They are the bravely accepted wounds of a great soldier. But as with the Mower cutting his own leg, so with Cromwell's scars: Marvell is uncannily able to suggest both body and mind cut into by the accidents and adventures of the unfortunate in the post-Arcadian world. Perhaps these wounds are even more dreadful than the wound of the Mower because Cromwell, now leagued with his destiny, is not heard to complain of what is being done to the life of a man who once lived quietly among his trees.

So the fierce and painful ironies of the poem's disbelief in Cromwell are not combined with some fair-minded praise to give the whole work political balance and moral urbanity. They combine rather with horrified sorrow to give something visionary in intensity and not graspable in purely political terms. Cromwell, a man of violence, is made of susceptible flesh that can be deeply scarred. An ungovernable, apparently free force that cuts through all sanction, he is none the less also beheld in the pathos of his bondage. His career, or the career of the power within him, is horrifying, and the poem's vision has bleakness enough never to retreat from that sense of horror. But it has openness and generosity enough too not to retreat from a humane knowledge of him as an unfortunate man marked by the gods for battles that will damage him as much as they will damage anyone else. Is it any worse to be a shrinking Pict than to be a man from whom people shrink?

This powerful tonal drama continues in the latter part of the poem. There is a great deal of sarcasm in the unlikely claim that the Irish, after Drogheda and Wexford, are now ready to praise the justice and goodness of their conqueror. There is heavy irony in the analogy of Hannibal's invasion of Italy, which ended after all in defeat. The image of Cromwell's dogs hunting the Scots is, as we have seen, fraught with violation and ransacking. The imagery of falconry is similarly predatory, and it also suggests the dangerous, unpredictable, never quite controllable will of the hawk once it is free. If it really does come back so dutifully to the 'green Bow' why does the falconer still have to 'lure' this precariously trained creature? The probing, disbelieving irony continues unremittingly.[10]

But so does the pathos evoked by Cromwell's own captivity, the violence done to him, his loneliness. We note the isolation of the 'one Man' who conquers Ireland, and of this man, doomed now to his restlessness and industriousness, who must alone fulfil so many different obligations. We note his lack of freedom in the falcon imagery, for if he is the hawk that kills, he is also the flaconer's captive, blindfold, tethered with jesses, released only to kill in a single flight before being caught again by its master and brought down from that 'green Bow' in a firm grip where the falconer 'has her sure'. We note the second 'strange collocation' in which valour is involved, 'this Valour sad', which is as profound and memorable as the first, activating both the available seventeenth-century meanings of the adjective, as 'steadfast' or 'sober', and as 'sorrowful', in a second, grim caricature of more romantic notions of valour.

By the end the unfortunate Cromwell is a figure of bleak power indeed:

> But thou the Wars and Fortunes Son
> March indefatigably on;
> And for the last effect
> Still keep thy Sword erect;
> Besides the force it has to fright
> The Spirits of the shady Night,
> The same *Arts* that did *gain*
> A *Pow'r* must it *maintain*.
> (113-20)

There is a kind of courage in such marching, such relentlessly continued application, just as there was in the image of the Unfortunate Lover grappling resolutely with the 'stubborn rock'[11] upon which a malevolent fortune had shipwrecked him. But the bleakness of the image is in the violence of that upright sword-blade, the power it has to 'fright', and above all in the weary unending sense of compulsion which pursues Cromwell all the way down to that emphatic 'must' in the final line.

None the less all the poem's disbelief, even its most drastic sarcasm, has still somehow not been enough to strip from Cromwell either his pathos or his battered humanity. The industrious and sad soldier-politician, unfree, impelled, wounded and self-wounded with deep scars, who, to the end, 'must' keep up his indefatigable march is looked at with an extraordinary mixture of drastic disbelief and unwithdrawn sympathy. He is 'the Wars and Fortunes Son', horribly deprived thereby of ordinary human parentage, but a 'Son' none the less, a human being described with a word which betokens a relationship of love. What kind of attitude, which, in Brooks' words, 'could be held by a human being' as opposed to a mere 'cold and detached honest broker',[12] is capable of containing such extremes?

The attitude, whatever it is, is unitary. The poem feels all of a piece. It doesn't split into prevarications or into the pros and cons of debate. It makes Cromwell palpable, indivisibly a human being, not a mere bundle of forensic questions. He has as much dramatic presence as the Mower, even though in the Ode we have not heard the hero speak directly.[13] But what unitary vision is it that can embrace the poem's sarcasm and its horror and still keep faith with the figure who is exposed to such profoundly undeceived scrutiny?

Cromwell has, on occasion, been compared with Shakespeare's Coriolanus,[14] and the comparison is fruitful. Both are warrior-heroes, both live out violent destinies and suffer extreme isolation. The violence of both men is appalling, and yet in spite of this both men inspire wonder and draw their beholders' emotions to the edge of empathy. Above all the vexed question of freedom and captivity is profoundly engaged by each figure, for Coriolanus shares with Cromwell the strange double sense of seeming, at one and the same time, to be a free agent acting alone and a captive, suffering product of the world's need for heroes, or of destiny's determination to drive men to extremity. The dramatic image holds such contraries within its unitary life. A tragic vision has both the disbelief and the generosity to embrace such complexity. With Cromwell as with the Mower, Marvell has taken his imagery of severance and loss to the level of tragic drama.

A second figure for comparison comes not from Nabokov (who never moved in quite these regions), but from his early Modernist predecessor, Flaubert. *La Légende de Saint Julien L'Hospitalier*[15] is another story of a warrior-hero whose life is full of violence and extreme solitude. He has the will and directness of Cromwell and he pursues his paths across the same fearful, unpeopled landscapes over which Cromwell marches at the end of Marvell's poem. Here again the simple fact of being selected by destiny (Julien is 'marqué de Dieu'[16] as enigmatically as Cromwell is singled out by 'Heaven' and 'Fate') makes an extraordinary life seem not so much like the life of the man himself as the life of an uncontrollable force within him. Again he seems free in his solitude and unfree as he follows the dictates of prophecy and destiny. Again it is a tragic vision which embraces the contraries of his life. It is, as with Marvell, a curious, impassive kind of tragedy which can see either sainthood or monstrousness in the hero's life and which, either way, apprehends a profound and irremediable sorrow.

A third figure for comparison is from Marvell himself. The Unfortunate Lover, the Orphan of the Hurricane, is Marvell's other unlucky warrior-hero, and the study of him seems like a prototype for this great study of 'the Wars and Fortunes Son'. The common factors are again violence, loss, isolation, courage, will, and wounding. In 'The unfortunate Lover' Marvell perhaps held the feeling of the poem just back from the tragic impassivity of the Ode. The poetry was slightly less personal, the central figure slightly more emblematic. The dominant tone of Blakeian indignation caught things more in the immediacy of recoil than in the aftermath of tragic reflection. But the change is not great. The one poem shades easily into the other, and it takes most of its indignation with it, for the sense of outrage in the Ode is still markedly strong.

The common vision is a tragic one. From Shakespeare's Coriolanus to Marvell's Cromwell is not a large step. From Marvell's Cromwell to Flaubert's Julien is an even smaller one, for the impassive, enigmatic tone, and the sharp, swift, sketching edge to the style mark both works as tragedy of an unusual kind, sombre and unsolacing. But it is tragedy none the less, not the disinterested, temperate debate of critical diagnosis.

It was the deepening of pathos in *Pnin* that first brought Nabovok's work close to the realms of the tragic. Then *Transparent Things* followed, with its impassive tone, its Sophoklean reference, and its sense of fearful depths beneath the surfaces of very ordinary things. It is a vision of tragedy rooted in the loss of Arcadia. With Marvell, Damon and Cromwell are the chief images of a great tragic vision with similar roots. It is tragedy seen, by writers with a strong sense of our Arcadian origins, as a condemnation to the pain and labour of perpetual exile.

In Nabokov's case the tonal deepening that began in *Pnin* was bound up with his development of the image of the father. His first image, his natural subject, was the son, the victim, the wanderer exiled from a world where fathers had lived secure. It was only when the simple dualism of this vision began to melt and when fathers were seen, like everyone else, to share the dilemmas of exile which are merely most apparent in victimsons, that the tone deepened. Tragedy emerged from a more exclusive kind of pathos when the image of the father emerged from categories provided uniquely by the son.

With Marvell, matters may well be very similar. He too has his first natural subject in the figure of the lost child, the abandoned lover, the bewildered and innocent victim whose world is invaded. The tragedy of the Mower is the tragedy of all such people. But the tragedy of Cromwell is different. Cromwell is a victim, but he is also a maker of victims. His is not a world invaded, for he himself is the invader, the great driving leader of all the 'wanton troopers' of the world. In this aspect he is an antitype to the Mower. As such he is not the natural subject for Marvell and the Ode's sympathy for him had to be found, and learnt, like Nabokov's sympathy for fathers.

It may well be that the Ode is in fact the very place that such sympathy is learnt and that the turmoil of its contrary impulsions, the violent drama of its sarcasm and its sorrow, is evidence of just such a turning point in the development of Marvell's imagination. It may well be too that, as with Nabokov, the new image of the father is at the heart of the matter. If the Ode is the place where the vital change occurs and Cromwell the key figure who inspires it, it becomes interesting to find that the later Cromwell is presented as a paternal figure, the father to Eliza.[17] It also becomes interesting that the other battle-scarred soldier-politician of Marvell's world, Fairfax, for whom he also clearly developed strong feelings of devotion, is in his turn also presented as a paternal figure, the father to Maria.

Each of these paternal figures in Marvell has lived in the world at its least Arcadian. One has eventually had his fill of it, has resigned his military command and retreated to the gardens, woods, and waters of his Yorkshire estate. The other still marches 'indefatigably on' in 'An Horatian Ode', and will still be tirelessly building, binding, and fastening the structure of the state in 'The First Anniversary of the Government under O. C.'[18]. But each now, regardless of their opposite decisions, can be regarded with the same non-exclusive generosity.

The literary word for the new range of feeling is tragedy. In personal terms, the poem's moment is that of the genesis or discovery of love. It is a particular kind of love, learned with difficulty and taken possession of slowly, as the paternal figure emerges from the simplistic category where the son had placed him, to command a full, open response in his own right. This, as background model, may account for the fighting turmoil of contradictory feeling given, and finally possessed, in the Ode.

The Cromwell-figure lives amidst the non-Arcadian world's violence. His valour is industrious and sad, his masculinity powerful and in some ways threatening. In his maturity, when he has left behind his gardens and his pear-trees, he is granted little respite from his labours, perching only briefly on the green bough before being reclaimed by his duties. He is battle-scarred by the world and by his own relentless will. His fortunate son is not yet thrall to the world, still idle, contemptuous of the kind of 'forward Youth' who, in order to 'appear' on the world's stage will, in his turn, push his way into the fighting. He remembers Arcadia and the plenitude of its complex, undisturbed colours. Beholding the indefatigable march of such a father he is appalled and sarcastic, though he may also be tormented by the dawning knowledge that he owes his ease and idleness to his father's work. His wit and insight can and must destroy the mystique of this mature figure in whose shadow he lies. He cannot go back on the critique to make it fair or balanced, for that would endanger his own still precarious insight and thus his own still precarious existence. But what he can do is to keep faith or, perhaps to his own surprise, find that he simply is keeping faith, willy-nilly, and that he cannot do otherwise. This is thus the moment of the genesis or discovery of love. Love is caught at a critical moment in the process of a mind's growth. The derogatory insights will stand uncancelled. The mature man will not be saved from the son's need to keep himself free by his wit. But he can be loved, across the gap of independence which the wit keeps open.

Eventually the strain will diminish and the expression of such love will be easy. The son will take possession of his feelings and move freely in the company of the great paternal Cromwell of the poem on his death or the paternal Fairfax of 'Upon Appleton House'. He will then even be able to return to the language of his ironies with the sting taken out of them. A Fairfax laid out his garden like a fort because he too 'could not cease' his 'warlike studies',[19] but the terror has now gone out of the idea of impulsion. Cromwell, on the first anniversary of his government, is praised as self-sacrificing:

> For all Delight of Life thou then didst lose,
> When to Command, thou didst thy self Depose . . .
>
> Therefore thou rather didst thy Self depress,
> Yeilding to Rule, because it made thee Less.[20]

But the old penchant for irony has left such phrases.

Perhaps this is to speculate groundlessly as to the structure of images in Marvell's mind. But there is one more factor which supports the speculation. In *The Rehearsal Transpros'd* Marvell speaks of his own father and of the father of Samuel Parker. He also speaks of how, in early life, sons relate to fathers and to figures of authority in general. He sees the whole business as normally fraught with lamentably unresolved feudings, and one of the things he finds most ridiculous and immature in Parker is his failure to have come to terms with early authorities, tutorial and parental, from whose opinions he now differs. Hence Parker's disorderly venom. Hence his remaining locked in the 'juvenile petulancy' of 'Boyes against their Schollmasters or Tutors'. Hence his aptness

to curse solemnly his Father and Mother for having educated him in those Opinions, to animate his new Acquaintances to the massacring of his former Camarades.[21]

This, like much else in *The Rehearsal Transpros'd*, is written by a man now completely at ease with such changes and traumas and able to play at leisure with the imagery of youth and maturity while Parker snarls and flails. It may well be that 'An Horatian Ode', together with the other poems on the parental figures of Cromwell and Fairfax, is, in fictional transposition, the nearest thing we have to documentary evidence as to how and when Marvell became the mature man who was later to ridicule that 'forward Youth', Samuel Parker.

PART FOUR

Arcadia Preserved

15

A SUBJECTIVE HOSANNAH

If 'An Horatian Ode' catches Marvell's mind at a critical moment in its development, *The Gift*[1] is, similarly, a key work for Nabokov. Here, as there, all the lines of a developing imagination seem to pass through a single work. There is clarification, and afterwards renewal.

The renewal was not immediate. The long pause in his career as a novelist was still to come and it would be twenty years after the writing of *The Gift* before the second, American phase was fully launched. But the careful irony and self-parody of *The Gift* already does a great deal of the work which will, in the end, make possible such things as the deepening and sharing of *Pnin* and the perfectly judged mingling of sympathy and mockery in *Transparent Things*. It is *The Gift* that first exposes Nabokov's natural subject of the bewildered, exiled son to continuous irony, and that first sets up for full exploration the contrasting image of the father.

After the severance from his boyhood Russia, Nabokov dwelt at great length upon his theme. He nourished within himself the nostalgia for Arcadia which was the spiritual centre of his being, fraught though it was with dangers. He knew where the centre was:

The nostalgia I have been cherishing all these years is a hypertrophied sense of lost childhood.[2]

Isolated in his cold room in Cambridge ('Scholastically, I might as well have gone up to the Inst. M. M. of Tirana') and in the long spiritual winter of refugee Berlin ('my secluded years in Germany') he hung on to his memories. He refused to surrender what had been torn away.

It was a saving grace, the source and centre of all his imaginative distinction. But such sustained cherishing of a single vision may also be a withdrawal and a form of self-love. The long-nurtured sense of loss, and the long-pondered efforts to redeem it, tuned his ear wonderfully to the voices of the displaced heard in his Russian books of exile, and opened his mind generously to the efforts of people like Martin (or like Cincinnatus in *Invitation to a Beheading*) who try to redeem their loss and remake their lives complete. His own life is creatively relived in all their lives. But as the line of exile-heroes lengthens we may begin to wonder at an element of repetition and thus of narrowness. Is the pattern of severance and nostalgia the only human pattern deserving of attention? Are exiles from Arcadia the only imaginative men, the only poets? Are they indeed always, so exclusively, poets? If imagination is 'the supreme delight of the immortal and the immature'[3] what about the rest of us mature mortals? Is this the only hunger in the world, the only loss, the only need, the only source of redemption? What is the difference between paradisal longing and regressive infantilism? What is delicacy and what is preciosity? What is purity and what mere self-with-holding? Were there really so few people worth meeting and valuing in all Cambridge and in all Berlin?

Irony, caution, and reserve are the modes of the intelligence which investigates these questions in an act of clarification. Such powers bring cleansing and self-discovery. Nabokov is always to some degree ironic of course; but *The Gift*, in which, at the end of his Russian phase, he subjected his most treasured themes to sustained disbelief, is more steadily ironic, or self-parodic, than any other of his books except *Ada*. There are games enough else-where, but nowhere so much as here. Here, the elaborate layer-ings and veilings of continuous irony play quietly, cautiously, and at length over his most cherished theme. *The Gift*, the final product of his Berlin exile and winter, is scrupulously enigmatic; *Ada*, coming after the long-postponed American spring, is ironic-ally tricky at effortless and merry length. Both books are slippery in the extreme.

Nabokov is known, probably too much known, as an ironist and games player. But in spite of this *The Gift* has, oddly enough, often been read as a fairly straight and respectful Portrait of the Artist as a Young Man. There is the hero, a young writer, a Russian Dedalus, with all the classic equipment of the artist-hero and all the classic Nabokovian nuances of Arcadian memory. He keeps faith with his imaginative origins in the childhood from which exile has severed him. His first works are poems of childhood. He clings in painful nostalgia to memories of his Russian family in its rural house. He finds wherever he can the hints and remnants of Arcadia in the leaves and shadows of a city's parks. Gradually he comes to write his first major work, *The Life of Chernyshevski*, a brilliant quicksilver attack on Philistinism. He finds his mistress, Muse, and soul-mate in Zina Mertz:

What shall I call you? Half Mnemo*syne*? There's a half shim*mer* in your surname too. In dark Berlin it is so strange for me to roam, oh, my half-fantasy, with you. (Ch. 3)

In the end he brings all the threads together in the sun, forest, and water of the Grunewald. All the Nabokovian themes and images are here: colour, childhood Arcadia, severance, exile, nostalgia, distinction of spirit, and poetic genius heroically maintained in isolation, then forest and forest waters as the proofs of triumphant arrival.

Fyodor has all the right credentials. He holds on to his childhood in his poems. He holds on to his family, to his beloved mother and sister, and, in memory, to his magnificent dead father. In exile, another Orphan of the Hurricane, he toils alone in a boarding house in Berlin, trying to hold on to the idyll. He develops the right literary views. He loves rhythmic delicacy and verbal play. He loves Pushkin, Gogol, and Fet. On the other hand, he has nothing but scorn for social novels full of cliché and general idea. He pours forth his scorn upon the likes of Chernyshevski who harnessed Pushkin and Gogol to crude notions of art as progressive social propaganda and who thought Fet was an idiot whose poems could have been written by a horse. He cuts the gross pundit to shreds with the verve and levity of his intelligence. He likewise fends off and stands aloof from all the junk writing of his exiled compatriots, like the monstrous metaphysical tragedy of Busch, the apocalyptic cries of Shirin, the clichés of a host of babbling critical theorists and lachrymose poets. He holds himself aloof from the grossness of Shchyogolev and of beflagged political parades in Berlin.

And thus he holds true to his spiritual, artistic, and intellectual integrity, slowly to be rewarded by the achievement of *The Life of Chernyshevski*. His Muse recognizes and loves him, and the Grunewald is the lyric apostrophe to his achievement. Forest, glades, thickets, rowans, and firs; brilliant-coloured birds like orioles, jays, and woodpeckers; lush grass 'primevally green'; a 'primeval paradise' where the sun 'licked me all over with its big, smooth tongue', browning the body into harmony with the natural world; the waters of the green world. He seems like Marvell leaving the house at Nun Appleton to find, at the end of his explorations, bright, easeful ecstasy in the green and light of the forest:

> Oh what a Pleasure 'tis to hedge
> My Temples here with heavy sedge;
> Abandoning my lazy Side,
> Stretcht as a Bank unto the Tide;
> Or to suspend my sliding Foot
> On the osiers undermined Root
> And in its Branches tough to hang,
> While at my Lines the Fishes twang![4]

But it is all in fact quite different. Everything in *The Gift* is mined from within and eaten through with rottenness. This apparent greenwood will snap at the slighest pressure. The hero is a modish, narcissistic, cruel, and withdrawn youth; his poetry is risible; his biography of the wretched Chernyshevski is as humanly impoverished as it is brilliant and his motives for writing it far from pure; his heroic father has feet of clay; his beloved Zina is mostly, if not entirely, mirage, made in his own self-loving image out of a not very wonderful woman whom he hardly knows. In addition it seems possible that he is in love with his mother, and perhaps his sister too. Sustained, elaborate, mining irony crumbles the whole tale to dust.

How can one look as straight as most critics have done, with equanimity even if not with enthusiasm, at those feeble verses about childhood which Fyodor writes, and then, having written, caresses and recaresses supine upon his bed at the novel's beginning? He writes a slender encomium of his lost ball, another of his bicycle, another of his monogram (*sic*). He writes of the snow in its 'immaculate whiteness' and the sky 'a blue that was bluer than blue'. The poems are precious, stilted, mandarin trifles, as nerveless as their creator. As the young bard contemplates their fineness, tasting the justness of his words and rhythms, imagining a reviewer in ecstasy at their 'harlequin iridescence', and further titillating himself with the notion that they contain a 'special poetic meaning' to which even the most laudatory reviewer will not be able to do justice, we should know at once that this is a novel to read with the greatest suspicion.

One might think of Joyce's humour at the expense of Stephen Dedalus, that 'priest of the eternal imagination' who 'had known the ectasy of seraphic life'.[5] But this is really far short of Dedalus, for the langorous, horizontal Fyodor has none of the fiery, combative intelligence of Stephen, none of his speed and nerve, none of his Shelleyan fire, nothing remotely approaching either his lyric gift or his philosophical sharpness. Ezra Pound's aesthete, Hugh Selwyn Mauberley, is the more relevant comparison from the classic era of Modernism, with his 'questing and passive' pre-Raphaelite dreaminess, his drifting

> Amid the precipitation, down-float
> Of insubstantial manna,
> Lifting the faint susurrus
> Of his subjective hosannah.[6]

So the novel begins with the 'faint susurrus' and 'subjective hosannah' of a horizontal bard. If the humour of this has passed some readers by it is not surprising that the slower, quieter disbelief of the rest of the book should have tended to slip through unnoticed. But everywhere Nabokov has mined his text and set his booby-traps for the unwary.

He has strewn Fyodor's narrative with numerous, precious little cameos of observation which are taken by the poet (but why by us?) as supreme evidence of a higher poetic sensibility. He has filled his narrative with the windings and *longueurs* of a young sensitive, drawing his trifles out to unconscionable length. He has coloured all Fyodor's recollections of mother and sister with hints of erotic thrills. He has haunted Fyodor, and rather upstaged him, with the tale of Yasha's death and of his father's subsequent grief, giving the tale a weight of human substance which makes Fyodor seem tinsel by comparison (howsoever poor a poet Yasha may have been). The slippery text cannot be trusted anywhere. The four major sequences (Fyodor's dreams of his father, his biography of Chernyshevski, his affair with Zina, and his ecstasy in the Grunewald) are all full of irony.

What do we make of Fyodor's father? What kind of ideal loving husband is this who hardly spends any time with his wife and who dismisses her with cruel humiliation ('You go home') when once she dares to seek him out on his travels? What kind of ideal loving father is it who, returning from his travels, is busy looking at his watch while his daughter tries to embrace him? What kind of patriarchal domination is it that makes him educate his son to all his own enthusiasms and opinions, with his experience as surrogate for the boy's own life, leaving the son to recall later how he

trained my very thoughts, as a voice or hand is trained, according to the rules of his school? (Ch. 2)

What sort of human being is it who has only his indifference, his contempt, or his gun for any humans, as opposed to butterflies or lichen, that he might meet with on his travels?[7]

One of his fellow scientists praises him as a 'conquistador' and the word sounds more apt than he seems to realize. There is his 'power over everything that he undertook'. There is his desire to 'imprint his force on everything'. There is his fascination with a species of butterfly which moulds a corneal chastity belt on to its mate. There is indeed the style of his lepidoptery in general as this relentlessly cataloguing man 'rakes noctuid after noctuid into the killing jar' and spends his little time at home in a museum 'full of crucified butterflies'. What has he done to the young wife who idolizes him as a hero? To what effect has he exercised his power over his son and imprinted his force upon him?

Fyodor's encomium of him is all breathless admiration and, reading unwarily, one might be carried along by him. But the breathlessness, as it continues, comes to smack of a determination to praise, a need to praise, a pained desire to find his father praiseworthy. From the half-shadows of Fyodor's text there gradually emerges not the ideal father of a child's Arcadian youth but a much grosser presence. We begin to construe Fyodor's father as an unloving, domineering patriarch in whose fearful shadow the helpless son seeks for solaces in dreams, fantasies, and deceptive fictions. Here and there there are traces of questions he trembles to ask but dare not:

Oh, don't look at me, my childhood, with such big, frightened eyes . . . Why then do I feel so sad . . .? (Ch. 2)

What should we make of such a father? What should we make of his supine son who now deceives himself with poems about an idyllic childhood? What should we make of his abandoned wife, abandoned first on their honeymoon when she was reading, ominously enough, Maupassant's *Une Vie*, the story of a tyrannical husband? Everything turns sour with irony. Dissonances are heard whenever the theme of an Arcadian childhood is played.

Fyodor's work on Chernyshevski is similarly flawed. The encomium of his father could not be taken at face value. Neither can this denunciation of another man, another father, another traveller (this time an unwilling one) to the furthest Eastern reaches of Russia's Asiatic territories. The parallels are not enforced but they will slowly dawn and do their work, inviting a reader to wonder and reflect.

N. G. Chernyshevski was one of the radical Russian 'men of the sixties' (with Herzen and Dobrolyubov, followers of Belinski). He was admired in the 1930s by the *émigré* progressive intelligentsia. He was also very highly praised by the ideologists of the Soviet Union as one of the great pre-Marxist materialist philosophers who, as such, also afforded welcome assurance of Russia's own national contribution to radical and materialist thought. His. Dissertation on *The Aesthetic Relation of Art to Reality*[8] was heralded as a triumph of pre-Bolshevik neo-Marxism. It was felt to constitute a useful corrective to the erring Menshevik ideas of Plekhanov and was a useful ideological justification of Zhdanovism. His materialist philosophy, with its militant scorn for Kant in particular and for all 'idealists' in general (Plato, Schopenhauer etc.) was similarly seen as a highly useful part of the Great Tradition.

He is in fact a very minor, clumsy philosopher and a feeble

aesthetician with coarse and narrow views. One should not be surprised to find Fyodor in the 1920s or Nabokov in the 1930s being ready to show their dazzlingly witty disrespect. Nor, on the face of it, should one be displeased at their readiness to cut down to size a second-rate pundit who was not only thought to be a great philosopher (a foolish but harmless error) but whose works were also used as an ideological weapon in the barbarous treatment of Soviet artists. The witty and brilliant debunking and general field-day are intrinsically to be welcomed. Other things, however, complicate the issue.

Chernyshevski, though no great philosopher, was a social reformer of some courage, a man of humane and generous will, a campaigning opponent of the Czarist exploitation of the Russian peasantry. He also suffered a long, punitive exile in Southern and Central Siberia. Gradually some parallels are established between the Chernyshevski story and the story of Fyodor, though Fyodor himself seems completely unaware of them. Chernyshevski was something of a ponderous pundit of a father, as Fyodor's own father has turned out to be. One of his sons, Sasha, tormented his practically-minded parent by becoming a rather feckless and bewildered aesthete, as Fyodor has turned out to be. His exile in Central Asia was the scene of Fyodor's father's travels in contemptuous indifference to what, humanly, may have gone on there. Certain poignant parallels are established. They never occur to Fyodor. They are never heavily accented in Nabokov's text. They are left quietly to dawn on the reader as the various parts of the book are laid together in silent juxtaposition.

It is a marvellous achievement of quiet irony slowly revealing itself. Intellectually, Chernyshevski deserves much of what he gets. The brutal sage created by Soviet hagiography deserves all of it. But there are other things stirring with more urgent human substance beneath the surface of his tale. Fyodor's Chernyshevski is a poor buffoon whose bubble needs pricking. Nabokov no doubt endorses the general intellectual line of it (who wouldn't?) and delights in its wicked brilliance (again, who wouldn't?). But where Fyodor is hasty and convinced, Nabokov moves slowly and circumspectly. There is room in Nabokov's non-directive text for one to wonder at the cold-bloodedness of what is going on in Fyodor's work and at the repellent venom of this destruction not only of Chernyshevski's theories but of his person too. We find more time than does the hurrying Fyodor to catch something humanly substantial and humanly forlorn in Chernyshevski, a figure who comes in many ways to seem a little like Luzhin about whom Nabokov, not Fyodor, wrote a profoundly compassionate book. There is room, outside the savage cleverness of Fyodor's work, for such second thoughts about its stature as the work of a young genius. There is room for thought about its performing surrogate functions for a bewildered young man flailing with unconscious violence at the image of his domineering father.

Perhaps Fyodor himself, outside the heady and self-opinionated world of his *Life of Chernyshevski*, has momentary intimations of this. He seems briefly to sense a genuine heroism in Chernyshevski's political battles; and, late in the novel, when the work is finished, a brief confession of the less than human tenor of his ungenerous effort seems to brush through his mind:

Oh, let everything pass and be forgotten—and again in two hundred years' time an ambitious failure will vent his frustration on the simpletons dreaming of a good life. (Ch. 5)

But by then it is far too late. By then the work is complete. Juvenile superciliousness has been mistaken for a high disdain.

Zina is suspect too. Perhaps her association with the leaves and shadows of Fyodor's Arcadian dreaming:

... like a shadow leaving its kindred element ... of night's own colour ... (Ch. 3)

is a kind of lyricism. But it comes more and more to sound like the language of fantasy and surrogate. Does she really exist at all? Did their night-time trysts ever take place other than in Fyodor's trembling, virginal imagination? Is her apparent praise of his work any more real than that which is offered by the various phantom reviewers whom he conjures up to console himself? Everything about her is insubstantial, unreal, suspect. Why can he not meet her at their 'real' home? How does that unprepossessing young woman who is thought by Kern to have 'character' because 'she looked down her nose at everything' suddenly become transfigured into the Arcadian Muse of Fyodor's night-time fantasies? At lunch-time she declines to eat or speak, contenting herself instead with flicking ash into an ashtray beside her plate. Is that consistent with being a Muse?

Zina as Muse and soul mate is a mere creation of Fyodor's self-love and hungry need, belonging only to his world of fantasy. Perhaps he does meet her and conduct some halting kind of affair; or maybe it is all the invention of a boarding-house lodger dreaming of his landlady's daughter. It matters very little which. Either way, the much-blazoned affair is a very frail fiction. Its real substance is nearly negligible. There is hardly any conversation between them, hardly any mutual knowledge, no sex, and, from Fyodor at least, no love. In his fantasy of her he sets up a great image of his own glory; with the real woman he feels only 'emotional constraint'. When her door is closed upon him he is subject to thoughts of masturbation.[9]

Finally there is the Grunewald, the apparent return to Arcadian origins and to the deepest and richest recesses of the imagination harboured there. The classic journey is given. He leaves a house. He passes by a series of gardens. He passes through a gate into the wildwood itself. The wood has its waters, its lake. Ecstasy brings the book to a triumphant close and Fyodor inherits his Gift. But here too, everything is flawed. Fyodor is not Marvell and the Grunewald is not Nun Appleton forest. A profoundly suspect, dissonant celebration of 'Nature's Cradle' and 'the Nursery of all things green' brings *The Gift* to an appropriately limping end.

In the wood there are orioles and woodpeckers, but there is also an old mattress and a lamp-shade frame. You can see the cars whizzing past through the trees. A small plane recently crashed here and strewed its wreckage about. There are picnickers in the primeval paradise. There is a party of five nuns mimicked by a small boy. There is a schoolgirl lying in the grass while two youths and a dirty old man try to look up her skirt. There is a possibly voyeuristic photographer who babbles on about the weather in extremely unparadisal tones:

Herrliches Wetter—in der Zeitung steht es aber, dass es morgen bestimmt regnen wird ... Da kommen die Wolken schon ...[10]

The newspaper is right too, for Fyodor later gets drenched. By then somebody has stolen his clothes while he is swimming. Ecstasy has a hard time of it in such surroundings.

But it is not just the surroundings, not only the seedy and derelict Grunewald which brings the book to such an off-key ending. It is even more the seedy and derelict Fyodor. He too looks up the schoolgirl's skirt and is by no means content to confine his fantasies to Zina. He is irked to find that he came too late to see the wreckage of the plane. He is pathetically full of notions that in this squalid little wood he is experiencing 'something akin to that Asiatic freedom' found by his father on his travels. He, the self-confessed stylist, thinks in clichés and silly giggles:

Farther on it became very nice: the pines had come into their own . . . I felt myself an athlete, a Tarzan, an Adam, anything you like. (Ch. 5)

The seediest thing of all is the meanness of his imagination. Marvell at Appleton House has a mind and an imagination that move outward, with wonder and fluidity. He is receptive to sensation and turned outwards to its sources in quickness and delight. But Fyodor is quite without wonder. He hugs things to himself to satisfy a private, selfish, and rather static mind. He carries all his opinions, and all his opinionatedness, with him. The fragmented and episodic narration of his highly selective ecstasy halts and stumbles from one greedily sought sensation to the next. There is no lyric play. All the flights of his imagination are quickly aborted. The whole Grunewald passage reads like a sad and ugly parody of Marvell's forest journey. The delighted mind of Marvell could declare that

> Out of these scatter'd *Sibyls* Leaves
> Strange *Prophecies* my Phancy weaves:
> And in one History consumes,
> Like *Mexique Paintings*, all the *Plumes*.
> What *Rome, Greece, Palestine*, ere said
> I in this light *Mosaick* read.
> Thrice happy he who, not mistook,
> Hath read in *Natures mystick Book*.[11]

But in Fyodor and the Grunewald there is no such fancy and weaving, no such fluid and whimsical play of intellectual faculties. He is 'mistook' again, just as he was about his father, his Muse, his inept poems, and his humanly inept though very clever work on Chernyshevski.

So the book's complex layerings of irony and unaccented juxtapositions do their work of clarification. It is a fine achievement and a fascinating process to observe. As Nabokov traces all the deceptions and falsities of Fyodor's life, which is so like and so unlike his own, he is drawing all sorts of difficult lines of distinction with perfect exactitude. The artist's Arcadian hosannah of exile and memory is mistrusted throughout for its mere subjectivity. As one of Pound's critics excellently put it in the case of Mauberley, he is making, in a sense, 'a mask of what he feared to become'.[12]

16

THE SOCRATES
OF SNAILS

The fourth Mower poem, 'The Mower against Gardens',[1] is unlike the other three. They were songs, animated by the primitive voice and music of a suffering man. Here the Mower makes a speech and conducts an argument of some sophistication. We are not here attending, with rapt exclusiveness, to the plight of a naïve victim, bewildered and outraged by the doings of more worldly men. This voice does not fill our imaginative world with such poignant and haunting candour. The poem is full of play and verbal ingenuity. Its intelligence creates the space for thought. Here again there is irony and clarification. The Arcadian theme is again treated circumspectly. It is deliberately mistrusted.

This Mower's voice is still real enough. It may still haunt, to some degree. But it creates none of the feeling of hopelessness and loss that came from Damon's singing. This Mower can look after himself. His belief in his own world of 'wild and fragrant Innocence' is still intact and unshattered. He is quite sure that the gods dwell with him and his kind. The plural 'us' and the confidently established 'dwell' of the poem's last line are a world away from Damon's isolation and deracination. This complaint against the violators of the world comes out of confidence, even contempt, not blight.

This talkative Mower is witty, skilled, and nimble. He would probably have held his own against Damon's shepherd, and might even have had an answer for Juliana. He is allowed to have his say, but the poem's atmosphere of ingenious debate creates a space between us and him and leaves room for other perspectives. The emotional temperature here is much lower. The speaker's viewpoint is important, but not as overwhelmingly compelling as Damon's. One might call this Mower a mask of what Marvell feared his Damon might become if he had his way for too long.

The place from which the voice comes is none the less beautifully celebrated at the end of the poem. It is a place of effortlessness and freely-offered beauty, without the toiling intricacies of
labour and mentality, where nature, man, and the benign gods
live together their unsevered lives. It is Arcadia, untormented by
restlessness and division:

> Where willing Nature does to all dispence
> A wild and fragrant Innocence:
> And *Fauns* and *Faryes* do the Meadows till,
> More by their presence then their skill.
>
> (33-6)

The poem's rhythm quickens with the life of this image, which
gives urgency as well as grace to the Mower's witness to his
world. For a moment this has something of the vision and music
of Damon.

But this closing lyric, strong though it is, does not have everything its own way. Before it, the Mower has said so much, with
such assurance, such complexity, and with a certain tendentious-
ness, that by the end of the poem we have taken the time to turn
aside and look askance. He cannot completely command our
assent. In particular, the sexual imagery of his complaint has its
suspect as well as its serious side.

Why, after all, is he so prudishly obsessed with make-up, with
tainting, with 'strange perfumes' and 'forbidden mixtures'? Why
does he harp so much on lasciviousness, vice, seduction, allure-
ment, adultery, and the *seraglio*? Isn't the idea of rape, which is
the final burden of the complaint, given in the word 'enforc'd', a
trifle heavy as a moral comment upon gardening?

A serious anxiety about our busy interference with nature is
still there, to be sure. When man is said to stupefy nature, to
make it 'double' and 'uncertain', and to 'vex' it, the Mower is
touching the note struck by Damon with his 'wandring' and
'displac'd' mind. But that was a man's mind. It is harder to be so
engaged by the theme when the bewildered victims of our pruri-
ent attentions are plants and when the means of our corruption
are tree-grafts, ponds, and manure.

The Mower does make his witness. His Arcadia has its life and appeal. Man, 'that sov'raign thing and proud', is to some degree chastised by his complaint. Substance is given to his arguments by the elaborate and intricate ornamental gardens of the mid-seventeenth century which tended to strangle nature and reduce everything to airlessness and constriction; and by the unprepossessing details of contemporary make-up like the thick-layered painting of the face and the use of heavy, malodorous greases and gums for the hair.[2] One hears the argument. But one still hears it being slightly overplayed. The genius of the poem lies in its capturing this sense of overplaying while being just attentive and charitable enough to let the Mower eventually get through to the beautiful lyric with which he is allowed to close. Marvell here backs away gently from what elsewhere engages him with the utmost poignancy. The brevity and presto of the piece are perfect for giving both disbelief and lyric in splendid harmony.

There is a kind of *naïveté*, full of primitive resonance, which speaks profoundly to our innermost sense of division and spoliation. The songs of Damon have it. But there is another kind of *naïveté* which speaks to much less disturbing reveries. This rather eloquent Mower evokes these less troublesome thoughts. His wittily elaborate poem is reminiscent (as Damon's songs could not possibly be) of some of Wallace Stevens' agile lyrical arguments in which more minor reveries are contemplated. The chastising Mower recalls that loquacious expert lecturer on 'the first idea', spokesman for the 'effortless weather', who, in Stevens' 'Notes Toward a Supreme Fiction',[3] issues a rebuke to a young man and advises him, as tutor, that all the skills of man amount to no more than a capacity for caparisoning elephants and teaching bears to juggle.

Marvell was a tutor. So was Nabokov in his time. There were, no doubt, a few excessively verbalizing, explanatory, and exegetical ghosts of their creative selves which had to be laid. Marvell knew how to catch out the *'easie Philosopher'* in himself that still stalked the great poet in the woods at Nun Appleton.[4] Nabokov could catch himself using 'easy art' to bring the great fifth chapter of *Pnin* to a conclusion perhaps too elegant for the terrible matters that it contained.[5] Such things are evidence of a poise born of patient, ironic self-clarification.

The writer of 'The Mower against Gardens' catches Damon in the act of becoming tutorial. The Mower has his point, but he harps on. He sounds a little like one of Stevens' amateur poets talking about aesthetic matters in a high tone—a Comedian as the Letter m, perhaps, or a Mower as King of the Ghosts.[6]

17

VAN THE PENMAN

The Gift must have had to struggle hard for its balance. Its enigmatic reserve and silent juxtapositions testify to an extreme caution, as Nabokov worked over his most cherished personal beliefs.

His next long work of irony, parody, and game is *Ada*.[1] Now he is very confident. His games are leisured and easy. But unfortunately the ease is not entirely convincing. *Ada* is Nabokov's most otiose work.

An author who writes seventeen novels in two languages and several other works besides is entitled to his mistakes. Even the mistakes of an author as fine as Nabokov will not be without their qualities and interest. So good a writer is incapable of pure failure. But he was capable, on this one occasion, of following a promising fictional line with a single-minded assiduity which in the end let him down. He follows wit into fancy, fancy into whimsy, and whimsy into vapid *longueurs*.

It is a great pity, especially since the fictional line which it follows to a vanishing point is in itself so attractive. The ambition is laudable. It commands ready imaginative assent. The reader starts with high hopes and all his prejudices in favour. But gradually things unwind and dissipate. For once, Nabokov loses his poise, and with it loses the whole tone of a book.[2]

Ada is a tale of pastoral fantasy. What if nothing mattered? What if everything were always for the best? What if our problems could just be dreamed away, fancied out of existence? What if Arcadia could be found in youth and sustained throughout a long, unsevered lifetime? What if brimming sexual delight were to begin effortlessly in childhood and parkland and go on unstinted until one approached a century of leisured years? What if gravity (as ever, in both senses) could be overcome, physical gravity by magic carpets ('jikkers') and moral gravity by endless wit, fun, and repartee? What if incest, the taboo of taboos, didn't matter? What if Terra were really Anti-Terra? What if Estoty were a woodland, parkland, water-rich state with a 'halcyon climate', covering huge areas of the globe, unthreatened by the hordes of Tartary, where effortlessly wealthy and effortlessly polylingual sybarites, living simultaneously in the nineteenth and twentieth centuries, could enjoy sex forever without fear of law, taboo, complexity, or cloying? What if one were born in a garden world without work and could stay there for ever in perpetual play?

It would be as if the brief, whimsical postulate of Marvell's 'The Garden' could be stretched out to the length of a long life of a hundred years and a long novel of 450 pages where one could always escape the 'busie Companies of Men' and find a solitude which would always be 'delicious'.[3] It would be as if the heroes of Nabokovian novels did not, after all, lead severed lives, but could instead come here to cash 'a blank cheque signed by Jupiter'.

It would be as if many other literary lives, from the works of other authors gathered together in *Ada*'s copious anthology, could also have their dreams realized and could share in Jupiter's hand-out as well. Chekhov's bewildered and becalmed provincials would make it to Moscow and the big time. Ophelia would not drown. Hamlet would have none of those irksome hang-ups of his about incest and other matters and would get on well with his rakish father. Marvell's garden would be full of very sexy melons, glimpsed at their pleasure in the grass.

Emma Bovary (since French literature is the book's major source of anthology material) would be provided with elegant tartan-clad lovers in Romantic landscapes and grand palaces instead of just Rodolphe in a wet wood and Léon in a dingy hotel. Frédéric and Madame Arnoux could meet whenever they wished in their parkland pavilion drenched with light.[4] They would all live to a comfortable old age, as would Chateaubriand's René and Amélie, with never a worry about incest, never a fear that the effects of the passions might lead to sin, or to the repudiation of sin in religious withdrawal.[5]

Rimbaud's *Illuminations*, filled as they are with the imagery and memory of childhood, would be the bright pictures and visionary moments in which his entire life consisted, without so much as a single season in Hell.[6] Mallarmé's fawn could have both of his nymphs, any afternoon, without their ever escaping him and without his ever being left with a sense of crime and blasphemy. Proust's prose would gather up time and memory into the complexities of its folding and unfolding but his book would be mercifully shorter. Marvell, a French poet and associate of Rimbaud, could write *Le Jardin*:

> En vain on s'amuse a gagner
> L'Oka, la Baie du Palmier,
> (Pt. I, Ch. 10)

and he could strew not only his sexual melons about the grasslands of Estoty, but the exotic fruit of his 'Bermudas' too:

golden globes of the new garden lamps that glowed here and there in the sudden greenery. (Pt. I, Ch. 34)

A dreary realist, by contrast, would get nowhere. Maupassant would be laughed out of court every time he approached with a vulgar tale of unhappiness and ill-luck in love and the miseries of poverty.[7]

Not only literary works but literary lives too would all turn out well. Shelley's *ménage à trois* with Mary and Claire Clairmont would last longer than it in fact did, and many of the ruffles would be smoothed out of it. Byron and his half-sister Augusta (their daughter was called Ada) would last a lifetime together off and on. There would be no drowning for Shelley in the Gulf of Spezia, no fever and rain for Byron at Missolonghi.[8] The young Romantics would live to be old Romantics, combining easily in their lives the Don Juanesque worldliness of Byron and the piercing purity of Shelley's imagination.

The pastoral dream of such a Land of Cockayne, Utopia, or Big Rock Candy Mountain is initially attractive. The ambition to write a Utopian fantasy of *Arcadia Maintained* (albeit a rather irritatingly literary one specially designed for initiates) gets one's assent. It promises to smile at many ponderous things, to defuse the problematic, and to make merry with the traditions of the novel from the Great House Romance of Sidney's *Arcadia* to the Dynastic Romances in many volumes of more recent years. It promises to be a splendid, light-hearted festival of erotica in full colour.[9]

So it gets one's assent well enough; and it probably gets it even more when one realizes that it will look with irony as well as with fantasy at the ever-Arcadian lives of Ada and Van. It seeks to give the fantasy, with its lyricism, fluency, and silvery delight, but it seeks to qualify it as well. It seeks both to give and to ironize the dream, both to celebrate and to repudiate. Some of the ironies will be light enough, presenting the central pair as rather precious and opinionated people. Some will be graver, making the reader recoil from the insensitive cruelty of the two lovers who make and maintain their Arcadia at the expense of other people. Notable amongst these is Lucette, the lesser light of the two nymphs, reminiscent of the nymphs of both Marvell and Mallarmé, and perhaps of Claire Clairmont as well, who is teased to distraction by both Van and Ada until she kills herself by jumping from an ocean liner, so that Ophelia, and maybe Shelley too, will have to drown after all.

But things go badly wrong. Celebration and irony soon get out of touch with one another. The irony becomes harmless, marginal, and rather self-protective. Its tone seems self-deprecating only to be the more winning, while the celebration of sustained Arcadia, freed from all resistance from gravity, runs endlessly on and on. One can imagine a fantasy of Arcadia without resistance, without irony; but it would have to be brief, slight, miniature, leaving its reader, who may be presumed to know enough about the pull of gravity anyway, to take the offered fantasy in the light of his own sufficient knowledge of its inevitable brevity. Marvell's 'The Garden' is, after all, not unlike that. But *Ada* is long and slow. It is as if 'The Garden' were writ very large and very copious, so that quick and whimsical delight finally gives way to boredom.[10]

Worse still, much of the book reads like a kind of self-justification, which now seems quite unnecessary from the successful, acknowledged, and masterly author of *Lolita*, *Pnin*, and *Pale Fire*. One wonders what is being indulged or gratified, and why, in the book's evocation of

a very old man looking back at a life of unrecognized endeavour.

(Pt. V, Ch. 3)

One wonders what it is that still rankles enough to make V. V. Nabokov give V. V. (Van Veen) so much room to discourse predictably on the acrobatic wonders of art which are

utterly and naturally unknown to the innocents of critical appraisal, the social-scene commentators, the moralists, the ideamongers.
(Pt. II, Ch. 8)

One wonders how far V. V. Nabokov is participating himself in Van Veen's declaration that

this is my sweetest revenge for all the detractions my lifework has met with. (Pt. I, Ch. 38)

Nabokov is not Veen, of course. But nor is he free of Veen, and there is now very little life in the weaving debates of author and narrator, or author and *persona*, which had once given his prose wonderful and complex texture. Where the ironies of *The Gift* were still functional and alive, solving and clarifying, the same things here have gone dead. The genius of the novelist has long ago moved on elsewhere in the American books. *Ada*, the most Russian of his American books, is a curious throw-back, a curious personal re-run of some old and now otiose themes. It pretends to the delicate and cunning irony of *The Gift*, but here irony is never allowed to do much damage to narcissism and nostalgia.

In this disappointing and slightly unbecoming Portrait of the Artist as an Old Maestro, the irony works, as it has sometimes been said to work in Joyce's *Portrait*,[11] as covert, self-protective endorsement of what it apparently deflates. The more Van Veen is deflated by irony the more Nabokov is seen to be doubly excellent. He is excellent as the creator of the beautiful dream itself and then excellent again as the source of a smiling intelligence which knows better.

In the case of Joyce, such criticism is far from fair. *A Portrait of the Artist as a Young Man* has a fine edge and sharpness both in celebration of Stephen's considerable powers and in mockery of him. But in the case of *Ada* it is much better placed. When all is said and done, when all the elaborate games and smokescreens have been forgotten, Veen is still allowed to function as artist-hero and general genius, howsoever he may, in the meantime, have teased Lucette to death with his charms and bored the reader to death with his uninteresting opinions[12] and his unlovely girl-friend.

There may be room for speculation as to why. Why, when Nabokov was at the height of his powers with *Pnin* and *Pale Fire* behind him and *Transparent Things* still to come, was he led away into the airy emptiness of *Ada*? What drew him so far along a line of fancy which tapered to such thinness? A possible answer may well be connected with a Joycean portrait of an artist-hero, though not with the portrait of Stephen Dedalus.

The Joyce of *Finnegans Wake*, (or *Winnipeg Lake* as it is dubbed in *Ada*) may well have caused the trouble with his portrait of an older artist in the form of Shem the Penman, Festy King, the Gracehoper and many more. Nabokov's novels frequently make play with parodic allusions to other works, of course. Like Marvell he frequently gets the germ of an idea from parodic contemplation of another author's work, and though the parody is usually kind there is often an element of competition or even rebuke involved. In *Ada* it may be Joyce's turn, specifically the turn of *Finnegans Wake*; and it may well be that this time Nabokov has been fatally drawn not only into the familiar parodic play of reference and glancing allusion but into direct imitation and contest.

Finnegans Wake is, like *Ada*, a book which sets out to defuse all problems with ever-benign laughter, tracing out 'the byways of high improvidence', rambling slowly through a wide world 'overlorded by fate and interlarded with accidence', ever-reassuring about the time and space we have for everything from birth to death and from the 'wildering of the nicht' to 'cockeedoodle aubeus Aurore'. Like *Ada* it is at bottom a gigantic pastoral, a sunlit 'funferal'.[13]

Both books place incest at the centre of the problems which they wish to defuse by refusing to take them seriously. Both books present all the alleged problems of intra-familial life as non-problems, or problems which can easily and merrily be negotiated by those who have not allowed themselves to be intimidated by Freud. Both books play their long, slow games of time and narration. Both are conspicuously unurgent. Above all, both present (and somewhat lionize) a carefree artist-figure who is always suspected of being fraudulent but who is none the less apt to be allowed to steal the show, merrily and at some length, in comparison with more leaden-footed, less frolicsome rivals—a Gracehoper amongst the laborious Ondts of the world. Both books provide this artist-figure with a father who is at once a portentous paterfamilias and a terrific sinner.

There are other, smaller likenesses: but it is the comic conflation of Gracehoper-Artist, Father and Family which matters, along with the airily anti-Freudian tone and a manner which may be called pastoral in so far as it presents, with steady acclaim and celebration, a world more pacific, sunlit, spacious, and painless than the one which we are unfortunate enough to inhabit. In *Finnegans Wake* Joyce made perhaps the greatest effort ever attempted to solve all the world's problems in terms of pastoral comedy, defusing everything with ease, relating everything to everything else and everyone to everyone else,[14] so that the very *principium individuationis* itself would at last succumb to the endless healing and solacing combinations of his puns.

A book which defied gravity on a scale like that must have tempted Nabokov. His declared love of Joyce by no means extended to *Finnegans Wake*. He found it indeed to be hardly ever redeemed from 'utter insipidity'.[15] But he may still have been inwardly drawn to imitation and competition. He had equalled Joyce in the most obvious form of notoriety, since *Lolita* had stirred the same sense of outrage as *Ulysses*. But with *Finnegans Wake* Joyce had achieved something more esoteric and perhaps even more attractive. With *Finnegans Wake* he had become the ultimate Modern who gave absolutely no quarter to his readers and with whom critics tangled at their peril. It was perhaps the role of polylingual, multi-referential, incomprehensibly intelligent super-artist that tempted Nabokov.

He was interested in that sort of notoriety as well. He was fatally capable of the sort of self-lionization as maestro that Joyce himself produces in the figure of Shem the Penman. So in *Ada*, Nabokov/Veen looks back with fondness on the scandal caused in Middle America by *Lolita*, just as in *Finnegans Wake* Joyce/Shem looks back with fondness on the scandal caused in Ireland in particular and the world in general by *Ulysses*. Shem rejoices to think of himself as a

semidemented zany amid the inspissated grime of his raucous den making believe to read his usylessly unreadable Blue Book of Eccles, *édition de ténèbres*.[16]

So Nabokov likewise is delighted with himself for having caused a town in Texas to change its name from 'Lolita' after the appearance of his own Blue Book under the *imprimatur* of a wicked French publishing house.

But *Lolita*, though as Blue as *Ulysses*, had not achieved the even finer notoriety of being 'usylessly unreadable'. The author of a best seller after all is denied the pleasure of being thought of as incomprehensible. So perhaps *Ada* would not only allude to *Finnegans Wake*, but imitate it, and compete with it ...

The result is unfortunate. For once, Nabokov is lost. For once the precision of lyrical and ironic tone deserts him. There are fine things in the book, and as a Nabokov enthusiast one will happily gulp it down along with all the rest. But it isn't hard to understand why other readers, innocent of an obsession with its author, find it 'usylessly unreadable' in the simplest of senses.

18

PALE FIRE AND GLORY

Marvell, by contrast, is able to handle with ease an ironic whimsicality as relaxed as that which is attempted in *Ada*. There is a mood in him which casts doubt upon the most cherished dreams of the human imagination with such lightness that one begins to wonder whether doubt has been cast at all. He can leave hardly perceptible traces of disbelief around the imagery of the 'halcyon climate',[1] the imagery of Arcadia preserved.

The secret is probably brevity. The short poem, unlike the long novel, can achieve an air of near-weightless suspension for a brief period. Images will simply hang there in unurgent stillness, separate and brilliant. There will be space around the image in which the reader may move circumspectly. The image itself, with its curious motionless suspension, will not quite sponsor the reader's doubts and enquiries. But it will permit doubt to arise.

This mood of suspension is apt to enter Marvell's writing when he contemplates the idea of religious purity. Where is the line between purity and preciosity? Between innocence and blankness? Between chastity and self-enclosedness? Between other-worldly exultation and self-deception? His mind plays over such questions with a scepticism so delicate as to leave a reader wondering whether it really is scepticism or whether he has simply lost Marvell's thread and wandered away into doubts of his own.

Part of Marvell's mind is distinctly cosmopolitan. The travelled, urban, poly-lingual man, at home in the diversity of 'the Animated City Throng',[2] came eventually to dominate. His is the voice that ridicules the mawkishness and ignorance of Samuel Parker whose head is set in a ludicrous whirl when he leaves the libraries and quadrangles of Oxford for the open world of London.[3] But another part of Marvell is private to the point of secretiveness. The withdrawing, meditative part of the man (most of whose poetry was seemingly never intended to be read by others at all, and who describes himself in *The Rehearsal Transpros'd* as reluctant to be drawn out into the world of writing and publication[4]) is as strong as the cosmopolitan part. He is one of the earliest writers for whom privacy is problematic. The private and public realms are separated by division and tension.

One of the effects of this is that he can look and speak from very different angles. From the sanctuary of the private realm he may look askance at the public world of political, military, and ecclesiastical careers. Alternatively, from the perspective of the public and political world of the city he may look at, and be less than completely impressed by, the inward, withdrawn spirit of private sanctuary.

Nothing could be further from, for example, George Herbert, where the individual Christian and the public churchman move in complete harmony. His poems are laid before us, his public, with the unguarded intimacy of private speech. Nor could anything be further from Henry Vaughan, whose poetry is highly personal and whose typical landscape is one of solitude, but who gives his personality and his solitude undefended to the world at large. Marvell, half at home in the city and half at home in the secrecy of his withdrawals, will not be as unproblematic as Herbert and Vaughan when so private a virtue as religious purity is under consideration. He invites care, suspicion even, where they have a candour which promotes complete trust.

Hence for example 'On a Drop of Dew',[5] a poem about religious purity and the paradisal longing for a return to unsullied origins. It is a carefully studied poem, written twice, once in English and once in Latin, like 'The Garden', which shares some of its themes and some of its elusiveness:

> See how the Orient Dew,
> Shed from the Bosom of the Morn
>   Into the blowing Roses,
> Yet careless of its Mansion new;
> For the clear Region where 'twas born

Round in its self incloses:
And in its little Globes Extent,
Frames as it can its native Element.
How it the purple flow'r does slight,
    Scarce touching where it lyes,
    But gazing back upon the Skies,
    Shines with a mournful Light;
    Like its own Tear,
Because so long divided from the Sphear.
    Restless it roules and unsecure,
    Trembling lest it grow impure:
Till the warm Sun pitty it's Pain,
And to the Skies exhale it back again.
    So the Soul . . .

(1-19)

Does it read like Vaughan? Or does it read more like a parody of
Vaughan, a parody in the gentle sense of Nabokov, for whom
'satire is a lesson, parody a game'?[6]

The cosmopolitan mind looks at the round, translucent dew-
drop soul and sets it in suspension. At first it looks like an object
of transcendent beauty and purity. But then, with hardly a shift,
it comes to look more like a doleful, sentimental, self-enclosed
little creature for whom, in its narcissism, all the pleasures of the
world are corrupt and inferior. It is one thing to have no time for
the world's corrupt blandishments, but quite another to be
'careless' of a 'Mansion', or to shrink from roses, or to shun
'sweat leaves and blossoms green' and to slight 'the purple
flow'r'.

Why, one finds oneself wondering, is this soul so enclosed in
itself? Why does it look no further than 'its little Globes Extent'?
Is there not a perceptible vibration of self-love in its 'scarce
touching where it lyes', and another in its 'trembling lest it grow
impure'? And what of its curious touch-me-not blend of the
prudish and the coquettish:

In how coy a Figure wound,
Every way it turns away?

(27-8)

The language of purity, hermetic and platonic, is quietly but
wickedly played with in this poem. The poem's apparent praise

of purity manages to leave behind a sense of preciosity, timidity, and withdrawal. It also leaves behind a touch of that suspect connoisseurship of exquisite sensation for which Marvell ridicules the '*Suttle Nunns*' at Appleton House. We crave the preservation of our paradisal innocence, perhaps. But it needs preserving alive, not in aspic,

> White, and entire, though congeal'd and chill.[7]

There is no firm emphasis to make a sceptical reading secure. But the very suspendedness of the poem seems to create an air of equivocation in which the platonic soul, round, light-filled, uncorrupted, and self-complete, gradually appears like a coy little mite by whom the cosmopolitan poet is far from impressed.

A different sort of religious purity, with 'an holy and a chearful note', is sought, and thought to be found, by the boatmen of 'Bermudas'.[8] The irony that surrounds them is even more airy and elusive. Why should their song of naïve and frank gratitude for the Arcadian haven provided for them by God not be taken at face value? Why should one suspect that there is irony or whimsy in the poem's atmosphere? The song is full of wonder. It has a lovely and graceful lyric rhythm. Does it not celebrate a mellifluent accord between religious men and the exotic world to which they row over the calm ocean while the winds listen?

The centre of the poem, with the island's scents, its fruits, and its colours, gives the main substance of the boatmen's song as a genuinely exultant lyric. But the centre is, so to speak, put in parenthesis by a certain wariness that precedes and follows it. The men are in a boat on a benign sea rowing 'along'. Then they arrive, but not so much in reality as in imagination, at an exotic, heaven-blest, Arcadian island. Then, at the end, after the parenthesis, we find them still in their boat, still rowing, though now the sense of rowing 'along', making progress and getting somewhere, has gone, to be replaced by the earily becalmed stillness of:

> And all the way, to guide their Chime,
> With falling Oars they kept the time.
> (39-40)

Men who are rowing seriously will sing to keep their rowing in rhythm. These men do the reverse, rowing only to keep their singing in tempo. Also, rowing is a strenuous activity in which oars are lifted and pulled, whereas here oars are said only to be 'falling'. It all has an odd air of slackness about it.[9] As the poem distances itself from its intense centre in their vision of an earthly paradise, it leaves us with a closing image of a tiny '*English* boat' in the vastness of the Atlantic Ocean, lonely, dwarfed, and not making much headway.

Before the lyric parenthesis there was already trouble. Is there a faint air of coyness about being 'unespy'd' in the ocean's bosom? Is there a faint air of emptiness or lassitude in their beginning 'What should we do . . .'? Is there a touch of the naïve in their conviction of the special 'care' which Providence has for them, as shown by the kindly arranged 'daily Visits' of comestible fowl? Perhaps even the boatmen themselves seem, after their song of exultation, a trifle embarrassed at their certitude, sobering themselves up with the self-deprecating brackets of '(of which we rather boast)' and '(perhaps)'.

Do they, moved to add these little hesitations as to Providence's special eye for their little boat, have something of what would seem to be Marvell's disbelief in their holy and cheerful chime? It would be as well if they did, for the chances of such a chime arriving at heaven's vault and, rebounding thence, echoing beyond the Mexique bay seem slender to say the least. There is little chance of such rowing in such a boat bringing them safely to their island paradise. The seas that cast the ambergris on shore are 'Seas, that roar', seas big enough not only to contain but even to destroy 'the huge Sea-Monsters'. These seas were renowned, of course, for their roughness, as Marvell well knew, having lived in the house of John Oxenbridge, a former resident of the isles. Will such chiming and such rowing be any match for the tremendous percussions of the Atlantic and the Caribbean? They may, miraculously; but all good miracles are considered with a certain reserve by cosmopolitan minds like Marvell's.

But this may be wrong. All may be well. Certainly, even if all is not well, both poems still leave something behind besides airy disbelief. They are far from being unkind or slanderous, and the possibility of the authentically miraculous leaves its trace in each, irony notwithstanding. At the end of 'On a Drop of Dew' we see the platonic soul

> run
> Into the Glories of th' Almighty Sun
> (39-40)

with a powerful surge and uplift, triumphant perhaps, to tease the cosmopolitan unbeliever who has hitherto been teasing the platonist. And the famous incandescent colour of the Bermuda oranges,

> Like golden Lamps in a green Night
> (18)

may be enough to justify the boatmen, who have minds which are at least capable of wonderful imaginative intensity, even if in reality they may be sadly deceived.

Both platonic exultation and the honest singing of Puritan plain-heartedness engage the human imagination and tempt it to flights which are known, but not trusted or shared, by the urban intellectual and private thinker. He has his reserve and his intelligent games to play. But the platonist and the puritan may well survive his disbelief, leaving behind the power of their dreaming whatever his mind may have done to invalidate it. It is not unlike the dilemma of Flaubert, though in a very minor key. He, another man both cosmopolitan and private, found the exaltations of religion both to contain the highest and most excellent flights of the human imagination, and at the same time to be completely unbelievable.[10]

19

ENDGAME WITH KNIGHT
AND BISHOP

Working with an irony less incorporeal, Nabokov is always capable of the poise that *Ada* lacked. *The Real Life of Sebastian Knight*,[1] following *The Gift*, is another slippery, untrustworthy book about an exiled writer. Matters deepen here. This sadder and more sombre book stirs some profound personal doubts. The ironic author whose narrators cannot be believed has played his games with the pretensions of the yound bard, Fyodor. Now he will find himself playing some more disturbing games with the life and work of an artist whose career is finished but who none the less may never have got past the Fyodor stage of lonely immaturity. There is a distinctly sombre self-confrontation and confession buried amidst the narrative games of his first non-Russian book. It halted Nabokov's career in a deep crisis of self-doubt.[2]

V, the narrator of *The Real Life of Sebastian Knight*, gives himself away even before he begins to tell his story. His very title is a presumption for, as the scruples and perspectives of Modernism might have taught him, there is no such thing as the real, or definitive, life of anybody. His first paragraph reveals him as an idle, haphazard researcher and thick-skinned breaker of confidences. His second paragraph reveals him as a self-preoccupied man and a poor, vulgar performer in the Nabokovian realms of memory. His third paragraph confirms his self-involvedness and invites us to suspect that his story is all fantasy anyway and that he himself is a mere 'garrulous imposter'.

Our mistrust is wide awake at once. We are ready to take nothing at face value, to query his authority and his motives throughout. We are also ready to piece together what we can from his rambling, evasive tale, hoping to pick up something of him and his subject where we may, making the most of little things that he lets slip and reserving the right to listen to other witnesses, perhaps especially when he appears to be telling us not to.

On the face of it this is a story about genius, or at least about great spiritual distinction. It is the life of a man who has kept faith and gone his independent way as a fine artist, embodying in his work the purity, accuracy, and succinctness of perception which we Philistine blunderers lack. V presents his hero as a successful author of five books with all the Nabokovian attributes. Sebastian Knight is a games-player, a maker of labyrinths, a stylist, a parodist, an individualist, a brilliantly witty deflator of the portentous. He is admired by the discerning and (perhaps even more importantly) misunderstood and abused by Philistines like Goodman. The tragic ruin of his short life is eventually brought about by a shallow woman who exploits him ruthlessly, another Juliana to another Damon.

But that is only V's version of Sebastian Knight, V's book. Nabokov's book is quite different. Nabokov's book holds V's book suspended within it in silent invitation to a reader's doubts. In Nabokov's book V's version of Knight cannot survive for one moment as an even remotely adequate account of him, let alone as his *Real Life*. Fyodor's version of his father's life was hopelessly distorted by his determined adoration. So here with V, a highly interested witness, hero-worship, strained identification, and hungry adoration from a distance distort his version of his half-brother's career. The author's involvement with his subject is just as disabling, just as deep-seated, just as intense.

There is sibling rivalry in the involvement, intensified in the case of half-brothers who, in competition, have different mothers to defend. The national, cultural rivalry between Russian V and English Sebastian complicates matters further. The strongest vitiating factor of all, dating back to childhood, is V's desire to be noticed by a gifted and aloof elder brother. This desire was there in their divided childhood household and it grows later into a curiously intense envy of his brother, almost a desire to become his brother, passing into his body after his death. Behind the prose of V's story of his impressive and famous brother one can detect something similar to Fyodor's sad and thwarted longing to accompany his magnificent father on his Asiatic travels. Such things will be detected again when, in *Pale Fire*, Kinbote longs in vain to join up his life with that of the famous and respected John Shade. Each man offers himself as the definitive commentator, uniquely equipped with special insight. But in each case truth is swept aside by a desperate involvement with another man's being.

In *Pale Fire* we always want to believe Kinbote, even against all the evidence, even when it is clear that he is fabricating everything. But V is a singularly unattractive man, even an obnoxious man, whom a reader will always find himself ready and willing to resist. In the case of V we are all too ready to disbelieve. He thinks of himself as fastidious and as having high taste, but he is at the same time a pushy person in hardly much less of a hurry than the entrepreneurial Goodman to get out a book on Knight while the market is right. The biographer's role of prying intruder seems never to embarrass him as much as it might, for he is a mawkish man with a gift for barging in and no sense of what a clumsy nuisance he is. He is selfish, mean with money, and a man who finds it easy to lie or break his word. He is unpleasantly free with his comments on other people's appearance. Sometimes the world rebuffs him, leading his researches up blind alleys and keeping vital clues or documents just out of reach of his greedy hands. He is the sort of man who makes one maliciously pleased when such things happen.

What emerges from a mistrustful reading of the book is a much less beglamoured story about Sebastian Knight and his lonely distinction or artistic genius. V obfuscates and blurs everything, but there will slowly emerge to the patient eye, from behind V's obfuscations, a sad and sombre tale. As this hidden tale emerges we first see Sebastian as a young boy in a broken, divided family, resentful of his father, resentful of his stepmother and half-brother, feeling himself stranded in the alien world that his family has now become. He clings tenaciously to the memory of his own dead mother whose last visit to him was, poignantly enough, on his birthday. He has her last present to him hidden away in his room for a long time afterwards. He holds himself aloof from his pestering half-brother. He is not popular at school. Aloofness and solitude are the keynotes of his life from the start.

As his life goes on the aloofness hardens into a regular manner and the solitude deepens. An inherited illness will further increase his misfortune.

He is the young witness of many deaths at the time of his exile from Russia. Once exiled he wastes no time in breaking free from the unwanted stepmother and half-brother. He will see his stepmother only once more in the three years that remain before her death. After that, in the further fourteen years that remain of his own life, he will see his half-brother only twice. On both occasions he will hardly be able to get away from him quickly enough. He seems to have had only one friend, with whom he quickly loses touch.

However, he meets and sets up house with Clare Bishop; but knight-moves and bishop-moves do not link up very well and we would be advised not to have too many hopes of so awkward a union. The basic weakness of the combination will always become apparent in the endgame: Clare is better matched with the other Bishop whom she later marries. In the endgame too, when the board is clear, the knight's unique ability to jump over other pieces is a dwindling asset. Only in combination are knights powerful at this stage of the game and this Knight is alone.[3]

None the less the meeting of Knight with Bishop is at the start auspicious. Sebastian's first book was written quickly in the summer following their meeting and it sounds bright and playful, even if contrived. Thereafter we can feel the heat and momentum gradually go out of things. The later books are put more slowly together as Sebastian retreats. Clare becomes more and more marginal to his life. Their eventual separation will then lead him into humiliation and ever deeper loneliness.

His writing also retreats as the titles of his books suggest. After the colour and brilliance of a *Prismatic Bezel* and the glitter of *Success* things darken. *Lost Property* is an ominous title for a book which V says is autobiographical in character. It is also an ominous title for a book written immediately after his separation. His last work, *The Doubtful Asphodel*, does nothing to dispel this sense of darkening, for the asphodel was a flower of Elysium associated with healing[4] and for such a flower to become 'doubtful' for a young man with a fatal disease means that hope has dwindled further. His own final verdict upon himself, in a letter written at the end of his life, confirms our suspicion that all has gone awry:

I am fed up (*osskomina*) with a number of tortuous things and especially with the patterns of my shed snake-skins (*vypolziny*) so that now I find a poetic solace in the obvious and the ordinary which for some reason or other I had overlooked in the course of my life. (Ch. 19)

What a haunting confession that is.

Mme Lecerf, the apparent Juliana of the story, can hardly be as much to blame for all this as V tries to imply. Sebastian Knight seems to have made himself an insufferable, arrogant presence in her not very fortunate life. What he suffered in the affair with her seems mostly to have been of his own contriving. It is hardly her fault if a snobbish, aloof, unhappy minor novelist gets hurt while setting up a literary image of her as an object to adore and revile. She surely has the right simply to be uninterested in the aesthetic affectation of Sebastian's idea of passion:

He told her bitterly that she was cheap and vain, and then he kissed her to make sure that she was not a porcelain figure ... he would come à *l'improviste* and plump down on a pouf with his hands on the knob of a cane, without taking off his gloves ... and say that she was vain and cheap, and that he could not live without her.[5]

Knight's own sad verdict on himself as a failed, unhappy man who has overlooked 'the obvious and the ordinary' begins to sound authoritative. Mme Lecerf's growing impatience with his snobbery and affectation begins to seem well-founded:

she found out that she had had quite enough of hearing him talk of his dreams, and the dreams in his dreams, and the dreams in the dreams of his dreams. (Ch. 16)

So does her charge that he was always

much too preoccupied with his own sensations and ideas to understand those of others. (Ch. 16)

An English businessman whom V meets in a hotel foyer seems to sum it all up very cogently:

the author seemed to him a terrible snob, intellectually, at least. Asked to explain, he added that Knight seemed to him to be constantly playing some game of his own invention, without telling his partners its rules. He said he preferred books that made one think, and Knight's books didn't—they left you puzzled and cross. (Ch. 18)

One is tempted to think that that might be about the size of it. It sounds very close to Knight's own dissatisfaction with 'tortuous things'.[6]

There has gradually emerged a very sad tale of severance, displacement, and unfulfilment. Many lives are involved, not only Knight's. The father of the two half-brothers was killed in a pointless duel leaving an already precarious family to disintegrate further. A strange, wraith-like English woman lived a life of exile in an unhappy marriage in Russia and lost her son when the marriage broke up. Another woman widowed by the duel, took her son and stepson into exile in her turn.

Nobody lived very long. The father probably died in his early forties, his first wife in her late thirties, his second wife at maybe about fifty. Sebastian Knight himself died at thirty-six. Clare Bishop killed herself at about the same age. Alexis Pan, another dubious-sounding writer whose path had once crossed Sebastian's, enjoyed a couple of years of fleeting fame and then killed himself too.[7] Neither V's pose nor Sebastian's seems capable of handling that sort of human material, the one riddled as it is with self-deception, the other given over to the sterile elaboration of 'tortuous things'.

Nabokov, sharing many qualities with Sebastian Knight, was interrogating himself searchingly. Sebastian, after Fyodor, is another mask of what he feared to become. But while Fyodor's languid aestheticism prompts, for the most part, one's amusement, Sebastians coldness, aloofness, and sterility are much more troubling. *The Real Life of Sebastian Knight* is still a work of irony, even of ironic game; but its tone is distinctly sombre. This artist is no festive penman lionized and indulged by an author at his ease. He is an unhappy, sterile, lonely person, too readily convinced of his own superiority and distinction, leading his short and disappointing life through from solitary childhood to broken adulthood.

After *The Gift* Nabokov was immediately renewed and ready to write again, even to write again in a new language (English), in a new country (France), in flight from Hitler's Germany and in a tiny flat where he hardly had room to work. But after the self-reckoning of *The Real Life of Sebastian Knight* came the long pause in his career, right through to the mid-fifties with only *Bend Sinister* in between. There was a deep and sombre warning to be read in this mask of himself. The patient disbelief of irony had uncovered some extremely chastening possibilities.

20

ARCADIAN ARTEFACTS

Marvell's thinking about the preservation of Arcadian innocence produced two great poems which, like *The Real Life of Sebastian Knight*, take irony back into less etherial realms. 'The Garden'[1] looks with belief and disbelief at the possibilities of preserving innocence and peace in a sanctuary or retreat. 'The Coronet',[2] sombre and regretful in mood, full of profound religious scruple, mistrusts the sacramental images of a religious art made from Arcadian materials

> That once adorn'd my Shepherdesses head
> (8)

and sees them as betraying the artist's 'Skill' and 'Care' to polluted purposes.

Did Fyodor, Van, and Sebastian Knight set up in their lives and works valid images of preserved Arcadia? Did Cincinnatus's paradise-rug of memory guarantee in its folding patterns the maintenance of connection from innocence to adulthood? Or was it all a matter of mere 'tortuous things'? Did all that 'Skill' and 'Care' produce a mere 'curious frame', like the false garland of 'The Coronet' whose winding complexity is hopelessly bound up with the 'slipp'ry knots' of the serpent of Eden? Is the solitude of 'a green Thought in a green Shade' deep and creative? Or sterile and empty like Sebastian's solitude?

Throughout his work Nabokov pondered the opposed images of art as genius and art as trickery, art as the product of imaginative excellence and art as the product of deceit. The imagery of the creative artistic imagination was placed repeatedly alongside the imagery of forgery, conjuring, illusionism, cardsharping and all the subjective hosannahs of idle wordsmiths. The enquiry remained ever-open, ever-inconclusive.

So it remains in 'The Garden' whose juxtapositional inconclusiveness is highly Nabokovian. The poem engages awkward issues. It engages the themes of solitude and sterility, with the idea of Arcadian hope turning to dust in a dreamer's hands; but then it ends fancifully, untroubled by the inconsistencies and irresolutions around which it is content to play. 'The Coronet' on the other hand is extremely serious. The Calvinist in Marvell is ready to see all his most treasured images shattered, withered, and trodden under foot if it can be shown that they serve only falsehood and pollution.

'The Garden', though in the end it is a fanciful poem, has great urgency behind it at the beginning. The opening stanza, in knotty, powerful complexes of imagery, sees men of the active world as sterile, narrow and crazed ('themselves amaze') by their 'uncessant Labours', just as 'restless *Cromwel*' was in 'An Horatian Ode'. The fifth stanza, with equal power, sets up an opposite imagery of fruitful, easy riches in a highly sexualized garden paradise. The tension between the two is at first very great. There is a strong recoil from the sterile, a palpable hunger for the 'wond'rous Life' of grapes, nectarines, peaches, and melons.

In the Latin version of the poem[3] the issue is left as simply polarized as that. The madness of active men ('praecordia' and 'furor') is opposed by the sanctuaries of spring ('penetralia veris') whose green powers heal and preserve the man who flees there. The garden sanctuary symbolizes the union of artefact and nature and the combination of sexuality with innocence or harmlessness.

But the English poem plays around the statement which the Latin poem is content to make straightforwardly. In stanzas 6 to 8, which have no equivalent in the Latin, complexity and hesitation veil the basic polarity. The pleasure of the sexualized garden suddenly becomes a 'pleasure less' beyond which there is now further retreat. Even in gardens it seems there are problems. Even in protected gardens there are further, deeper shades, protected even from the colours and juices of sun-filled fruits. In a purer, darker, recessed greenery 'Mind' and 'Thought' take sanctuary even within a sanctuary. But then, in the most famous of all Marvell's tantalizing ambiguities, this very retreat may bring its doubts. The 'green Thought in a green Shade' sounds like a profound centre of life, deep and fertile. But

> Annihilating all that's made
> (47)

sounds an ominously destructive and disappointingly single-minded way of getting there.[4] The duplicity of things is having its way with Marvell even here, turning the 'penetralia veris' into a questionable place. Is this deep shade, after all, so different from the 'short and narrow verged Shade' of the first stanza, which mocked striving men and enclosed all their efforts in littleness? Was 'annihilating all' what the retreat from the violence and sterility of the world was supposed to produce?

Criticism should not try to answer these questions for the poem itself does not try to do so. It pursues them, traces them out, but then leaves all the different findings of its pursuit open, intact, and calmly juxtaposed in the unpressured composition of the whole poem. It is a very open poem, content to leave behind both the urgency of its questions and the whimsicality of its non-answers. As the poem winds down in its later stanzas, the soul in sanctuary takes on the brilliant light and colour of a bird; but, like Marvell's dew-drop soul, it is not without its self-regard and even dandyism as it 'whets, and combs its silver Wings'. Even at the world's green beginning in Eden there was troublesome sexuality and the interruption of solitude, for the green thoughts of the solitary Adam were gravely disturbed by the creation of Eve. But why have we wandered so far back in retreat, back before even the creation of Eve, to find so strict and extreme a notion of celibacy or singleness, when 'single', in the opening stanza, was used to describe a state of poor, celibate sterility from which the riches of the garden were to rescue Marvell?

There is no answer, only the steady working of doubt beneath the surface of what is still a kind of celebration. The doubt and the celebration will simply have to inhabit the mind together. The garden of the celibate Adam, wandering 'solitary' and 'alone', simply stations itself in the mind alongside one's memory of the 'Luscious Clusters of the Vine' which, a few stanzas before, welcomed the garden wanderer with rapturous profusion.

Confidence in sanctuaries of preserved Arcadia gradually dissipates. Certitides vaporize. Expected rewards look less fine in the achievement than in the pursuit. Even when the poem returns to the patterns of the Latin, to close with a praise of garden-making, gentle dissonances continue to be heard. In the Latin, the gardener ('opifex horti') and the careful bee ('sedula ... apis') work in unison. But in the English there are light hints of division even here, for here the bee 'computes its time' without benefit of any artefact, not even the Arcadian artefact of a flower-clock made in a sanctuary world by a 'skilful Gardner'. The bee surpasses every artificer in effortless industry and spontaneous computation. He annihilates nothing and needs no redeeming artefacts or saving retreats. We unfortunately, even the gardeners amongst us, are still condemned to some kind of labour, just like the striving, competitive toilers of the first stanza.

This dissipation of what seemed Arcadian is wonderfully gentle. It is done with half-tones and half-smiles, with tiny linguistic hints and pressures. It makes doubt and disappointment seem painless. The seeker after sanctuaries is as kindly treated as were the dew-drop soul and the Bermuda boatmen. Dreams are respected and the defects of dreams not cruelly insisted upon. But it does begin to look as though Arcadia simply cannot be preserved. It looks as though all images of innocence and all sanctuaries are bound in the end to disappoint us. It looks as though the solitary pursuit of perfection will, as with Sebastian Knight, produce sterility rather than saving Arcadian artefacts.

'The Coronet' would seem to reinforce such sobering conclusions. From another more troubled perspective, the painless disappointment which gently dissipated longing in 'The Garden' might turn to acute anxiety. The mind yearns after innocence and holds perfection in high regard. So it sets up symbolic artefacts to satisfy the yearning and to embody the regard. It makes gardens. It seeks 'Garlands of response'. But the disappointments inherent in the effort may not always be painless. In 'The Coronet' garlands again are sought:

I seek with Garlands to redress that Wrong
(4)

and gardens again will supply them:

> Through every Garden, every Mead,
> I gather flow'rs . . .
>
> (5-6)

But in this profound, sober, and Calvinist poem the sense of sterility, disappointment, and guilt of Sebastian's 'tortuous things' is very painful indeed.

The guilt of the poem's opening aches profoundly in the confession of duties neglected 'long, too long'. Amends are attempted with a moving mixture of modesty and haste. Forlorn confessions are heard in the parenthetical '(my fruits are only flow'rs)' and '(so I my self deceive)'. Complex omens of guilt and difficulty echo in the idea of 'Dismantling . . . fragrant towers' to make this belated sacramental garland.

When disappointment comes now it comes as sudden pain, unmollified by the slow, gentle pace of the transitions in 'The Garden'. It is recorded with the note of lament, and as in the bitter lament of 'The unfortunate Lover' we can again hear the urgent voice of Blake:

> Alas I find the Serpent old
> That, twining in his speckled breast,
> About the flow'rs disguised does fold,
> With wreaths of Fame and Interest.
>
> (13-16)

No levity will disperse such fears and make such disappointments acceptable or painless. Their dissonances are sharp. The word 'debase' follows quickly on in the next line to fix this unhappy sense of irremediable pollution.

From here there can be no whimsicality and dispersal. Resolution now is immediate and stern, for there follows at once a weighty, dignified, and courageous eight-line sentence which takes the poem to its end in a single rhetorical sweep. It negotiates its complex structure with deliberated certainty, pressing on from the opening 'But' through 'Either', 'Or' and 'Though' to a clearly foreknown, and inevitable self-sacrificial purpose:

> That they, while Thou on both their spoils dost tread,
> May crown thy Feet, that could not crown thy Head.[5]

Calvinist scruple about the pollution of arts and sacramental ornaments has a clear and powerful voice in Marvell. This kind of writing makes one think of him along with Milton and Bunyan, the other great Calvinist radicals of seventeenth-century literature, in whom the images of the paradisal and the polluted were equally powerfully developed. The paradise lost by Milton's Adam and the paradise re-entered at last by Bunyan's pilgrims were separated by a world of mist, mire, and deformation in between. Marvell too has his share of this vision with its extreme poles of tragic calamity and exultation. It is by no means the whole of his mind, nor even the centre of it, but it is there none the less. It must have made its contribution to his strong sense of irrecoverable loss, deepening it, extending the range of its images. In this single poem it declares itself with sure and dignified power. The numbing self-doubt that stirred those images of the total failure of art in *The Real Life of Sebastian Knight* finds its Marvellian equivalent here in the regretful recoil from all 'tortuous things', all 'curious frames'.

But maybe at the last there is just room for doubt, just room in afterthought for residual queries which might turn the poem back again, away from Milton, Bunyan, and Blake and towards the more familiar areas of reserve and irony. The dominant note of the poem is, overwhelmingly, that of self-sacrificial readiness to see the falsities of art shattered and withered. The rhetorical certitude of the poem's ending depends upon the great courage of that conviction. But there may still be some room for manoeuvre.

A less awesome alternative is kept open by Marvell's offering Christ his 'Either ... Or ...', the 'Either' being that He should not necessarily shatter garland and serpent together but rather 'untie' and 'disentangle' the one from the other. So a tiny crack opens in the rhetoric of courage and self-sacrificial conviction. But what if the crack should close again and Christ should follow the second course of shattering serpent and garland together, and treading on both their 'spoils'? Even then all may not be lost. The careful wording of the last two lines keeps the spoils of the serpent just separate from the spoils of the garland and leaves the garland, even at this extremity, to 'crown' Christ's feet if not His head. A crown, set at the feet of Christ, is still a crown, still triumphant.

There is a trace of his lighter, ironic nimbleness in Marvell's retrieving so much at the end from what is otherwise a cogent declaration of readiness for self-sacrifice. The gravity of the poem's religious courage still remains. Its fear of sterility and pollution remain. But even when Marvell is grave, he is phenomenally quick, darting in at the last moment to retrieve a saving paradox from beneath the feet of a theological certainty.

PART FIVE

Comedy and Carnival

21

THE ENCHANTED HUNTER

The matters discussed in the previous section have been the stock-in-trade of studies of both Marvell and Nabokov. Irony, ambiguity, equivocation, parody, self-parody, and game have, in one way or another, dominated discussion of the two authors. Critical terminologies have differed, but in this tonal area the witty poetry of the seventeenth century and the ironic prose of Modernism have provoked some similar responses. The sophisticated games-playing intelligence of the artist has frequently stood at the centre of things.

Such critical languages have done their work well. But they have perhaps by now done it a little repetitiously and they have certainly done it a little exclusively. Marvell and Nabokov are both, evidently enough, masters of the most delicate irony and subtle play. But both are masters of a good deal else too, and the dominant critical vocabularies, concentrating exclusively in one area, may well be obscuring other things.

When the era of Modernism at last discovered Marvell, the lyric poems very quickly found an audience which Modernist art itself had educated to the right expectations. Once Modernist art had greatly increased the breadth and depth of uncertainty which readers could tolerate in literature the way was clear for the great enigmatic ironist in Marvell.

But not everything was gain. Seventeenth- and eighteenth-century readers of Marvell may not have been able to assimilate most of the poems but they had known how to laugh at *The Rehearsal Transpros'd*; and nineteenth-century readers were still laughing at a poem like 'The Character of Holland'.[1] There is an area of Marvell's work that is humorous but not in the way that the dominant critical language of his modern discovery can catch. *The Rehearsal Transpros'd* and a group of poems including 'The Character of Holland' have this humour. It is not elegant wit or ironic reserve. These works are, simply and boisterously, very funny indeed. They used to make people laugh aloud and that is certainly what they are for.

Nabokov too is known as a humorist, but rather too much known as a humorist of delicate shades. A more boisterous laughter is essential to him too, a vital part of his creative life. The earlier Nabokov is apt to use his laughter rather directively, in for example the mixture of fantasy and derision which animates the cartoon portraits of Berlin philistines in *King Queen Knave*, *Laughter in the Dark*, or *The Gift*. It is never pure satire, never purely corrective or purposive, but it has a basis in satiric directionality and animus.

But there is also a cartoon-making quality to this spirit, rejoicing in a kind of overplus of comic performance and displaying powers of fantasy far beyond what would be necessary for a pure satirist bent only on destroying his victim. In that overplus where laughter tends to become gratuitous, celebratory, and undirectional, the truly creative spirit of Nabokov's humour is to be found. Satire shades into saturnalia as this element comes to prevail over the power to deride.

Once in the earlier work this element breaks free to produce the portait of Alla in *Glory*.[2] Elsewhere it is more an incipient power in Nabokov's mind, heard fitfully, caught occasionally in this or that image or remark, but never quite becoming the dominant mode of his writing. With Alla, his subject was the growth of sexual pleasure content with impermanence amongst the accidental collisions of the world. That was the subject that first gave his laughter its rein. Much later, when this new comic spirit firmly established itself beyond directionality and animus, it was again the link with sex and accident which prompted its freedom. *Lolita* is the key work again. Telling the tale of the impermanent and ludicrously unlikely sexual collision of Humbert and Lolita liberated Nabokov's humour from satire and distaste. His bent for the freer comedy of Saturnalia was set free.

Lolita, *Pale Fire*, and *Look at the Harlequins!* see the later Nabokov exploiting this new vein of fully liberated comedy. In each, the comedy is high-spirited, more boisterous than ironic game and less aggressive than satire. In each, the new romance form prevails. Romance is the traditional form for narrations of sexual adventure and misadventure. In addition, romance, with its amiably loose-limbed structure, determined at bottom by the shape of a journey which may have as many digressions as it wants, is ideally suited to the world of accident and impermanence to which this comedy is attuned.

The moment of liberation in *Lolita*[3] is one of high confidence. The book begins exuberantly and the *brio* of performance stays with it almost throughout. Finding the mode of romance Nabokov has also found a confident voice. Finding the comic-romance theme of a man in love with a child means equally that he has found an ideal transposition of the Arcadian theme into newly bizarre realms, full of fictional potential. From the beginning, *Lolita* is breezy with that sense of discovery.

Matters come quickly to a head. When Humbert meets Lolita it is his immediate and irretrievable undoing. The banal suburban talk of Mrs Haze goes on as she gives him a guided tour of house and garden. But suddenly he is not following her. He is sidetracked, both physically and linguistically, and left stranded, gaping, not at her flowers but at her daughter:

'That was my Lo', she said, 'and these are my lilies.'
'Yes,' I said, 'yes. They are beautiful, beautiful, beautiful!'
(Pt. I, Ch. 10)

Humbert has done his best these many years to act like an example of *homo sapiens*, even *homo civis*. He has had jobs ('thinking up and editing perfume ads'). He has been married (to 'Valeria the comedy wife'). He has more or less behaved himself. He has kept his sex-life 'practical, ironical and brisk' and buried his lusts and fantasies like a 'law-abiding poltroon'. He has attached himself tangentially but harmlessly to 'the world of love and work'. He has had one breakdown, but the 'robust outdoor life' of a lust-chilling polar expedition has set him up again in viable imitation of a 'housebroken' citizen.

Then, when he meets Lolita, all is immediately lost:

there came a sudden burst of greenery—'the piazza,' sang out my leader, and then, without the least warning, a blue sea-wave swelled under my heart and, from a mat in a pool of sun, half-naked, kneeling, turning about on her knees, there was my Riviera love peering at me over dark glasses. (Pt. I, Ch. 10)

His 'aging ape eyes' are riveted and his imagination begins to race towards improbable, fairy-tale consummations:

as if I were the fairy-tale nurse of some little princess (lost, kidnapped, discovered in gipsy rags through which her nakedness smiled at the king and his hounds). (Pt. I, Ch. 10)

Time collapses and the life of childhood and pubescence joins with the adult present in perfect accord:

The twenty-five years I had lived since then, tapered to a palpitating point, and vanished. (Pt. I, Ch. 10)

The greenery of the 'piazza' and the water of the blue wave of unfolding memory have from the beginning set matters in the inevitable Arcadian mode. Now, as the vision holds and intensifies, the two classic elements recur:

while ... I went down the steps into the breathless garden, my knees were like reflections of knees in rippling water ... (Pt. I, Ch. 10)

It is Arcadian promise too brilliant to be resisted. The dissolving, easy, green, and liquid world of *homo poeticus* has stirred in the memory of a man who has never been able fully to abandon it. From back across the gulf of severance a magic salvation seems to offer itself. The worlds of child and adult seem to offer to re-join. The hungry, precarious adult of the severed world is rendered powerless by so miraculous an offer of release.

It is Arcadian, idiosyncratically Nabokovian. But it is also much more ordinary than that. This is a scene of Love at First Sight and the story which it begins stays faithfully throughout to all the commonplaces of romance both high and low.[4] The book is a classic, first-person account of doomed romantic love from dazzling revelation to fatal end. The rhythm of its prose follows in a single sweep the rapid blaze of Humbert's passion and then its long, sad fading. In Part One the momentum of romance is sustained *crescendo*. Part Two then traces the collapse of romance as Humbert's life is followed all the way down to its final desolation, regret, and confession.

But if *Lolita* is deliberately commonplace in romance structure it is, of course, decidedly odd in matter. It follows the commonplaces obediently only to contrast them with the highly unclassical persons of the hero and heroine. The comedy of the book is built on a continuously incongruous lack of *rapport* between the rhetoric of romance on the one hand and, on the other, two unusual lovers: lumbering, bulky Humbert, '*Berthe au grand pied*', *aetat* 37-42, and his stepdaughter Lolita, 'chest circumference twenty-seven ... figure linear', *aetat* 12-17.

Part One of this off-beat yet orthodox romance introduces the Hero and his Quest (chapters 1-9). Then comes the the great moment of Vision when he first beholds the Heroine in a suitable setting of sunlight and flowers (chapter 10). There is then his long hunger for The Unattainable (11-23), who is however miraculously attained in a crowning Consummation aided by a beneficent Fortune (24-33).

Part Two then traces the declining fortunes of Passion beset by The World to the point where She is finally Lost. The first transcontinental Journey is a Bid for Freedom (1-3); Thayer Street is a precarious sojourn in the ordinary world where Obstacles and Taboos loom large (4-14); the second trip is a dejected shadow of the first where the Rival comes ever closer and the beloved is revealed as Deceiver (15-22). There is then Sorrow, Abandonment, and a fruitless attempt at Consolation with Another Woman (23-7). Finally there is Reunion and Repentance (28-9) and the fatal Revenge (30-6).

Everything from romance, both high and low, is here. It reaches as high as the myth of Tristan and Iseult and as low as the kind of show-down ending in which Decency Wins Through and a Heart of Gold is revealed in an erstwhile Monster. It is both the story of a Grand Passion and the parody of such a story. Such a passion transfigures the commonplace world by adding magic, or merely glamour, to the humdrum. The romantic hero of such a story disdains the humdrum world of law and taboo from the height of his illicit dream. He makes an inordinate, but splendid, demand for freedom. He is daring enough, foolish enough, reckless enough, immature enough, lucky or unlucky enough to demand that dreams shall be made real and that the bits and scraps of the ordinary, unillumined world shall be transmuted into brilliant colour and harmony.

It is as romance and as parody of romance, as a book both of dream and of the world that resists dream; that Lolita reveals its

Modernist belongings. As with *Pnin* in the realm of pathos so here in the realm of comedy, Joyce is behind Nabokov and Flaubert behind Joyce. *Lolita*'s comic dealings with romance make it a bizarre, latter-day relative of Joyce's *Ulysses* and of Flaubert's *Madame Bovary* and *L'Éducation sentimentale*. It looks with kindly, patient, and inventive humour upon what happens when an extraordinary hunger for romance is set down in an ordinary world which is unlikely to give it any quarter.

Humbert is like Emma and Frédéric in having his exotic dreams, with most of his being invested in them. Like them he derives much of the rhetoric of dream from romantic literature. Like them he cannot cease being immature. He is like them in pathos and absurdity. Above all he is like them in that, despite his absurdity, he is able to leave behind a curious sense of actual heroism or integrity as after-taste to his fundamentally ridiculous quest for transcendence. To that extent he is like them in being a descendent of Don Quijote, that pathetic, absurd, and yet endlessly admirable hero of Flaubert's favourite book.[5]

Madame Bovary, L'Éducation sentimentale and *Ulysses* are, like *Don Quijote* behind them, amongst the very greatest of books. Nobody would want to claim the same stature for *Lolita*, fine though it is. It has its pathos as well as its comedy, but not remotely to the degree that the endlessly poignant *Madame Bovary* does; and while its comedy is often hilarious it is hardly so probing and disturbing as the muted, chastened, dead pan comedy of *L'Education sentimentale*[6] nor so comprehensive as that of *Ulysses*. It does not have the emotional intensity of *Madame Bovary*, nor the vast scale of the other two works; nor can it match any of them in the haunting conjunction of what is foolish to the point of the absurd with what is painful to the point of the tragic. But its belongings are here. It is a late, bizarre, idiosyncratic miniature of a literary mode in which Flaubert and Joyce produced the classic Modernist achievements. (Perhaps some of this is declared by Nabokov's providing Humbert with a shadowy pursuer with whom he is vainly trying to compete and whose name is Gustave.)

Emma dreams of high society and illicit love. Frédéric dreams of a saint-like and transfiguring devotion. Mr Bloom dreams of almost everything, from being the amiable sage of Flowerville, to being a vengeful 'dark crusader' bent on ridding the world of sin.[7] In each case a great Modernist comic romance sets its hero's prowess as dreamer against the commonplaces of the humdrum world. He exhibits thereby both his folly and his greatness, for the humane powers of Modernism characteristically lie in ambiguous images. A simpler, purely romantic attitude to such confrontations would deem the world well lost and produce therefore heroic or transcendent tragedy. A simpler, purely anti-romantic attitude, on the other hand, would see the world's victory as a merited triumph over folly and would produce therefore cautionary tales. But most of us would feel our intelligence to be insulted by the first and our generosity by the second. We would thus prefer, with Modernism, to compose our minds as best we might in an awkward, shuffling combination of both.

So it is with the great comic romances of Modernism, as of course with *Don Quijote* before them. A difficult, divided loyalty is beautifully given in the generosity and humour of such books. Nobody should be so foolish as to imagine that Emma or Frédéric is an authentic hero; but nobody should be so tardy in imagination as to find no authentic witness to the desire for liberty in their doomed pursuits of transfiguration. Flaubert's famous impassivity, his unreadiness to conclude or to take sides, is the only possible attitude.[8]

Humbert then is the typical dreamer of comic romance. He is also distinctively Nabokovian, an adult of the world of severance seeking to escape from his *homo sapiens* or *homo civis* self and return to his *homo poeticus* childhood. The keynote of his dream-self is magic, but a magic which is happy to shade off into mere glamour and luxury as well. His hunger for the 'perilous magic of nymphets' is given in a language of dazzling, pyrotechnic colour in which magic, glamour, and luxury combine as something both wonderful and ludicrous. His dreams derive from an opulent, pampered Old World upbringing in which 'ruined Russian princesses' were wont to lavish their attentions on the young scion of a family made rich by trade in nothing more gross than silk, wine, jewels, and perfume. His first experience of love was in a mimosa grove beneath 'an arabesque of lighted windows' and 'a cluster of stars'. In this gem-laden 'princedom by the sea' he first offered his beloved

the tingle, the flame, the honey-dew ... the sceptre of my passion.

(Pt. I, Ch. 4)

His later fascination with nymphets is always a search back in time for that first grand, lascivious magic. A nymphet is always magical. She is a 'fateful elf' with 'fey grace'; she casts a 'spell' and a 'charm'; she is 'mysterious'; her power is 'fantastic'; she evokes possibilities of life as 'an enchanted island' situated in 'entranced time'. This may all be wild nonsense whereby a pervert seeks to add glamour to his lusts. But comic romance thrives upon leaving such unelevating thoughts to linger, obstinately, about what looks, equally obstinately, like a genuine if off-beat rhetoric of passion. Thus our desire for magic must get along with our knowledge of the real; but on the other hand, however sober our knowledge of the real may be, we cannot quite break ourselves free from the imaginative dream that Humbert pursues. This pampered, veering madman who thinks that nymphets are 'maidens' beckoning to 'bewitched travellers' is strangely difficult to shake off. However bizarre he may be he still keeps some kind of contact with the high romances of chivalry and with the low romances of glamour which are alive in all the ordinary tropes of delight used by the most unillumined minds, from 'wonderful' or 'fantastic' or 'mysterious' or 'marvellous' to merely 'enchanting' or even 'charming'. Nobody who has ever used, or even thought such words has quite the right to deny the imaginative appeal of Humbert.

To find oneself not quite immune to the perverse and wild talk of the likes of Humbert is a disturbing and amusing experience. In this case it is more amusing than disturbing since *Lolita* is a fairly light, airy book whose imaginative trip is quite easy to enter and leave freely. Humbert does not take one remotely as far in the realm of spiritual adventure as either Emma or Quijote and there is no problem, closing the book of his life, in returning to the normal world. But the trip has been made none the less, with great gusto and fire. We are taken by Humbert's magic and even more by his outrageous comic *hauteur* as he looks down disdainfully from the heights of his fantasy at the dismal, unmagical world below.

The descent of this dreamer and disdainer upon the suburban household of the person he is pleased to call 'the Haze woman' is a superbly sustained passage of this outrageous humour. Just as his dream blazes ever more radiantly, so, in consequence, ordinary life, where mature males 'wield' mature females in 'that routine rhythm which shakes the world', is dismissed with ever more reckless disdain. Poor Mrs Haze ('fat Haze', 'the fat cat', 'phocine mamma', 'she of the noble nipple and massive thigh') is overwhelmed by the riot of Humbert's ever-more-licensed wit. Her droopy cigarettes, her houseful of 'Mexican trash', her 'black rubber headgear' for swimming and the pink cosy on her toilet lid are all overwhelmed along with her.

But the anti-directional shift in Nabokov's humour means that this onslaught is quixotic rather than satiric, Saturnalian rather than vengeful. Mrs Haze is more the foil to Humbert than his victim and the aim of the humour is not so much to annihilate her as to celebrate the comic genius in him. It also celebrates the comic genius of the world itself, whose freak series of fortunate accidents and incongruous coincidences wonderfully aids Humbert's progress.[9]

The earlier books had set up many images of genuis, as spiritual distinction and artistic or intellectual eminence. But nowhere did Nabokov capture the nature of imaginative genius more perfectly than in this comic celebration of its luck and licence. Nowhere before this is there any portrait of genius as convincing as that of Humbert the Wizard, Humbert the crafty spider, Humbert the gliding ray, Humbert the cunning, manoeuvring his stealthy way through all the impeding trash and able, in a crisis, to produce false alibi and argumentative getaway car in a trice. His endlessly ramifying networks of stratagem, his *blasé* humming and strolling, the teetering precariousness of his perilous but relentless progress, the ever-increasing brilliance of his lyrical dreams of gold and magic, the miraculous transformation of 'Humbert the hound, the sad-eyed degenerate cur' into one who moves levitationally through his *seraglio* in 'royal robes': it is all beautifully managed as a celebration of genius and imaginative power. The humour of it curiously endorses romance by finding such fertility of mind in even so ludicrous a romance hero.

Poor Mrs Haze would seem to stand little chance against such an invader. Her own competing dreams of domestic bliss ('sun and shadows of leaves rippling on the white refrigerator') and marital content ('where pink mountains loom') seem helpless against Humbert's sarcasm. The Saturnalian world itself conspires against her too, most unfairly of all when the local newspaper prints her name as 'Hazer'.[10] The world eventually conspires with him so far as to remove her at the moment of her greatest menace, and to deliver thereby, with complete romance improbability, the object of his dreaming into his all-licensed hands.

By the end of Part One the radiant freedom of romance has conquered all. The glistening, mirror-lined room of The Enchanted Hunters, where 'level upon level of translucent vision' is stacked, makes the ordinary, impeding walls of reality give way to Humbert's vision and ego in endless, reduplicating succession. The 'magic ammunition' of his pills, each one a 'microscopic planetarium with its live stardust' will give him his 'beauty and bride, imprisoned in her crystal sleep'. The magus is in complete command.[11]

That it is not in fact Humbert's pills which do the trick but Lolita's highly un-magical lasciviousness learnt at summer camp, is the first intimation of the real world's curious and complicated revenges. But for the moment no matter. What will soon prove to be the very different curves of two highly dissimilar lives collide and run together for a brief while. They will stay together, more or less, throughout the year-long journey of this most errant of knights. As in all romances, high and low, extravagant hopes are invested in the brilliant, total convergence of two lives. Their convergence will be temporary, but the trick, for the time being, is not to think forward to when the banal facts of individual difference will reassert themselves in the real world where long and complex lives must be spent, each pursuing its own unique trajectory.

Lolita first became popular of course in the anticipation of its being a dirty book. It has probably remained popular, surviving the good fortune of that initial misconception, because of this extravagantly romantic comedy in Part One. The main work of the book is done here, creating the momentary miracle of an impossible dream coming hilariously true. It is a *brio* performance of great energy, with all the speed and confidence of that moment of liberation in the novelist's career.

In Part Two the ordinary world will punish so immoderate a demand for liberty. It will retake, inexorably, all the ground which romance had seized in a tumult of brilliance and luck. Part Two is the payment. Humbert thought he had found 'a brand new, mad new dream world' where 'everything was permissible' and where life could be lived without impediment, 'all blocks removed'. Gradually the blocks are put back, impediment and obstacle return.

Some of the impediments are very ordinary facts of nature and society. Some are decidedly unlovely facts which the romantic can hardly be blamed for fleeing, pointless though his flight may be. Some of the more interesting, however, are facts about the different lives and alternative dreams of other people. These facts, less obvious than the others, and less often recognized, make *Lolita* a larger, subtler, and more generous book than it might otherwise have been.

This third kind of fact prompts the recognition that Humbert is not, after all, the only dreamer. He does not have the monopoly of dream, romance, glamour, and magic, just as Pnin does not have the monopoly of the pain of severance. Though Humbert may dream brightest he certainly does not dream alone.

Mrs Haze herself is an alternative dreamer and it may not after all be true that all her dreams are quite bested by Humbert's. She it was who gave her daughter the glamorous name of Dolores, and a kindly afterthought might see a sort of clumsy fancy both in that and in her insistence that her garden paving shall be called a 'piazza'. Her 'Mexican trash' may be trash to Humbert, but his word may not be final. It is, in its way, an attempt to transfigure the real world of drabness. It may be that her interest in cretonnes, chintzes, and red candles may compare not altogether lamentably with Humbert's interest in silks, perfumes, and robes. Even her pink toilet-cosy may be redeemable, for who is Humbert to lay down the laws of dreaming?

And who is he to gainsay her version of a Grand Passion, whereby her imagination runs the same kind of riot with the exotic figure of Humbert as his does with the exotic figure of Lolita? She makes of Humbert 'an image . . . to adore'. She says he is 'her ruler and her god'. She thinks of him swimming at her side as 'her merman'. She says she is bewitched by his 'dark romantic European way'. Who is he to object, who not only loves a magic infant, but also fancies himself as an oriental potentate lolling in a convenient suburban *seraglio*? He may have finer words than his rivals to express his dreaming; but if it is dream that counts and not just words then other people's dreams will have to be respected too.

That means Mrs Haze; but also many others. Somebody must once have called that undistinguished stretch of water 'Hourglass Lake'. Other suburban parents have given their daughters such names as Grace, Stella, Lucinda, Rosaline, and Viola. *Lolita*, it turns out, is rather a generous book as regards the human desire for glamour. The generous idea that even the kitschiest forms of glamour might be fairly close relatives of 'higher' forms of romance was first found in *Glory*, in the figure of Alla. Here that idea flowers in gaudy profusion.

The spirit which tries to transfigure a group of cabins and garages by calling them Sunset Motel, Green Acres, or Park Plaza Court, claiming them as 'landscaped' and enjoying a 'gracious atmosphere', is ridiculed by Humbert. But again, his word may not be final. It is perfectly easy to see in such things the same itch for romance and luxury as animates him. The same itch has been at work in naming the various Scenic Drives, Painted Canyons, and Gateways to This, That, and The Other that pop up everywhere on the trans-American journey. The adman's imagery of paradise and the movieland imagery of glamour are not after all so easily to be ousted by Humbert's own particular dream. Readers of *Lolita* who are willing to share the flights of his peculiar fancy have no very good right to be peevish about such marvels as a Magnolia Garden advertised as 'a foretaste of Heaven', an imitation of the Grotto of Lourdes in

Louisiana, Lincoln's home faked up for tourists or a splendid-sounding zoo in Indiana

> where a large troupe of monkeys lived on a concrete replica of Christopher Columbus' flagship. (Pt. II, Ch. 2)

We come to see more zest than mawkishness in such efforts to transfigure. Disneyland may at least be a minor province of paradise, one of the patchy paradises of the earth such as the author of *Glory* wished to celebrate. Who in his right mind, or his right imagination, would not wish to accede to a faked effect of Venetian sun 'when actually it was Pennsylvania and rain'?

There have been readers of *Lolita* who have taken all this as satire or animus. Some of them have gone on from there to wonder about the mean-spiritedness of Nabokov's response to the culture that adopted him. But this is not the laughter of satire, nor even of parody or reserve, and its portrait of America is far from mean. *Lolita* and *Pnin*, Nabokov's first American books with American settings, are both full (as well they might be) of a mellowed warmth towards the country which had given this difficult, much-exiled writer a generous welcome to its omnivorous, polychrome culture. From *Lolita* onwards none of Nabokov's books can be trusted to give special privileges to spiritual élites and his humour can never be trusted to be straightforwardly directional. Consequently, Humbert's wanderings in this 'lovely, trustful, dreamy, enormous country' must get along as best they can with other men's desires and with the most garish products of them.

Lolita too has her alternative dreams. Their real direction is to be found in her wish to be a drum-majorette, or to make it to Hollywood or Broadway, or to be showered with coloured belts, blouses, sundaes, Indian curios, and copper jewellery. Again Humbert, gracing the New World with his silk-clad and perfumed presence, is in no position to object. Nor could he object to her desires for escapist, romantic movies offering

> an essentially grief-proof sphere of existence wherefrom death and grief were banned, (Pt. II, Ch. 3)

since his own predilections ('never grow up') are uncomfortably similar. Whatever it is that makes Quilty 'the only man she had ever been crazy about', shutting out thereby both romantic lover and prosaic husband, it is, stubbornly, a human fact. As in all Modernist comic romance such a fact, however unlovely, will have to have its existence respected. It must be allowed to take its quietly resistant place in the pattern of the whole book.

Once again Joyce and Flaubert lie behind this unpeevish acknowledgement of the cluttering diversity of different people's desires and of the world's multitude of stubbornly resistant facts. The Dublin of *Ulysses* and the Paris of *L'Éducation sentimentale* are the classic ancestors of Nabokov's idiosyncratic America. Joyce's picture of Dublin gives all its citizens the right to independent lives and desires recorded in the random criss-crossing of their paths and ambitions. The streets of Flaubert's Paris contain a similar, randomly-moving mass of diverse people, meeting or missing each other as chance will have it, each trying to get along in his own way, preoccupied alone with some never quite edifying but never quite despicable attempt to make humdrum life less humdrum. Their lives serve to make the romance hero lose the exclusivity he would comfortably enjoy in a book where the world was more conveniently designed for him.

Lolita is not built on that scale, but the idiosyncratic debt to Flaubert and Joyce is there none the less. In such a world the lucky blaze of Part One of *Lolita* will inevitably be followed by the reassertion of the ordinary in Part Two. Such immoderately romantic dreams are bound to be curtailed, sad, comic, and doomed to failure. The rapture gives way steadily to a lamenting sense of 'my poor joy'; then to the 'cry of lone disaster'; then to a maudlin, confessional awareness of 'dreadful cumbersome sins'.

The ordinary social world of Pratt and Cormorant, of 'tight-zippered Philistines' and a 'federal law and all its stinging stars', will easily soak up all Humbert's sarcasm. Then, just as easily, it will retake all the territory that his sarcasm had invaded. The natural world likewise will lose its momentary romance bloom, returning from transfiguration to

soggy old pastures, the wind, the bloated wilderness . . . (and) . . . yucca blossoms, so pure, so waxy, but lousy with creeping white flies.

(Pt. II, Ch. 2)

What had seemed like a return to Arcadia will come up against awkard, spiky, venomous things on the forest floor of the beautiful but 'never Arcadian American wilds'.

The final dismal reckoning records the desolating completeness of this reassertion of the real. An untransfigurable landscape of provincial, industrial poverty stares back at the dreamer's gaze. The trappings of his ease and glamour (silk shirt, nacreous buttons, cashmere tie, gossamer handkerchief) intrude ludicrously in such a place. Two young men here are already the mutilated veterans of a war. In unenchanted Hunter Road, 'last house', the scene is

all dump and ditch, and wormy vegetable garden, and shack, and grey drizzle, and red mud, and several smoking stacks in the distance.

(Pt. II, Ch. 28)

The human world has further rebuffs in store. The callous prose-package of their lives concocted by John Ray Jnr., Ph.D., will make privacy public and turn unhappiness and pain into a best-seller, a promotion, a career. The natural world too has further revenges, in the shape of Humbert's fatal heart attack and in the fact that

Mrs. 'Richard F. Schiller' died in childbed, giving birth to a stillborn girl, on Christmas Day 1952. (John Ray's Foreword)

A feckless dreamer of eternal childhood, seeking to remake Arcadia in the 'never Arcadian American wilds' and to live an adult life in the state of homo poeticus can be no match for such overwhelming opponents. His triumphs are ever more fitful. Soon they are no more than brief halts in an otherwise continous decline. His victories are ever less actual, ever more merely verbal. They are either desperate tirades of sarcasm or flimsy edifices of romantic words, like the lyrical encomium of Lolita's tennis which makes a great blaze of words about what is in reality a feeble performance.

The tennis-game is a tour de force, Humbert's last, bright, futile poem. But by now his lyricism has all but faded to colourlessness and such brio is rare. The book's comedy cools. Muted ironies and dead pan sardonic smiles replace the earlier hilarity. The accents of humour are flattened and then Humbert's regret, despair, and weeping sense of guilt begin to colour the ending with a kind of poignancy of which Joyce and Flaubert are again the masters. It is a halting poignancy, part authentic and part kitsch, part tragic part maudlin. It represents strong feeling in the impure form to which such feeling is apt to be reduced in the ordinary world where clumsiness and incongruity intrude everywhere in our finest thoughts since our eloquence is never any match for our desires.

It is this beautiful but infinitely difficult tone, incomparably achieved in *Madame Bovary*,[12] that Nabokov attempts in the latter stages of *Lolita*. Humbert turns from dreamer and comedian to confessing sinner. His narrative is punctuated with regret and guilt:

> '*Lolita, qu'ai-je fait de ta vie?* ... my poor bruised child ... I saw Lolita's smile lose all its light ... the absence of her voice from that concord ... even the most miserable of family lives was better ...
>
> (Pt. II, Chs. 29, 32, 36)

But it is at this point that the reader of what has been an offbeat and airy book is likely to feel some strain in the attempted transition of tone. There are voices in Flaubert and Joyce which can pass easily, in the turn of a phrase, from comic to tragic. There are lives there to which a reader's response is, from first to last, a perpetual vacillation between one feeling and another. But *Lolita's* hero is a simpler figure than the heroes of Flaubert and Joyce. He is painted with great surface gusto but with no great depth. It is hardly possible for the hero of such an exuberant work of fictional artifice to turn, at the last, into the weeping figure from whom these fragments of regret are torn.

Emma, Frédéric, or Mr Bloom could have done it. They can make such transitions with complete naturalness. But it is hard to hear such things said by the much simpler figure of Humbert. Such depths of sorrowing self-accusation cannot convincingly be found in a figure who has hitherto played a role more straightforward and stylized than theirs.

At the very end therefore, the book's new, free kind of comedy has run out of creative power. It worked beautifully in the earlier, often hilarious account of Humbert's outrageous romance demands. It worked beautifully in turning the comedy of America away from the animus of satire. But it cannot quite manage this last turn. Instead of hearing Humbert speak we seem to hear Nabokov speak on his behalf, adding and appending things which could not have come from his fictional creature, squeezing sentiments out of him that could not possibly have been there.[13]

None the less, in spite of this final problem, the new start has been made. Nabokov's next book in this vein was *Pale Fire*. Here there is no such trouble. Kinbote is the equal of Humbert in romance and comedy, but in addition he far surpasses him in a genuine pathos, integral rather than merely appended, which allows these difficult turns and modulations of tone to be made with unfailing facility.

22

I, THAT WAS DELIGHTFUL

Marvell has a word for the mood of this celebratory, non-directional laughter. The word comes in 'Fleckno, an English Priest at Rome'[1] which is one of three poems giving his boisterous comedy at its best.

In the earlier part of the poem Marvell has had his fun with the figure of a very thin man in a pinched room at the top of a narrow staircase in a tall house. Half-way through the poem a second source of amusement presents himself in the form of a friend of Flecknoe who meets Marvell on the narrow stairs and is soon blustering, in 'gathring fury' about his right of way. Marvell was capable of hot temper himself and on another occasion might have risen to the bait. But now his mood was, he says, 'delightful', and so he replies with good humour and high spirits, parrying the blusterer's threats, calming him down with some high-flown banter, flattering him into submission and thus surviving to enjoy more sport, at the newcomer's expense as well as Flecknoe's, in the poem's second half. A Marvell who is 'delightful' (full of delight, merry, in the mood for fun) is the comic poet of 'Fleckno', 'Tom May's Death', and 'The Character of Holland', and later the comic pamphleteer of *The Rehearsal Transpros'd*.

We know Richard Flecknoe better, of course, from Dryden's 'MacFlecknoe'. But Dryden's more famous poem is satire, with a serious political and ideological purpose, while Marvell's poem is 'delightful', a more or less purposeless piece of laughing verse. In Nabokov's terms Dryden's 'MacFlecknoe' is a lesson, Marvell's 'Fleckno' is a game.[2] If we accord pure play and fantasy their rights we will surely find finer poetry in Marvell's work than in Dryden's. His work is much the more generous of the two and much the more quick-witted. It also reaches deeper into what humour is all about than could any work of directed, destructive, or corrective comedy.

The humour of 'Fleckno' depends upon its evocation of a world ruled by accident and random collision where people are buffeted about by the quick operations of chance. It is that Saturnalian world which made the lives of Humbert and Lolita collide to form so unlikely and preposterous a union. It is the power of chance that makes Marvell 'oblig'd' to visit Flecknoe in the first place, drawing him absurdly into the orbit of this curious man and rendering him less free than we are (or think we are) in ordinary life. It is chance that then, with fertile genius, keeps him captive in myriad ways. He is seduced by a devil, allured by music, seized and held by a tyrant or tormentor, impeded by the narrow confines of space, thwarted by the laws of physics, 'oblig'd' again by Flecknoe's determination to involve him in a new friendship, drawn along as hapless bystander in two other men's altercation. Like Nabokov, Marvell has a wonderful eye for the improbable obstacles and tiny nuisances of the world which, howsoever improbable or tiny, are enough to take away all our freedom and dignity and deliver us over into the mere whirl of things.

In 'Tom May's Death',[3] May similarly finds himself delivered up as the hapless victim of mischance with no more control over, or awareness of, what happens to him than 'one put drunk into the Packet-boat'. Drunkenness is, of course, a rich source of the comedy of mischances since a drunken man loses his footing and his freedom not only on banana-skins like the rest of us but on non-skid surfaces as well. May is a classic case of such involuntary propulsion, 'hurry'd', 'amaz'd', and 'uncertain' as the poem's story takes its grip on him, looking about himself 'doubtfully', 'stumbling', finding himself incongruously 'translated' from one state to another. After the rapid whirl of the poem's beginning he tries to gather his wits, gamely enough one might think; but the massive figure of Ben Jonson bears down upon him, like some dreadful composite of all the world's myriad oppositions and obstacles, overwhelming the hapless victim with his towering rhetoric and driving him from the poem as helpless as he entered it, carried away 'in a Cloud of pitch'.

So too in the third of these poems, 'The Character of Holland',[4] whose laughter is again a matter of 'delightful' pleasure taken in mischance. Where Flecknoe was ridiculously thin the Dutch are ridiculously fat, for such in the end are apt to be the elemental simplicities of this sort of comic pleasure. Flecknoe was nothing but bony fingers and stringy guts, the Dutch are all butter and beer. In addition their country is absurdly prone to mischances because it is so precariously exposed to inundation, condemning them therefore to a perpetual 'mad labour' of reclamation. The comedy at the expense of their labour again trades in the elemental simplicities, laughing simultaneously at the smallness of what is involved:

> Collecting anxiously small Loads of Clay,
> (13)

and at the hugeness:

> How did they rivet, with Gigantick Piles,
> Thorough the Center their new-matched Miles.
> (17-18)

But all these furious extremes of effort, large and small, are to no avail; for the sea is to Holland as Jonson was to May, a giant composite of everything that overwhelms us, everything that sets our works in disarray. Three images of children's games (leapfrog, level-coyl, and ducks and drakes) catch the element of play both in the sea's easy victories and in Marvell's pleasure in the circumstance. Then a beautiful image of absurd, unexpected inudation sums up the classic dilemma:

> The Fish oft-times the Burger dispossest,
> And sat not as a Meat but as a Guest.
> (29-30)

In the nineteenth century that couplet seems to have made Marvell's few readers laugh. We, taught by Eliot and Modernism to read most of his verse, may still need to learn how rich the poetic fantasy of such humour is, forgetting satire, with its lessons, in order to enjoy again this sort of play which is supposed to make us, as it made Tennyson, laugh aloud.[5]

Nothing catches the non-directional spirit of play better than this once-celebrated couplet. It has all the speed and surprise of celebratory comedy, all its accidents and mischances. The fish's

translation from meat to guest and thus from plate (where it was
motionless, horizontal and dead) to chair (where it is animated,
vertical and alive) is spectacularly quick and it sets up a whole
world of randomly disruptive events. It is with wonderful sud-
denness that the solid burger, with his possessions, is 'dispossest';
and there is something splendidly disconcerting about the marine
usurper, whether he sits at table with the amiable bearing of a
true guest or with the more impudent look of an uninvited one.
There is also something excellent about the fish's ability to do
this trick 'oft-times', and about the way that the burger's good
fortune in finding himself with a dining companion turns at once
to embarrassment since his guest's plate is empty, necessarily,
for the guest was to have been the meat. Also, how does a fish sit
in a chair? How does it contour its limbless self to the shape of a
chair, and how does it prevent its slippery self from sliding to the
floor?

The fantasy of such laughter is as rich as the more famous lyric
fantasy of Marvell's other poems. Its life depends above all on an
unaggressive spirit, a 'delightful', pacific spirit that leaves fantasy
free from the burden of correction to ramify and develop as it
will. This is pure fun and very gentle writing. Dutchmen, and
burgers generally, should not feel themselves glanced at hurtfully
by it. The gentleness of the mood can be seen in its rhyme, which
takes all the sting out of the burger's being 'dispossest' by rhym-
ing the word with something as amiable as 'Guest'. How could
dispossession be made to feel less terrible? Would Dryden, or
any more purely satiric writer, have been capable of forgetting
the drive of his contempt and treating his victim so kindly?

The poem, though, does have its satire. It may well have been
written in two parts at different times in Marvell's career, with
more politics being grafted onto a poem that had at first been
full of fun.[6] Howsoever it came about, it stands on an edge between game and lesson, though it is all in the game rather than
the lesson that the quick wit of the great poet is to be found.

The same is true of 'Tom May's Death'. Critics have tended to
read the poem for political purposes, looking in it for evidence of
how Marvell's political opinions shifted between the late 1640s
and the early 1650s. But in the end a reader of poetry loses in-

terest in such matters for the fine poetry of 'Tom May's Death'
is less serious and more fantastic than any politically inspired
reading can catch. May, it should be noted, is rousted not by
Marvell but by Ben Jonson and that little shift creates a space
between the authorial voice and the voice of contempt and
dismissal. That space is enough to throw everything into the
complex jeopardy of play where any supposed messages or
revelations of political commitment are hardly to be trusted.

Marvell creates the room to withhold himself slightly from the
drive of Jonson's albeit magnificent destructive rhetoric. Room is
also created for disinterested fun at the sheer spectacle, which
presents us with the simple comic phenomenon of an enormous
man with a huge roaring voice confronting, with lamentable un-
fairness, a cowed, silent little person who can't get a word in
edgeways. We relish the spectacle, and our relish is a long way
from whatever pleasure might be found in satire. It is again less
sophisticated than satire. We are once more back in the world of
fat men and thin men, big men and small men, loud men and
silent men, confident men and their bewildered victims. And just
as Marvell's kindly rhyme took a little of the heat off the 'dispossest' burger, so this deflection of things into more elemental
regions of joking takes some of the heat off poor May. We have
the room and freedom to side with him in his misfortune if we
want. We might well be pleased that Jonson castigates Virgil and
Horace as well as May, which makes Jonson himself look less
perfect and which, just for a moment, provides a kind of reliev-
ing solidarity for May, a companionship in distress.

A true satirist like Dryden hunts his victims down more single-
mindedly than this. Satire is a narrower, more authoritarian
mode. But the true satirist in this poem is Jonson, not Marvell.
Jonson is the source of the poem's directionality. Marvell stands
slightly back from him, enjoying the fun. Jonson thus figures
in what is really a comic drama. Marvell has caught his tones to
perfection. Here is Jonson's crushing epigrammatic force, his
effortless manipulation of classical reference, his unhesitating
conviction of his own authority, his terrible anger, with trembling finger pointed in accompaniment:

> But the nor Ignorance nor seeming good

Misled, but malice fixt and understood.
(55-6)

Here is the lordly singing of his 'high and aloof'[7] tone, his bardic
tone, 'sounding of ancient heroes' and singing 'of ancient Rights
and better Times'. Marvell has heard him as well as he heard his
Mowers and his pastoral lovers, catching the nuances of his voice
and spirit:

> Return, Return,
> Where Sulphrey *Phlegeton* does ever burn.
> The *Cerberus* with all his Jawes shall gnash,
> *Megaera* thee with all her Serpents lash.
> Thou rivited unto *Ixion's* wheel
> Shalt break, and the perpetual Vulture feel.
> 'Tis just what Torments Poets ere did feign,
> Thou first Historically shouldst sustain.
> (89-96)

That is perfect Jonson. Who but Jonson could exhibit simultaneously such fierce indignation and complete self-control,
managing and directing his fury, judging tempo and balancing
effects? The sentence is, as Marvell says, 'irrevocable', and May
is caused instantly to vanish by the force of its breath. Jonson is
made to perform as superbly as ever he did in his own verse. We
relish the man in this marvellous representation of him. We
savour again his unique being. He is revered, perhaps loved. But
he does not quite fill the whole world. We can look around him,
and behind him. We can wander out of earshot. We can enjoy
him without having to be totally committed to him and without
having to be totally convinced by his lesson, howsoever elo-
quently it is delivered. We can see him as a player in a game; a
figure, along with May, in a very funny piece of theatre. There is
room enough to find him splendid but slightly unbelievable, a
larger-than-life character.[8]

'Fleckno' itself, to return to the most purely fun-centred and
innocent of the three poems, lacks any semblance of a purpose.
No one could mistake it for a satire on Catholics or *émigrés* or
minor poets. The elements of its humour are again unsophisticated and commonplace: a very thin man and general oddball; a
young, quarrelsome friend; both of them somewhat quixotic; a

ludicrous altercation between the pair, and Marvell as helpless bystander involuntarily embroiled. The poem is just a chapter of accidents enjoyed by a quick-witted, fast-footed poet whose brilliant linguistic powers delight to keep up with the flurry of surprise events. Speed, accuracy, and unconcealed ingenuity of invention are the hallmarks of this poetry of social and verbal escapade. Rhymes may meet perfectly in fluent couplets or fall unhappily on the wrong stress. Rhythms equally may run in powerful measure or hobble ineptly. Fast, complex trains of joking may delight us with their speed or awful slow puns (like the dreadful Italian one on 'stanza') make us groan with pleasure. It is the performance of a comedian who thrives on the fact that he can keep his feet in a world of collisions and buffeting chances.

He keeps moving. He takes pleasure in his own nimbleness. Warming to his game, and entering more fully into its 'delightful' mood he will even throw in some complicating factors of his own, as if the world's native complications were not enough of a challenge. Donne was as quick as this in his own not very satiric Satyres. Jonson often was, too, in his various social skirmishes. But if we move from here to Dryden, the speed of things slows dramatically. The quicksilver quality has gone, the 'delightful' quality. Things have become earnest, satiric, a lesson. The essence of humour has been cooled to bring it under control, so as to be able to use and direct its now diminished energies. It is a great loss. The world of Dryden's 'MacFlecknoe' is duller and more sombre than that of Marvell's 'Fleckno'. It is also more repressed, slowing the play of fancy and turning humour into the rather sad, authoritarian ability to display contempt.

The later verse satires attributed speculatively to Marvell have little of this quicksilver. They are genuine satires, with a strict and limited purpose. But the masterpiece of his later years shows him none the less to have retained all his powers of laughter even if verse was no longer the medium which could embody them. *The Rehearsal Transpros'd*[9] has the speed and mercurial playfulness of these earlier poems. The lessons of satire are again transcended by swift linguistic games. Comic invention is ever-fertile, creating a superabundance far beyond what strict argument or attack might require. The rousting of Parker is enjoyed, and felt to be enjoyed as a performance in its own right.

It had its satiric purpose, of course. What is more, unlike most satire, it seems to have achieved its purpose. But it achieved it not with the controlled contempt of satire, but with the recklessness of flyting, exuberant abuse, or carnival. It did it by being beyond measure, by being an inundation of words rather than a crisp dismissal. It is nearer to Nashe than to Jonson, nearer to Swift than to Dryden, nearer to Byron (on the 'tyrant' Southey)[10] or Shelley (on *Swellfoot the Tyrant*)[11] than to any more careful or organized writer of satiric rebuke. In modern literature one could better find an equivalent verbal carnival of excess or an equivalently torrential quality in Joyce or in the Joycean Nabokov than in any satirist. Marvell is as quick and as overwhelming as Humbert or Kinbote. His words have the same prodigious comic freedom to breed and swarm as do the words of *Finnegans Wake*.

Byron and Shelley both loosed such writing on men they considered petty tyrants. Southey and Swellfoot are little men, but ludicrously inflated, gross and portentous. The free play of such comedy is the natural enemy of tyranny and the sanity of its spirit is the natural enemy of petty self-inflatedness. In Samuel Parker Marvell found just such a man and just such a theme. *The Rehearsal Transpros'd* is profound and serious enough to be thought of as a great work in the history of freedom. But it is in the nature of things that freedom should be represented in it by fantasy and laughter, while tyranny is represented as solemn and portentous.

So Parker is given as 'a great ecclesiastical politician' of 'overweening presumption and preposterous ambition'. In accordance with the flyting spirit Marvell gives him as a despot, beating 'pulpit-drums', crushing the opposition beneath 'the wheels of his chariot', wearing the 'sacerdotal habiliments' as the uniform of a spiritual tyranny. He finds myriad images for his cruelty, his vulgarity, his noisome brutality, his censorious menace. He is a 'Scanderbag', an Emperor Julian, a Nero, a Caligula, a 'Dancehment Kan',[12] an oriental despot luring his victims to their doom in his 'garden of venimous plants'. He is also a figure of gross and ludicrous appetite, sexually rampant and cloacally obscene. He is in short a carnival figure, and the spirit of the attack upon him is a constant invitation to the open pleasures of laughter. The drive of the prose never narrows. Nothing ever turns to bitterness or to stridency. It always seems free, fertile, and content to progress waywardly.

But *The Rehearsal Transpros'd* also articulates a genuine idea of spiritual distinction, in contrast to the religious vulgarity of Parker. This aspect of the work, which makes it, along with 'The Coronet', Marvell's finest statement of his own religious opinions, is linked in easy harmony with even the grossest of its laughter. When, in contrast to Parker and Parkerism, Marvell brings forth either his own views, or the lives and views of Owen, Baxter, Milton, Bacon, and, above all, Calvin, the prose can always modulate easily to other, quieter tones. The coarsest joke is easily able to share his mind with the greatest delicacy, subtlety, and decency. There is room to doubt whether truly satiric laughter could link so easily with so considerable a statement of spiritual conviction.

Marvell begins with an introduction which, fittingly enough for a work in this spirit, he calls a 'Dance'. He sets forth Parker as a 'malapert Chaplain' bent on tyranny, making him look like an even more vulgarly pushy version of the 'forward Youth that would appear' at the start of 'An Horatian Ode'.

The 'Dance' contains a fine passage on writing and printing. Parker is an absurd stylistic despot, able to endure no 'man's Tautologies but his own', and a menacing despot of publication and censorship. Printing makes for freedom of information and argument, freedom of access to words; so, for Parker:

'Twas an happy time when all Learning was in Manuscript, and some little Officer, like our Author, did keep the Keys of the Library. (p. 4)

For the censorious Parker, the printing press is a dangerous invention, perversely diverting the original high purpose of iron letters which was for branding slaves and schismatics. No image could go more quickly and tellingly to the heart of the matter. The freedom not only to think, but to speak, write, and print what one thinks, is one of the main themes of *The Rehearsal Transpros'd*. It deserves the same recognition as Milton's *Areopagitica* as a great document in the history of uncensored writing. Dryden saw this at once, and at once took offence, comparing Marvell, as Parker himself had done, with Martin Marprelate,[13] in whose writings ecclesiastical authority had earlier been outmanoeuvred by the mobility and wit of the urban underground press. Liberty is served by opportunist 'rascally Operators of the Press' outwitting a ludicrous, inflated man

pearch'd upon the highest Pinacle of Ecclesiastical Felicity, being ready at once to asswage his Concupiscence, and wreck his Malice. (p. 7)

The fantastic sexuality of that Pinacle ('when a man's Phancy is up, and his Breeches are down') completes this wonderful opening portrait of the tyrant as a wallowing profligate. One can immediately hear the Joycean note, for the gross, sexual element in Parker's fantasies of power makes him look uncannily like the patriarchal and censorious figures of *Finnegans Wake*, grown monstrous with male authority and sexual self-congratulation.

Marvell then says he will leave his Dance and turn to 'more serious Counsels', but the comic and the serious never separate so neatly. Laughter and grossness will continue, however serious the subject. The sexual current goes on as Marvell affects astonishment at Parker's lavish praise of Bishop Bramhall, finding it hard to imagine a man

so sharp set, or so necessitated that he should make a dead Bishop his Mistress; (p. 13)

and the carnival spirit continues its depiction of the monstrous appetites of the powerful, like the Pope who, given the slighest opportunity,

would have swoop'd up the Patriarchate of *Lambeth* to his Morningsdraught, like an egg in Muscadine. (p. 18)

This is, as Dryden knew, the rhetoric of the Good Old Cause;[14] but in Marvell's hands the Good Old Cause is still finely alive and it still furnishes him with a deep, radical idea of liberty which easily survives Dryden's sneer.

We then pass from Parker as the praiser of Bramhall and ecclesiastical power to Parker as the scourge of Calvin. Here he is a 'Mastiff', toothed, ferocious. He is also a torturer

who shall persecute the Scripture itself, unless it will conform to his Interpetation. (p. 23)

He is a huge prodigy portended by comets. He is a beast who

'runs a Mucke' in vicious frenzy. Where before he had the dead Bramhall as his mistress he now has the grave of Calvin to make his 'constant Pissing-place'. Where before Bramhall rode like '*the Knight of the Sun*' or '*King Arthur*', now Parker rides demented 'by his growing too early acquainted with *Don Quixot*'. One of the great burlesque set-pieces of *The Rehearsal Transpros'd* comes here when Marvell, prompted by his amusement at a geographical error committed by Parker, takes off in an opportunist aside to write an allegorical encomium of the River Rhone, which fleets through the '*Lake perillous*' of Calvin's Geneva

and never thinks itself safe till it hath taken sanctuary at the Popes Town of *Avinion*.[15]

But here the modulation from carnival to delicacy comes into play, for Calvinism, rescued from Parker's ludicrous travesty of it, begins to make its contribution to the book's sense of what a real religious scruple might look like. The prose looks to an excellence beyond the philistine bluster of Parker yet does it with hardly an interruption to its veering ribaldry and flyting abuse. The unflustered voice of an adult decency can be heard along with the noisy verbal profligacy, just as it can in *Ulysses* and *Finnegans Wake* where the beautifully pacific voice of Joyce's tolerance emerges from a fertile chaos of words.

Then we come back to the 'forward Youth' and to another great set-piece on Parker's portentous advancement. The serious voice in Marvell is now the urban, cosmopolitan voice, unfussed and at ease in the city where diverse words and writings abound. Parker, by contrast, an ill-read, semi-educated provincial, finds his head spinning when he exchanges the square, narrow security of the university quadrangle for 'the *Town*' and 'the open Air'. The long set-piece on his arrival in the Great World where he instantly flies into crack-brained giddiness is a masterly portrait of an ignorant juvenile 'thinking himself now ripe and qualified'.[16]

There are men like this in Nabokov, arrested at adolescence and out to reduce the world to conformity with their simplistic notions. Chernyshevski in *The Gift* is one such, so are Paduk and Alexander in *Bend Sinister*, Edgar Wind in *Pnin*, Emerald and Pink in *Pale Fire*. Nabokov's hostility to Freudianism and to

Marxism is always a hostility to simplistic systems hatched in libraries and then sallying farcically and cruelly forth to reduce the world's diversity to a handful of wooden terms. Modernism at large, especially Joycean Modernism, is always apt to be the voice of diversity speaking against system and reductivism. It is apt to speak for what, in *Ulysses*, is called 'tenacity of heterodox resistance' against what, in *Finnegans Wake*, is called 'putting Allspace into a Notshall'.[17] The Modernist literature of heterodox resistance, enacting a diverse world in its linguistic and structural openness, is prefigured in the verbal profligacy and structural waywardness of great Renaissance comedy, nowhere more clearly than here in Marvell's extraordinarily modern defence of the right not to conform.

This then brings us, by way of some more carnival images of Parker as a beast of gross appetite, 'howling, yelling and barking' and falling on nonconformists with 'his chaps and his paws', to a contrasting passage on Richard Baxter and John Owen.[18] Baxter figures as a small boy who once stole plums and sloes from Bramhall's garden and must now 'be whipp't for't' by Parker. The whipping is schoolmasterly and punitive, but it is sexual as well, for boys in Parker's unlovely care must

down with their breeches as oft as he wants the prospect of a more pleasing *Nudity*. (p. 36)

Owen too calls forth this imagery of children and punitive schoolmasters. The 'juvenile petulancy' of Parker is a pupil's recoil from his teachers, the child's impulsion 'to curse solemnly his Father and Mother'. Hence this ex-University man's fury against Owen, the Oxford Vice-Chancellor. Hence his violent brandishing of

the *Publick Rods* if not the *Axes* against the Boyes, to teach them better manners. (p. 41)

The language of childhood is used by Marvell here in yet another way, portraying Parker as arrested in adolescence, while Owen, like Baxter, comes across by comparison as an adult of great dignity. By the time Marvell wrote this, in his early fifties, his poems' long contemplation of what is justly childlike, and what, in Fairfax or Cromwell, is justly parental, must have settled

deep in his mind. So must his own break with the probable politics and religion of his youth (for this passage is evidently personal). But unlike Marvell, Parker seems not to have looked into
his own psychology at all, so where Marvell is now the master of
such matters, drawing on the images of childhood, playing with
them and transposing them at will, Parker flails wildly, the ignorant victim of their working within him.

From here on, in the latter pages of *Part One* and throughout
Part Two, *The Rehearsal Transpros'd* rests easily on what Marvell
has already built. He has his carnival figure of the caricature
despot and yapping juvenile together with a seemingly inex-
haustible store of comic images in which to depict him. He has
his crude religious bigot and intellectual reductivist, hardly
capable of expressing an opinion without revealing the vulgarity
of his thought. He has his counter-sense of adult decency and
personal religious scruple, together with a clear conviction of
their social roots in the open, diverse city and the secular state,
cleared of the ecclesiastical controls of which Parkerism is the
menacing symbol. It is all clear and coherent, notwithstanding
the wandering, rambling unhurriedness of its highly imagistic
style which never follows a straight line when a zigzag one will
do and never rests content for long on the mere denotive surface
of words, preferring to burrow down speculatively into their con-
notive depths.

Now that the central figure has been so clearly set up, Marvell
can proceed to the central tenets of his gross philosophy. We
come to the six dramas of the playwright Bayes:

> First,   The *Unlimited Magistrate*
> Secondly,   *The Publick Conscience*
> Thirdly,   *Moral Grace*
> Fourthly,   *Debauchery Tolerated*
> Fifthly,   *Persecution Recommended*
> And lastly, *Pushpin-Divinity*[19]

The first would set up the King as a religious absolutist, flat-
tered and coerced by the priesthood into using his unlimited
powers for 'prolling and molesting the People'.

The second would make the priesthood into an inquisition,
diversely equipped with 'tests and picklocks' and other 'wayes of

compelling men' which Marvell finds 'brutish' and 'devilish'.

The third 'overturns the whole Fabrick of Christianity', draining it of all spiritual worth 'if Grace be resolv'd into Morality' and religion becomes of significance only in the realm of public behaviour.

The fourth portrays Parker's obsession with religious nonconformity as the supreme if not the only moral issue by comparison with which any other vice is nearly negligible.

The fifth returns to the images of tyranny, comparing Parker's pagan cruelty with that of Julian the Apostate, expressing gratitude for God's mercy 'that Mr Bayes is not Emperour', portraying the despot as a headsman as well as a user of '*Pillories, Whipping-posts, Galleys Rods* and *Axes*' (especially Galleys, upon the urgent need for squadrons of which Marvell is particularly lively), and depicting Parker as 'an excellent Tool' of a brutal regime, given to such characteristic lolling excesses as feeding 'of a Fanatick's Giblets' and insisting

that a Nonconformist's head must be wip't off as oft as (his) nose drivels. (p. 59)

The sixth offers Parker's strained theocratic punctilio as equivalent to a child's game of push-pin.

All six plays are then despatched together as works of mental and stylistic syphilis, for

the mind too hath its Nodes sometimes, and the Stile its Buboes.

(p. 61)

It is a splendid flyting and carnival demolition of the Parkerian spirit of ecclesiastical authority, concentrating on the menace of the powers it seeks for itself, and on its simplistic bungling when it turns its attention to moral or intellectual matters.

Marvell now ranges further afield, taking bits and pieces from Parker to prompt his excursions:

I will take a walk in the Garden and gather some of Mr. *Bayes* his Flowers. (p. 77)

He reviews the history of seventeenth-century religion and the calamity of the civil war, producing an increasingly persuasive, fair-minded, but radical view of high Anglicanism's 'incumbring

Churches with Superfluities' and 'reviving obsolete customs'. At its worst, the Church required

so many several Cringes and Genuflexions, that a man unpractis'd stood in need to entertain both a Dancing Master and a Remembrancer
(p. 131)

and delivered sermons which were

a very Mash of *Arminian* Subtilties, of Ceremonies, and Decency, and of *Manwaring*, and *Sibthorpianism* brewed together. (p. 133)

This is the Good Old Cause again, but presented with a fineness of discrimination which keeps all its radicalism alive and none of its bigotry, and which has no difficulty combining adult tolerance and calm with the burlesque spirit of laughter. At one moment, Marvell is weighing things quietly and judiciously; at the next, he returns to the likes of Parker, with the nonconformists beneath their chariot wheels, cutting and slashing like enraged warriors, hacking about themselves in argument

rather in a swashbuckler and Hectoring way, than either like Philosophers or like Christians. (p. 116)

He can step from dignity to Saturnalia and then back again in the turn of a sentence, so close does the centre of his whole imagination now lie to the freedoms which reside in laughter, as much as they once resided in the complex images of his lyric poems.

Of all the great comic writers of the Renaissance it is perhaps Montaigne of whom one is most reminded. He crops up several times in *The Rehearsal Transpros'd*, once clearly acknowledged, elsewhere as probable source.[20] It is highly appropriate. There is a personal note of moral and religious self-assessment in *The Rehearsal Transpros'd* as there is everywhere in Montaigne whatever his subject; and Marvell's prose style matches Montaigne's in its rambling patience, its density of image, and its perpetual playfulness. They share the ability to turn at will from playfulness to the deep, pacific seriousness of men who had both witnessed religious civil wars and who wanted no more of their ideological authoritarianism and their consequent violence in word and deed.

Part Two is simpler. When Parker was rash enough to attempt to reply, Marvell had little trouble completing the task that *Part One* had substantially achieved already. The image of the carnival grotesque again sustains the pamphlet. The opening of this second part is another of the great scurrilous set-pieces of the work, taking the figure again and dressing him in the highest colours as a noxious bundle of appetites, 'the Ecclesiastical Giant', whose guts are a swill of 'Slime and Choler' and whose lust is uncontrollable:

though he were on the Rode to *Canterbury*, let any female but cross his Way, 'tis odds that his Beast will stumble, and throw his Arch-deaconship in the Cart-rut, with his whole *Tridentine* Portmantle of Polity and Theology.[21]

After many pages on this, and on the violence and malignity of Parker as a kind of ecclesiastical mercenary, 'a Divine of Fortune', Marvell again comes to the six plays. But by now the ideas of Parker are of limited interest. The issue is quite clear. Marvell writes more on the first of the plays than on all the others put together, for *The Unlimited Magistrate* is the play about power, and it is power that has been the basic issue throughout.[22]

The matter in question is the power of the church, the ideological tyranny of a church demanding conformity and having the civil power to enforce it. The separation of ecclesiastical from civil power is a precondition of freedom, as well as of true religious feeling. The secular state is the source of freedom while the church that Parker represents is bent on

the invasion of all the Rights of Mankind and Privileges of Reason.
(p. 215)

This is the only topic that can now hold Marvell's interest and he writes on it with all the animation of *Part One* and with that Montaignian ability to move easily between laughter and seriousness. Parker's hectoring, punitive spirit seeks always to compel. Marvell's comedy will therefore see him as 'Mr. Necessity Bayes', or as an incarnation of the force of *anangke*, an authority even higher than Jupiter, wielder of 'the great Hammer' that drove the nail through the axle-tree of the earth. But there is also a real sense of outraged human feeling in the prose, accompanying the comedy. It surfaces when Marvell considers Parker's forwardness or ambition, when he considers his crude, reductive account of Calvin or his ungracious treatment of Milton.

Above all it is felt when Marvell considers the cruelty of unlimited power, its licence, its delight in outrage. In the passages on Nero, Caligula, and Julian the Apostate, all of whom had been treated with fatuous complacency by Parker, Marvell is at his best. A strong recoil from violence was native to him, and this prose, with its festal qualities and its unmalicious laughter, is a perfect medium for its expression. There are passages here that match the great writing about cruelty and war in the poems, and here such writing makes common cause with his laughter as easily as in the poems it made common cause with his lyricism.

That is the paradox of carnival laughter. It is coarse and primitive while satire is sophisticated. But that also means that carnival laughter is a kind of Mower amongst the Julianas of satire, an innocent amongst the world's more cruel adepts. It has never lost its innocence; and that seems to enable it to get along with both common decency and uncommon spiritual distinction.

PART SIX

Household and Woodland

BLUE INENUBILABLE ZEMBLA

Each author had his first subject. There was the child with his Arcadian world of woods and water; then the child-like man, *homo poeticus*, and his subsequent severance, exile, and deracination. This first or natural subject was caught in nostalgia, in precarious celebration and in lament. It evoked powerful sentiment and called forth a sense of emotional displacement rising to the level of the tragic.

But then each author had his disbelief. There was a secretive, scarcely perceptible irony, too wary and delicate to be traced with any certainty. Then there was a stronger irony of clear reserve and self-rebuke; then free-running, Saturnalian comedy, consuming all in its laughter or embracing all in its unaggressiveness. The first subject was still there, for the Arcadian genius of *homo poeticus* grades into the playful wit of the ironic intelligence and thence into the Puckish, boyish quality of the 'delightful' laughter. But the first subject no longer quite has the world to himself as his own exclusive playground or as his own exclusive theatre of tragedy and sentiment. The image developed, ramified, and met real resistance.

As this happened an opposite image began to claim a place for itself. The working father was not necessarily what his playing son thought he was. The father began to break free from the simple category to which his son's life-story sought to consign him. Another kind of man, older, rooted, worldly and weather-beaten, claimed an opposite place in the imaginative field. In Nabokov's novels the paternal image grew more complex and interesting. In Marvell's poems the mature, sceptical voice of a worldly man cast doubt upon the complaints of Mowers and upon the religious ecstasies of both Puritans and Platonists.

None the less, on the whole, this further image, with its opposite perspectives, is more an implied than an actual thing in the two writers' works. Its rebuke or resistance may be heard in the tone of a poem or novel or its presence assumed because of some perspective that a poem or novel might derive from it. The first subject has certainly been made to leave way for a man quite different from the lone, displaced fugitive. But we have not yet seen too much of this other figure. We have felt his presence, respected his implied point of view, and been made to know that there is a world which belongs to him. The first subject, however, has continued to hold our imagination, even if other perspectives have been opened.

Pale Fire[1] is the one exception to this rule in the whole run of Nabokov's works. Here the solid, worldly figure of John Shade matches the solitary, Arcadian genius, Kinbote, step for step throughout the only genuine two-person narrative that Nabokov ever wrote.[2] He is not just implied but visible, audible, and palpable as a second character who is always able to balance Kinbote, or rebuke him, or doubt him, or, perhaps most tellingly of all, simply to be indifferent to him. Everything that was implied or incipient in the broadening perspectives of the other novels is here brought to completion. The dreaming, deracinated, nostalgic man of Arcadian imagination must thus battle throughout with a quite different figure. This new figure is a husband and father whose marriage is secure, whose job is tenured and who lives his calm life in the same provincial house from birth to death.

Pale Fire is thus the broadest of Nabokov's books. It involves deferences to two worlds. One of these is the classic, Arcadian world of pained, nostalgic memory, given here as the 'blue inenubilable[3] Zembla' of Kinbote's childhood. The other is Shade's world of respectable work and duty, a world of houses and institutions rather than of greenery and water, where childhood is a theme relating not to labyrinth, dream and memory but to the plain needs of education and the ordinary love and care of parenthood. The two worlds are imaginatively present throughout. Two men confront one another, two lives are interwoven, two meanings of childhood engage one's attention as the stories are given together.

This may, curiously enough, give *Pale Fire* a certain resemblance to 'Upon Appleton House'. On the face of it one could scarcely think of two works which offered themselves less readily for comparison. Where *Pale Fire* is quixotic, idiosyncratic, and written with great *brio*, 'Upon Appleton House' is leisured and contemplative, moving 'with slow Eyes'[4] over every area of Marvell's thought, summarizing and gathering it all up into a single statement as nothing in Nabokov attempts to do. No seriously sustained comparison between such diverse pieces of writing could possibly be tried. Yet there remains a handful of intriguing parallels and no harm will be done if we list them and let them stir as they will in the mind as the novel and the poem are considered in turn.

In each case there is a house, sitting on its 'square of green'.[5] The houses have well-kept gardens, the one laid out by a Fairfax, the other tended by Sybil Shade. Beyond this domesticated greenery there are densely growing trees, the forest at Nun Appleton being matched by the fringe of trees at New Wye which stands between the gardens of Shade and Kinbote and leafs up in summer to make life difficult for spying neighbours. Near each house there is a stretch of water (a river at Nun Appleton, a lake at New Wye) which plays a key part in the drama of each work.

Each house is a centre of domestic bonds and family continuity. Fairfax is a husband and father who has returned to the family home where his ancestors had long resided, while Shade, as we have seen, is a husband and father who has lived in what was his father's house for the whole of his life. Both men are famous. Both are poets, of perhaps about equal minor distinction. Both have daughters (Fairfax's living and Shade's dead) who are the focus of their parents' love and thought.

In each case there is a new arrival who enters this rural scene of domestic continuity, parental care, and traditional living. Marvell has come to Nun Appleton to tutor Fairfax's daughter in various foreign languages, Kinbote has come to New Wye to tutor students at Shade's college in one foreign language, Zemblan. Each intruder is a travelled, cosmopolitan figure entering a static provincial world. Each is a single man (Marvell a bachelor, Kinbote separated from his wife) entering a family world. Neither is yet known as a writer and both are rather secretive about their writing; but each of them, Marvell and Kinbote, will write his greatest work as a consequence of this visit and this teaching-post. Each will prove to be incomparably more gifted with poetic imagination than the minor poet who lives in the house.

In the course of his visit each intruder will contemplate at length the life and career of the domestic man. In looking at him and his household he will be contemplating the whole subject of relations between the stable world of houses and work and the surrounding, exotic forests of nature, play, and dream. Both intruders will be seen among the trees while the heads of the two households sit secure at home; and each, moving among the trees, will have his head filled with thoughts and visions which would probably have astonished Fairfax and Shade had they lived to see the works of Marvell and Kinbote respectively in print. Neither, however, did so live, so that the more 'fantastical' qualities of their visitors' imaginations probably remained unknown to them to the end.

There are some tiny parallels too. Brilliantly-coloured birds fly in the gardens of the two houses, a waxwing at New Wye, a kingfisher at Nun Appleton; and a dethroned king called Charles figures in the painful past of both stories.

The key thing is childhood. There is the woodland childhood of Arcadia, magic, and memory which haunts the edges of two worlds of adult work and domestic care; and there is childhood in the ordinary world, childhood lived out within the care and confines of Shade's household or of the '*Discipline* severe'[6] of Fairfax's authority. Both worlds are given in *Pale Fire* as nowhere else in Nabokov. Marvell too gives both worlds in 'Upon Appleton House', leaving behind in the poem a magically rich presentation of the innermost visions of his private fancy together with a calm, generous portrait of the Fairfacian virtues.

Nabokov knew his Marvell, of course. He had worked hard on his verse for his commentary on Pushkin's *Eugene Onegin*.[7] But there is no need to surmise any fanciful connection between the two works on the basis of such parallels as are not too solemnly listed above. The shared images rise naturally and independently from the shared, lifelong concerns of the two authors. Houses, gardens, woods, water, parents, children, tutors, and solitary

travellers: it was virtually inevitable that such images would
come forth as a set when either of these two authors produced a
work which summarizes a whole life, as 'Upon Appleton House'
does, or which, like *Pale Fire*, presents, with a breadth and
balance all its own, a vision common to all the novels.

Kinbote, first, is the successor to Humbert. As in *Lolita* so in
Pale Fire a rakish cavalier from the Old World breaks loose in an
ordinary, slightly round-headed part of the United States. Again
he lives just long enough to tell his tale, in the first person confessional, with stylistic flourishes equal to the flamboyance of his
imagination. Kinbote moves more warily than Humbert and his
story comes out more haltingly and deviously. But in the end the
magic, glamour, and glorious disorder which Humbert foisted
on to the Haze household is matched by the equally highly-
coloured mayhem which Kinbote foists on to Shade's poem.
Hazy suburbs and Shaded provinces are drenched alike in brilliant, cosmopolitan colours.

Kinbote matches Humbert in lordly insouciance, in spectacu-
lar egotism, in polyglot culture and literacy, in imaginative richness, quick wit, and cunning, in cavalier opinionatedness. He is
like him in exile, journeying, and hiding, like him in steering
a precarious course between confidence and fear, aplomb and
grotesquerie, dignity and disarray. Like Humbert he is deracinated and severed from the world of his childhood, from his
'tender and terrible boyhood' in Zembla. Like Humbert he is
haunted and hunted by the brilliant memory of this childhood.
Like Humbert he is gripped by an illicit, insatiable lust in which
the hunger for childhood is transformed into perverse desire, for
while Humbert loved young girls Kinbote loves slightly older
boys.

This second Nabokovian romance is as comic as the first.
Now, however, the tonal complexity attempted unsuccessfully at
the end of *Lolita* is managed to perfection. Here comedy is
blended perfectly with pathos. Kinbote is as funny as Humbert
but he is also a figure of great poignancy, a romance comedian
but also a displaced man. His life is cut into by great chasms of
loneliness. He is haunted by guilt. The shreds and tatters of a
subtle and fine moral conscience cling to him in his dereliction

and make him feel this dereliction with shame. Moral concerns far beyond Humbertian comedy are engaged by such things as his religious beliefs, his battles to retain his honesty and integrity, and his recoil from all forms of violence. He is tormented by contrary impulses, wishing both to confess and to conceal, to tell all and to hide all, as his halting, back-tracking story gradually reveals itself footnote by separate footnote.

Like Humbert he is quixotic in comedy. But Kinbote has the mournful countenance of the original Quijote as well, and were it not for Nabokov's avowed dislike of Cervantes' work[8] one would have said that he had a half-rhyme or half-shadow of his name as well. Like his great predecessor he has a wonderful ability to create comic chaos in the provinces, but also the darkened mind of a man abused by enchanters. The depths of such a mind are given quite awesomely here as they never were in *Lolita*. Kinbote is capable of genuine despair and of the terror of damnation.

He is also capable of a love beyond his lusts. It is indeed his capacity for love which causes him pain, by making him think of his lusts as darkness, mud, and horror. He loves God in his own desperate way. He loves Shade to some degree. He loves Shade's poem with an overwhelming passion which survives even his disappointment at discovering its infidelity to him. Above all he loves his estranged wife. From somewhere in the deepest recesses of his mind comes what he calls his 'dream-love' for Disa, surviving all his sexual recoil from her. He loves her in spite of his appetite for boys; and this 'dream-love' may be said to survive the hosts of his catamites in so far as it is recorded, once and once only, in a footnote at the heart of which there is a declaration of belief unequalled by anything else he ever says:

I trust the reader appreciates the strangeness of this, because if he does not, there is no sense in writing poems, or notes to poems, or anything at all. (433-4n.)

The great figure of Kinbote is the central, memorable achievement of *Pale Fire*. This 'soft, clumsy giant' of a cavalier King Charles, 'above two yards high', prolific in lust and 'surnamed The Beloved', is one of the great comic creations of modern literature. The human core of the book is a celebration of the resources of his imagination, shot through with a moving record of his pain and loneliness. But this is now a two-person novel and there is not only Kinbote. He is shadowed from first to last by another man. The opposite, twin, *alter ego*, or *Doppelgänger*, John Shade is like Kinbote and unlike him at every turn. The two figures criss-cross, interlace or run parallel in innumerable patterns. Kinbote is still the giant of his book, the major human presence in it; but he is the least easily dominant of all Nabokov's major characters. The ordinary, domestic figure of Shade never leaves the field free for Kinbote to run as he will. He is a perpetural resistance, a perpetual complicating factor.

Kinbote, forced to fence at length with this far from negligible opponent, is himself pushed further than he might have been in a world like Humbert's where he would have been allowed to win with ease. He must twist, turn, dodge, and improvise with great skill and cunning to see his task through to the end where not only Shade and his poem but the whole world of New Wye and serious scholarship will have been held at bay just long enough for him to complete his Commentary and his Index, down to Z for Zembla at the geographical extremity of the earth and the mental and moral extremity of the mind. Had Humbert met the resistance of such an opponent he might have developed Kinbote's range and richness and the tonal modulation at the end of *Lolita* might have proved less awkward in consequence.

Pale Fire, then, is Kinbote's book, but also Shade's. They compete for the book, just as they compete for the words and meaning of John Shade's poem. But what *Pale Fire* has most been famous for is its idiosyncratic form. The formal idiosyncrasy is delightful in itself, of course, for to make a novel out of a Foreword, a Poem, a Commentary, and an Index is to sustain the games of a playful intelligence at marvellous length. The book also exploits the curious fact that in some sense we believe what we none the less know to be fictions, and it thus blurs the frontiers of fact and fancy at every point. The zest of these games quickens the prose throughout.[9]

But such formal games and tricks of perspective, even at the incomparable level at which Nabokov is capable of playing them, would not alone support a full-length novel that we read and read again both laughing and moved. The human stories of Kinbote and Shade come first and the novel's curious form in fact serves those stories in various ways.

Its discontinuity works to create unhurriedness and an air of suspension, leaving gaps, leaving things separate and free to relate as they will, declining any simple, sequential march to a meaningful Conclusion. It makes us read back and forth in the book, picking up bits and pieces about the characters with something of the fragmentariness of real experience. It leaves interstices between the passages of its narrative where what we may never know about one of the two characters may be presumed to lodge; or where they may realign themselves, out of our view, to come back in the next separate passage in yet another relationship to one another, yet another pattern. It creates the classic provisionality of Modernist narrative and the freedom that comes from the absence of pressure.

But it is also a discontinuity that sorts well with the character and dilemma of Kinbote. In the narrative's gaps and silences Kinbote breathes, reflects, plots, regrets, regathers his forces for another wrestle with the angel. Of all the qualities which the unusual nature of the narrative brings to *Pale Fire* the most obvious one, the halting and stumbling of difficult speech, may well be the most important. Possession of Shade's poem enables Kinbote to speak and to join the great world of the respected in Literature and Learning. By a lucky chance he has the poem and can use it to break out of the solitude of his life, to talk for once, even if only in notes and glosses.

That his talk should fumble along in a fractured anthology of footnotes, reminiscences, and asides is entirely appropriate to the human predicament involved. It is the speech of a man unused to speaking but desperate to speak; or the speech of a man who only half wants to speak and who all the way through is tempted by the call back into hiding and silence. The odd form of the novel lends itself perfectly to the speech of a 'lonesome man' holed up in his 'sad domicile' but with a tremendous fictional world in him craving release.

The strange central pair of Kinbote and Shade relate, oppose, and interlace in innumerable ways. The poet is the sun, brilliant with his own 'fire'; the thieving, parasitic commentator is a mere sterile moon, with no light or heat of his own. But the sun in this case is called Shade and neither his poem nor his life suggests that he is the fieriest of orbs. His commentator, on the other hand, is incongruously ablaze. From here the comic dance of paradox and dialectic begins.

Shade, though a poet, is a mere 'fireside poet', Kinbote, though a mere scholar, is a 'cosmopolitan scholar'. The poet is incongruously drab, the commentator incongruously plumed. The poet is the Fairfacian man, living in a provincial house, employed at a provincial college, preoccupied with domestic matters and occasionally dabbling in philosophy. It is the commentator who roves and veers at the edge of Shade's garden as he had once ploughed his way through the meadows and bracken of his childhood Zembla, precariously employed, negligent of worldly ties and duties, with an imaginative world in his head richer than a rural poet, a Shade or a Fairfax, could ever imagine.

From this reversal of normal roles everything seems to follow effortlessly. Nabokov has created a pair of figures who weave about each other in numerous patterns left in free play by the discontinuity of the form. In this richness of dualistic variation, based upon simple, opposed characteristics, Shade and Kinbote inherit much from the work of Nabokov's prose masters, Joyce and Flaubert. Joyce's Dedalus and Bloom and Flaubert's Bouvard and Pécuchet can be felt behind Shade and Kinbote; and behind all of them, of course, lie Don Quijote and Sancho Panza. In all these cases there is a rich play of like with unlike, similarity with opposition. Such pairs are apt to stand apart or move together as they play out all the elaborations of what seems like an archetypal contrast.

The basis of this archetype is probably what George Orwell said it was when he observed the shared pattern in the characters of Cervantes, Flaubert, and Joyce, together with Shakespeare's Hal and Falstaff and Conan Doyle's Holmes and Watson.[10] The basis, thought Orwell, was one of worldly man and otherworldly man, gross man and ideal man, typically represented in a pairing where one is fat and one is thin. In Kinbote and Shade we meet them again, inevitably together and inevitably out of step, with

the tall, lean Kinbote trying in vain on their evening walks together

to adapt the swing of a long-limbed gait to the dishevelled old poet's
jerky shuffle, (Foreword)

or crossing the university library in self-confessed splendour 'at a
military quick march from east to west' while his squat, fat friend
is rather less flatteringly remembered

squirming up the college hall stairs as a Japanese fish up a cataract.
(691n.)

Much of the breadth and richness of *Pale Fire* must come from
its touching this archetypal source, so that the book's mere possession of a second character is enough to make it qualitatively
different from all the other works.

In accordance with the archetype, Shade is round, 'pudgy',
even perhaps 'misshapen', but Kinbote is excellently tall and
straight. Shade is apt to be static, sitting and talking at home or
in the Faculty Club; Kinbote is apt to be caught in the full,
angular career of one who describes himself as 'a vigorous though
unorthodox skier'. Shade is a carnivore, Kinbote drastically
vegetarian. Shade has a happy, stable marriage, Kinbote a
restless and unhappy history of promiscuity with his hordes of
catamites and a sad, fleeting, unachieved marriage. Shade likes
Pope and writes in couplets, Kinbote likes the late romantic
lyrics of Tennyson, Hardy, Housman, and Frost[11] and when he
writes himself it is sometimes in fragments, sometimes in tor-
rents, often in tears, and often of sunsets. Shade's mind is
secular, Kinbote's religious. Shade's New World home is at a
Mediterranean latitude, provincial, inland, and lowland; Kinbote's Old World country of Zembla is in the far north, with a
cosmopolitan capital city and the constant presence of sea and
mountain. Shade is secure, as we have seen, and has always lived
in the same house; the precarious Kinbote has somehow fetched
up next door to him after a wild, improbable journey, reversing
his way through the geographical alphabet from Zembla to Appalachia, which he calls Arcady.

Shade's spirit is succint, rational, probing, sceptical; Kinbote's
is veering, divergent, associative, and romantic. Shade is 'meth-

odical', Kinbote 'impractical'. Shade is bourgeois, Kinbote aristocratic, even royal. Shade's poem has qualities of candour, honesty, and directness and in his public talk he seems to relish an image of himself as the local Dr Johnson, or the local Diogenes; Kinbote is always wily and devious and given to the courtly arts of flattery and insinuation. Shade has many friends and acquaintances and is a man much admired; Kinbote is lonely and much derided. Shade's character is reflected in his shabby clothes and his old saloon car, while Kinbote's taste for the dashing runs to 'lilac slacks hailing from Cannes' and a powerful, sporty car. Shade shaves (and makes a ritual of it, putting it in his poem as a feature of his life); Kinbote sports a big red beard. Shade is content to sit visible in his house at night with the lights on and the curtains open while poor Kinbote dodges about among the dark trees outside, braving the terrors of the night and of 'the nightfall of the mind'.

But the richness of such pairs depends not only upon the ramifying series of opposites which they present but also on certain likenesses which seem to draw the two partners together in spite of their unresolvable differences. Such a pair, in their polar oppositions, present to us the dividedness of things and the irreconcilability of the high with the low. But they will have points of contact too which gives them the power to suggest union rather than division, keeping alive our desire for the real and the ideal to merge. For this the pair must have things in common.

So Shade and Kinbote are both liberal in opinion. Both are haters of violence. Both are lovers of literature. Both are scorners of orthodoxy. Both are scholars of a sort and poets of a sort. Both love wine and word-games. Each has his own kind of arrogance and irrascibility, and his own little bundle of Strong Opinions, on trivial matters as well as on serious ones, for Shade loathes swimming pools while Kinbote, in memorable terms, scorns swans.[12]

Their deepest points of contact have to do with the centre of the Nabokovian world. They both lost their fathers in infancy. In each case the father was a man of some renown. Each searches back into memories of childhood with fondness, with care, even with trepidation, as if something sacred were harboured there.

Each has a strong memory of childhood associated with a particular toy. Each has his own kind of resemblance to the dead child, Hazel, Shade's physical, Kinbote's mental. They share the same birthday, July 5th.

So they are opposite and yet in some ways similar. The long list of their differences makes us experience them in all their hopeless polarity. On the other hand their similarities help to arouse dreams of an impossible, possible union. The archetype on which they draw has much to say not only about opposites but also about the union of opposites. Its creative power is tribute to the endlessness of division but also to the never quite abandoned dream of reintegration.

In the greatest literary versions of the archetype profound intensities of mutual need, loyalty, and love are thus apt to unite the partners, howsoever opposed. This is especially so with Quijote and Sancho, and again with Bouvard and Pécuchet. They are therefore among literature's greatest portrayals of friendship as well as of division. Their stories even feel at times like love-stories, that of Bouvard and Pécuchet being as much as anything a tale of love at first sight.[13]

In *Henry IV* and *Ulysses* it is probably this underlying promise of union which intensifies our response to the failed possibilities of the central relationship. We cannot help believing in these possibilities. We feel that Hal is more profoundly drawn to Falstaff, more bound to him in friendship and even in love than his cool explanation of the liaison suggests. We want to believe this, whatever he may tell us. Something makes it imperative that we believe it; so that then their final sundering feels as painful as it does, no matter what political and moral necessity may dictate and no matter how we may have been forewarned.

We feel such possibilities again, in spite of all the evidence to the contrary, in the relationship between Mr Bloom and Stephen. Hence the painful disappointment of their long, ineffectual meeting.[14] Hopes and longings of a general kind have been aroused in us and when they are not fulfilled no amount of rationalization, howsoever well founded in a realistic sense of division and difference, will console us. Some deeper sense of disappointment, outrage, and metaphysical violation will linger.

With Shade and Kinbote, similar things happen. Their actual contact is minimal. As the story develops it comes to seem less and less actual, more and more a figment of Kinbote's imagination. The final rebuff indeed banishes Kinbote to the remote background of Shade's poem, reducing him to the insignificant anonymity of 'some neighbour'. Perhaps therefore everything that Kinbote has claimed is mere fantasy. Nothing in the slippery, inomniscient narrative will gainsay this sad surmise.

But the archetype works to stiffen our resolve that so complete a débâcle shall not be all. It makes us determined that some part of Shade should be reserved for Kinbote, however fleetingly. It makes us need the two of them to make some sort of contact, lest the world should seem composed of nothing but discord. Then, when we are forced to see that their relationship has been nothing, or nearly nothing, we feel something of the poignancy evoked by the later pages of *Ulysses*.

The archetype may speak to many kinds of human relationship. Friendship is no doubt at the core of it, but it has things to say about brothers, about masters and servants, and about comrades in arms. At its deepest, perhaps, it is rich with things to say about old and young and, more specifically, about father and son. In *Henry IV* and in *Ulysses* this is so, for the fat and worldly man wants to be father to the thin, young devotee of ideals and duties. In *Pale Fire*, Shade has no such wish *vis-à-vis* Kinbote; but Kinbote, whose vague and distant father died when his son was not quite three, leaving him with hideous dreams about his father's violent death, looks very much like an anxious candidate for the paternal affections of a man who, after the suicide of his daughter, is an orphaned parent. Behind this version of the pairing, colouring our emotional response to the two men, lies another, richer, version of something already given in *The Defence* and *The Gift*. Here again we have the desperate search of an exiled, severed, displaced son for the recognition and affection which is not given by his inaccessible father. The ironic self-clarification of *The Gift* has done its work well. *Pale Fire* handles the theme with full inventive liberty.

Shade then is all-important. Kinbote cannot be allowed to run away with the whole book. We may begin with the poet as resistance and foil, before turning to his flamboyant commentator.

Clearly Shade is more than just the 'fireside poet' of Kinbote's jibe. His work deserves better than the rather brisk, lit.crit. pigeon-holing which Kinbote once offers for it:

an autobiographical, eminently Appalachian, rather old-fashioned narrative in a neo-Popean prosodic style. (1000 n.)

That is uncharitable; but it is hard, none the less, not to share Kinbote's briefly voiced disappointment that 'the sun does not rise' in Shade's verse. The poem is succinct and civilized, sometimes pleasingly tough, often droll, occasionally quite strong in sentiment. There is a genuine individual intelligence in it. But both his names suit him well, the sunless Shade and the commonplace John.[15]

As resistance and foil to Kinbote, however, he can claim to play over the Nabokovian themes in his own quiet fashion, depriving Kinbote thereby of any monopoly of the realm of the Arcadian. He thinks back to his childhood. He evokes his room, the house on its green lawn, the loss of his parents, his boyhood solitude, his favourite toy. There is lake-water and greenery in his world as well, sunlight through leaves, the bright flight of the waxwing. But these are rather unecstatic presences in a subdued world. Even when he is in the woods of his boyhood he never properly belongs there:

> I walked at my own risk: whipped by the bough,
> Tripped by the stump. Asthmatic, lame and fat ...
> (128-9)

There are echoes of the unfortunate Luzhin in the early life of Shade, and consequently hints that something vital may have passed him by.

His adult life is similarly subdued. He meets his future wife by a waterfall whose 'roar and rainbow dust' give some romance to the setting; but romance is flattened in tone by the prosaic facts of their encounter, on 'damp grass' in a 'tame park' during a break for lunch on a high school outing. In part Shade is a Nabokovian *homo poeticus* for the classic motifs are there. But the colours and movements of this domesticated world are so dulled as to create in addition the opposing sense of Shade as Luzhin, Shade as a man in whom the Arcadian element is weak.

As an adult he has the Nabokovian virtues. He is literate, inde-
pendent-minded, and candid. His wit and his curiosity are both
real. He lectures on

> childhood memories of the strange
> Nacreous gleams beyond the adult's range.
> (633-4)

He cites Goethe's great poem *Der Erlkönig* about a child horribly
wooed and destroyed. His values centre on a Nabokovian sense
of the patchy paradises of the earth as superior to any imagined
paradise, and of virtue as consisting in the ability to remember
and revere the fleeting excellences of this-worldly life:

> I'm ready to become a floweret
> Or a fat fly, but never, to forget.
> And I'll turn down eternity unless
> The melancholy and the tenderness
> Of mortal life; the passion and the pain ...
> Are found in Heaven by the newlydead
> Stored in its strongholds through the years.
> (523-36)

This is all authentic Nabokov. It summarizes Nabokov's own
secular conviction that the trans-human is less than the human.
But it is authentic Nabokov in an unmagical, unquickened form,
matching exactly that unmagical boyhood.

When things do promise to quicken and Shade moves and
speaks with untypical zest, his wife brings him back rapidly to
their more normal tenor:

> Stormcoated I strode in: Sybil, it is
> My firm conviction—'Darling, shut the door.
> Had a nice trip?' Splendid—but what is more
> I have returned convinced that I can grope
> My way to some—to some—'Yes, dear?' Faint hope.
> (830-4)

It is a humiliatingly swift victory for the domestic at the end of
his most far-reaching spiritual excursion, encouraging the feeling
that Shade's marriage is rather low-key as well. It is impossible to
be sure, of course, because most of the evidence has been doc-
tored by the highly prejudiced Kinbote. It is also true that the

enigmatic Sybil twice receives a poetic encomium from her husband. But poor Hugh was all encomium for his crisp, chilly wife and there may be something similar here. Sybil comes through, in spite of her husband's praises, as perhaps meriting Kinbote's scorn. She sounds like a careful, corrective woman, just a trifle too expert in emphatic putdowns, like Luzhin's wife a good manager of things, including husbands.

Kinbote towers over Shade in genius. Though a mere commentator, he blazes far brighter than his poet. The riches of his fantasy life are unbounded. If Shade is like Hugh in his love for a chilling wife, Kinbote is like the inner, unseen and unheard Hugh suddenly made eloquent. Something like the 'fantastic majesty'[16] that was kindly and whimsically surmised on Hugh's behalf, pours out of Kinbote as he seizes his one, strange chance to be heard, which possession of Shade's poem gives him.

Suddenly gifted with speech, he can at last take an exquisitely engineered revenge upon his tormentors and spiritual inferiors. He can take revenge on the philistines of the world like Gradus, a simian personage with uncouth habits, gross tastes, ludicrous clothes, and no mental equipment to speak of, who is despatched to oblivion, very slowly, in the long report of his odious life and bungling journey. He can take revenge on the brisk and efficient Sybils of the world by means of a scatter of dismissive jokes and the triumphant culminating index reference of '*passim*'; and on the pip-squeaks of the world too, by dressing them all in a succession of ridiculously flashy, ridiculously conspicuous, and ridiculously identical green jackets and then, at the end, leaving the whole pack of them out of his Index altogether.

But revenge is not really his business, delicious though his revenges are in their finely-timed modulation from well-savoured intricacy to drastic simplicity. He has more urgent and less violent things on his mind. His work is really a kind of desperate testament. Its characteristic tones are witty, lyrical, and also heart-breakingly distressed.

He begins quietly, alluding to his 'personal misfortunes' in the Foreword and to 'that carrousel inside and outside my head', but holding on to his poise, keeping these presences at bay. He even permits himself to relax a little at the beginning of his Comment-

ary, with the loquacious wit of his disquisition on robins and of
his remarks about Zembla's beautiful climate and taxation
system under his benevolent rule.

Confidence increases. Soon he is in full comic career with his
description of Gradus reading:

swinging down to the foot of the page from line to line as from branch
to branch. (17, 29 n.)

Then comes his marvellous invasion of the Goldsworth household. Kinbote in the house of Judge Goldsworth is as splendid a
figure of comic upset as was Humbert in the house of Mrs Haze
or Quijote in the inns of La Mancha. His summary removal of
the gourmet cat and his unreadiness to participate in Goldsworth's curtain-regatta have the authentic sweep of Humbertian
or Quixotic comedy, delighting us with a simple inability to conform which overturns the apparatus and routine of daily life. His
struggles in Goldsworth's garden, fighting a losing battle against
the summer leafing of the trees, replay some of Humbert's struggles with the uncomfortable American wilds, and Quijote's with
windmills, wineskins, and the rest.

But now there is the Quixotic pathos of the figure as well.
Kinbote's testament modulates, suddenly but convincingly, from
comedy to distress. The flitting garden figure, spying on his il-
lustrious neighbour from behind a 'bodyguard of black junipers',
is already far sadder and more disturbing than Humbert. His
subsequent plunge into despair and thoughts of suicide, following a sudden recollection of his 'tender and terrible boyhood', is
quite beyond Humbert's tonal range.

Suddenly, after the poise and swagger of his wit and the festival
of his misrule, his imagination is cowed. His spirit drops perpen-
dicularly into thoughts of his 'cheerless domicile' with its
'solitary double bed' where the 'nightfall of the mind' awaits him
in his insomnia on 'dreadful nights' when wine, prayer, and
music are all equally powerless against 'the cracklings of old
death'. Humbert could always remain more or less unbowed
and his fear was rarely more than the simple fear of being found
out, seldom the fear of being mined from within that Kinbote
experiences. Kinbote strides or cringes by sudden turns, now

sweepingly confident, now stopped short and reduced to terror or desperate prayer ('Dear Jesus, do something') by

that cold, hard core of loneliness which is not good for a displaced soul.
(62 n.)

This is a figure fully entitled to that word of Damon's, another night-time wanderer who will never find his home.

Throughout his confession we meet these steep pitches down from comic to near-tragic. He is always likely to be unmasked, revealed in his loneliness, watching and waiting in his emptiness, a 'desponder' like Swift, subject to 'excruciating headaches', haunted by the endless grief and weariness which he finds stated in Robert Frost's great poem ending with the repeated line:

And miles to go before I sleep.[17]

He finds himself confessing his 'distress and disappointment' and his sense of being one of those who 'burrow in filth every day'. He finds himself fading towards the end into resignation and exhaustion, consoled only precariously by the Christian hope

that salvation may be granted to me despite the frozen mud and horror in my heart. (802 n.)

He finds himself making movingly re-iterated references to Appalachia as Arcadia ('our sunny, green, grass-fragrant Arcady') as if to hold on to the precarious peace he has found in the stable world of New Wye and in the eloquent world of Shade's poem. He ends 'petering out'. His last paragraphs are sombre and fading, punctuated by thoughts of death and flimsy hopes of salvation:

I have suffered very much ... I pray for the Lord's benediction ... My poet is dead ... God will help me, I trust ... (1000 n.)

It may be, however, that his demise is not quite certain when his Commentary limps to its end, even if no less an authority than Nabokov himself has found it certain that Kinbote committed suicide on completing his edition of Shade's poem.[18] He still has his Index up his sleeve, wherein his comic self is once more going strong, and we know that he has recovered before from depths like these. Kinbote is not only a 'desponder'; he is also a man who rallies himself repeatedly to the exultations and festivals of his laughter.

The rallying laughter of a brave fighter against the dark is heard in all the comic passages of his story. In each of the set-pieces of his fantasy-life the desponder lifts himself from the miseries of his displaced soul. Each passage is a new flight of fancy, turning disarray into adventure. Each is lavishly embellished in the telling by a comedian of formidable gifts. Each is an extravagant poem, comparing wonderfully well with the drabbish verse of Shade, even if, like Humbert's poem on Lolita's tennis, it is a mere edifice of words, reared upon very little.

It took a poetic imagination much greater than Shade's to write the adventure of Alfin the Vague who mislaid an emperor and was killed by a malevolent skyscraper; or the anti-feminine tale of Fleur de Fyler whose ever-increasing proximity and nakedness were no match for the King's effortless immunity to women; or the homosexual epic of Oleg in the *Alice in Wonderland* tunnel; or the romance of the King's escape, with its hackneyed folk-yarn of Griff and Garh, which is his finest work of literary parody; or the nonsense story of the meeting between Gradus and Bretwit where no intellectual energy is detectable in even the combined cogitations of two men; or the erotic poem of metamorphosis whose strip-tease hero is called Gordon; or the cheery tale of Andronnikov and Niagarin which manages to seem both merciless and yet somehow good-natured about the 'elementary facial expressions' of Soviet cosmonauts.

Kinbote's mind is a cascade of invention. Guilt, fear, and despair grip him repeatedly and seem to hold him locked; but by the strength and resource of his fantasy he keeps unlocking himself and sallying forth on yet another fresh creation before the terrors close in again.

This is all beyond *Lolita*. The easy poise of such elaboration speaks of something completed or settled in Nabokov which was not there in the earlier book. The loose-limbed, discontinuous form of *Pale Fire* allows digressions and bellyings of the theme to be easily accommodated; the simple, archetypal pairing of Shade and Kinbote holds all the digressions and bellyings together in completely convincing unity. There is nothing in the book that does not belong to its characters, nothing appended by an intruding Nabokov. The archetype has helped him to bring everything together and hold it beautifully suspended between these two versions of his basic *homo poeticus*, the one content to be subdued in a sane and stable domestic world, the other mad and veering, incapable of being subdued or domesticated or contented.

Perhaps the greatest product of Kinbote's poetic imagination is not a work of comedy at all. This is the passage on his 'dream-love' for his wife which constitutes his note to lines 433-4 of Shade's poem. It is written in the melting, roseate style of his numerous sunsets, the style that describes his wife as:

my lovely, pale, melancholy Queen, haunting me in my dreams, and haunted by dreams of me,   (Index)

or that pictures her alone and abondoned on a 'blue terrace', standing with 'the listless grace of ineffable grief'. It is the style of one who is 'constantly quoting Housman' and who is made uncomfortable by Shade's addiction to the Augustan severities. But Nabokov is a master of bitter-sweet; and like Marvell, who listened so well to the overpowering sentiments of grief and disconsolateness, he can now catch to perfection what is authentic in modes of expression which limp along as best they can with the worn clichés of love and grief.

Such clichés in this passage, with melting and sobbing rhythms to match, manage to convey an extraordinary intensity of feeling. Successive waves of wonder pass through it. Comedy and banter interpose at intervals, as if some part of Kinbote still did not quite believe his feelings; but again and again another wave will come, bringing another still clearer memory of his wife's beauty, misfortune, humiliation, patience, agony, strained composure, and pathetic hopes for his redemption. Kinbote is drawn on further and further in almost hypnotized wonder, through and past each resistant piece of sarcasm or banter, deepening and intensifying as the note goes on his vision of his wife's continued love for him and of his own love for her in 'the heart of his dreaming self'.

In the end it fades and he lopes away into yet another 'vast sunset'. But for eight pages it has been a strangely powerful *cavatina* of buried and hopeless love. It is overwhelming in sentiment but, cliché notwithstanding, it has that extraordinary transparency which Nabokov and Marvell regularly achieve when writing monologues of lost love. It is the furthest point to which Kinbote's spirit reaches, easily matching and balancing Shade's own praises of his wife and easily surviving, in our eventual sense of the book, all the brilliant comic celebrations of his lust.

This passage, perhaps more clearly than any other, proclaims Nabokov's new ease in the comic romance mode and his ability to mix and modulate his tone at will. It sustains just that bittersweet tone of sentiment and regret which failed him at the end of *Lolita*. Humbert has grown considerably in becoming Kinbote. The poetic, coloured Arcadian voice is now wonderfully rich, not least because the prosaic voice of Shade's resistance has a far greater function than merely to be opposite and wrong. They are not pure opposites. They overlap and mix. They compose numerous complex patterns. Both are thereby heightened; and both are preserved in the gentle, negligent order of the complete work.

24

THE NURSERY OF ALL
THINGS GREEN

'Upon Appleton House'[1] also creates its air of unforced resolution by means of a form in which there is room for discontinuity. The poem is content to move through its various phases at an unhurried pace. The different sections are laid together in an unpressured sequence of quiet juxtapositions, to relate as they will, to work as they will in the mind. Marvell is as scrupulously withdrawn as any Modernist narrator, as skilfully patient with the multitude of tiny comings and goings which his open, flexible imagination finds in play in the world and thus wants to leave in play in his poem. The work has a curiously Modernist air of suspendedness about it and, in self-enquiry and autobiographical contemplation, a Modernist air of being ever-provisional, governed always by the quiet arts of experiment.

There is, however, unity to the poem, even amidst such careful lack of finality or conclusiveness. It touches everything in Marvell's world. It has a space, range, and completeness unlike anything else. It reaches out to the furthest extremities of his vision and then returns upon itself, unforced, to end with what feels like a profound settling. There is no rhetorical assertiveness. All the separate parcels of the mind are allowed to relate and come to terms with one another in loose unity, or even just to agree to leave each other alone.[2]

All of Marvell is here, and consequently most of Nabokov too. It is a poem about a house, then about a garden, then grassland and then woodland, each grading into the next as the house is left further behind on the poet's journey. It is about the '*Discipline* severe' of the house and about the 'wanton' windings of river and tendril in the water and woodland outside. It is about 'men who live in houses, 'Streight' men who live in 'strait' domestic confines; and about another man whose solitary, fugitive mind reaches out to the furthest, hidden recesses of the forest to find an adequate imagery for the full range of its needs.

It is about the work of architects who cut the earth to get stone for houses and cut down the live, green trees for wood. It is also about the tortoise, whose house grows with him, shaped to his body, the product of no work or cutting; and about the woodpecker, who is as fine a calculator and engineer as any human maker of artefacts but who does his skilled work by merely 'tinkling with his Beak'. It is about effort and effortlessness, strain and ease, work and play.

It is about flow as against measure, grass as against stone, 'wanton harmless folds' as against 'streightness'. It is about 'labyrinths', 'gadding *Vines*', the rippling crawl of caterpillars and the interlacing and curling of greenery in a world of wood and water where 'abandoning', 'sliding', and being 'undermined' feel free from all danger.

Running through it all is the theme of childhood. Maria Fairfax is a fortunate child brought up in the peace and security of a garden. Isabella Thwaites, by contrast, was seized and held behind a 'gloomy Cloysters Gates' by perverse adults who behaved

> Like Gipsies that a Child hath stoln.
>
> (268)

The young birds of the forest are like Maria in their security, for the forest is so kindly disposed towards infancy as not to threaten the open, trusting, 'shining Eye' of the fledgling thrush. The young heron is dropped unharmed from the treetops by its parents.[3] The young woodpeckers are fed by the forest as easily as they are housed by it, both food and nest being provided by that simple, musical 'tinkling' of the adult bird. Outside the forest, by contrast, in a more exposed, considerably less trustworthy world, the young rail is killed in the nest by adult men at their work.

Marvell is an adult, working as a tutor to a child and thus a part of Fairfax's '*Discipline* severe'. But there is a boy within him too, giving his playful fancy to the celebration of Fairfax's garden, looking up like a child at the huge figures of the Mowers, fishing in the forest's waters and climbing in its trees, to emerge and be gently upbraided at the end as a 'trifling Youth' caught at play with his 'Toyes' by Maria, a child supposedly in his tutorial care. The child's 'judicious Eyes' at this moment look down severely at her tutor who seems more childlike than she.

It is about the very childhood of the world, 'Natures Cradle', the 'Nursery of all things green', the first stirrings of life where sun and water quicken things into greenness, the 'Garden of the World ere while' from which some 'luckless Apple' has expelled adults if not children and men if not birds, but which we may perhaps approach again, in the mind at least, as we re-find and re-experience our childhood by wandering in a wood.

It is about the violence that has 'negligently overthrown' that once green world, specifically the violence of war. Arcadia is threatened by many things in the adult world but by none so much as war. War is the supreme instance of all the forces of severance, the supreme destroyer of the young. It killed the young Villiers, wrecked the life of the Unfortunate Lover, armed the chariot-wheels of T. C.'s destined cruelty, casually destroyed the Nymph's fawn. It was led 'indefatigably on' by the uplifted sword of Cromwell in 'An Horatian Ode'; and in *The Rehearsal Transpros'd* it will still sum up for Marvell the typical condition of the post-lapsarian world:

> But alas! that state of perfection was dissolv'd in the first Instance, and was shorter liv'd than Anarchy, scarce of one days continuance. And ever since the first Brother Sacrificed the other to Revenge, because his Offering was better accepted, Slaughter and War has made up half the business in the World.[4]

Here, in the countryside of central Yorkshire, a great soldier has retired to peace and solitude in a traditional English house in an apparently unravaged landscape. But Marston Moor is not far away; nor, for that matter, if Marvell ever cast his mind back to earlier civil wars in England, is Towton. His poem, with its imagery of massacre and pillage, will carry intimations of Drogheda and Wexford, even in Wharfedale. Retirement, for an adult, would seem to be a complex and difficult business. We take our world with us and its images are deep-rooted in the mind. Only in the forest, the poem's central 'Sanctuary' of 'yet green, yet growing' life, is all memory of war finally shed from the mind. Here a great image of unending pacific life is set up in a green hide-out less cramped than the 'penetralia veris' of 'Hortus' and more sunny than the 'green Shade' of the English version, 'The Garden'.[5]

Finally it is about sex. The wood is peaceful in contrast with war, labyrinthine in contrast with straightness, a place for a boy to play rather than for a man to work. But it is also an erotic place, suggestive of sex-play rather than of children's play. It is a place of seduction, caressing, licking, holding and clasping. It is full of the rhythms of desire, ecstasy and satisfaction. In one sense it is therefore quite different from the world of the virgin-child Maria, the virgin-child Isabella and the boyish Marvell. But in another sense child and adult meet in this erotic wood. Play, in the wood, feels simultaneously like the romping of a boy and the sex-play of adults. The embraces of the wood and the river feel like those of a sexual partner and like that of an adult nursing a child. The sanctuary of the wood is really a place where the two worlds, the two parts of the mind, may find each other at last and connect again, picking up all the broken threads of severance.

For Nabokov childhood graded effortlessly into sexuality in a birch-wood in the security of his Arcadian Russia where children's play gave way to sexual play with undeflected ease. The world of politics and violence then intervened and the adult was left on the other side of a divide. Marvell's life was also led in the midst of political violence, the life of Fairfax even more so. Similar contraries are involved, similar images of severance seen, similar images of healing pursued. In the woods at Nun Appleton there is enacted a sacrament of re-joining. The boy and the man meet and converse. There is common ground. Such a reunion cannot, of course, be made in triumph and held on to for ever. Man and boy, and public and private, will still have to go their separate ways. But there is a genuine re-joining and recognition in the mind. No later adult sense of severance or solitude will be quite so painful after such a forest communion of all the mind's memories.

A poem concerned with such diverse matters cannot be expected to be a single, closely unified meditation following some linear argument to a logical conclusion. Its articulations will be more supple. It will deal in the provisional, and in quiet, laconic juxtapositions, without the forced march of a thesis. The author will listen to himself as much as he will speak, just as he has listened attentively to others in monologue and dialogue. His readers must overhear him, as they have overheard his other speakers, without itching to be addressed with any bolder rhetoric. We must wait as he waits, pause as he pauses. He normally has time to walk slowly and stop frequently, meandering and changing tack.

But though the poem meanders freely its route is afterwards left quite well signposted. The signposts are thematic as well as geographical. First he is in the house and its hall, talking of the present inhabitants. Then he is in a doorway or at a window, looking out to the 'Neighbour-Ruine' of the old nunnery and considering the house's past. Then comes a three-phase journey taking him further and further away from the house. First there is the garden where nature is dominated by man, worked, shaped, and designed. Then there is the meadow further out, where men still work, cutting the grass and raising cattle, but where extra-human things begin to be approached. Then there is the wood, unworked, untouched by man, of endless age, beyond the boundaries of the economic world where a working adult is turned back into a playing child. Then there is the return, to reconsider the human world of households, education, and marriages, and the poem closes with Marvell moving back through the garden in the evening, making for the house which he left in bright daylight.

House, nunnery, garden, meadow, wood, and return: the six phases of the walk are marked clearly enough.[6] But as with romances and picaresques the pattern of a journey lends itself to the most wandering, easy-going kind of narration. Journeys are not necessarily pilgrimages and they do not necessarily have goals. They may provide a very loose-limbed structure for a narration, as here, where there is no continuous drive or push through the poem and the separate disconnected details are not overridden by the composition of the whole. The poem's end is nothing like a goal. It is distinctly unemphatic and wistful.

Two further structural patterns profoundly rooted in our imaginations work succinctly to hold everything together in quiet relation. One is the cycle of the day, which traces Marvell's walk from the morning through the midday heat to the cool air and fading light of the evening. The other is the cycle of leisure, refreshment, or holiday, the cycle on which Shakespearean comedy is based,[7] which begins with a house, moves out to woods and fields and then comes back to the house again, renewed or chastened by the woodland experience.

The shaping presence of each lessens the need for a more limiting, linear argument. They help the poem's unrhetorical air of provisionality too, by tacitly reminding us that this is only one day among many, or only one holiday interlude before the confinements of work and discipline create the need for another. The wistful, unemphatic ending, in accordance with such structures, tells no consoling lies about the ever-recurrent nature of disruption and re-formation.

Finally, of course, there is the structural relation of Marvell to Fairfax. Once more there are two men and two worlds. Once more they are opposites, yet connected, and once more the pairing is very rich. Marvell is the solitary figure, the outsider. He has joined the Fairfax household and is closely involved with it, but he is still able to regard the house and the family with an observer's detachment. As the poem unfolds we will be given as detailed a view of the rich interior of his mind in solitude as ever we are given of Kinbote's.

Fairfax, on the other hand, is a social being, the centre of a network of social relations. Many readers of the poem have been misled by the known political circumstances of Fairfax's life and have placed too strong an emphasis on the issue of his resignation and retreat. But in the poem that is a very minor matter, mentioned in only two stanzas. For the rest he is an active man, a man of '*Magnitude*', 'the *Master* great' at Nun Appleton, a solid man in a functioning social world, albeit a provincial one. He represents the world of work and institutions, as lord, as head of a family, and above all as educator of his daughter.

In as rich an opposition as that between Shade and Kinbote, it is Marvell, not Fairfax, who is the figure of solitude. His retreat is not *to* the house of Fairfax but *from* it. He retreats to the

'Sanctuary' of the forest and it is between house and forest that the poem moves.

The poem's first phase, praising the present house, is elegant and in some ways conventional. The house is modest and traditional. The gentle countryside of central Yorkshire has not been ravaged to provide materials for a vast edifice. Forests have not been hewn down, quarries have not hollowed the earth into desolate 'Caves'. A small house, fitted to the size of a man as a nest is to a bird or a shell to a tortoise, reflects the domestic sense and sober imagination of a man who knows he is a mere 'Mote of Dust' and who does not wish to be 'superfluously spread' in arrogant absurdity. At the start of the poem the Fairfacian world of houses, domesticity, and education looks very handsome indeed. Marvell's praise of it is full and generous.

The voice of Ben Jonson can be heard in this praise of Fairfax. Jonson was the principal maker of the tradition to which this passage belongs. At Penshurst he had celebrated a similar domestic propriety which he saw as imaged in a traditional, native style of architecture, eschewing such exotic and alien materials as toushstone and marble.

But the Jonsonian voice was bigger and more formal than the intimate voice heard here. He gave his praise in a magnificent, ample rhetoric on the heroic scale. Marvell, as we have seen in the poem on 'Tom May's Death', was ready to relish that rhetoric and take pleasure in the voice and presence of the maestro. But Marvell was the watcher and listener at Jonson's rousting of May, not the giant speaker himself. He kept his distance from Jonson; and so here, as Jonson's tradition comes down to Marvell two generations later, it changes. Marvell adds some distinctly unconventional elements of his own.

As soon as this tradition becomes Marvell's it tends to become Arcadian. What is here, but was not in Jonson, is the perspective of the Mower's 'true survey'. The Fairfacian world is excellent because it has retained something of that easy rapport between man and nature. In this Arcadian variant of the voice of Jonson animals are 'exprest' by their dens, birds have nests which are 'equal' to themselves, tortoises have 'cases fit'; and when 'dwell' is made to rhyme with 'Tortoise-shell' it at once takes on a very different colouring from that which Jonson gave it when his heroic humanism packed all its weight behind the word at Penshurst ('their lords have built, but thy lord dwells') and at the estate of Sir Robert Wroth:

> Thy peace is made; and, when man's state is well,
> 'Tis better if he there can dwell.[8]

One cannot easily imagine the great-voiced Jonson deriving models for human behaviour from 'low roof'd Tortoises'; but with Marvell the gentle, Arcadian vein works its way into the conventional rhetoric from the outset. It will still be there at the end, when the salmon-fishers go home in the peace of the evening with their leather coracles upturned on their heads making them look *'Tortoise like'*. A poem about a great man's estate is oddly and delightfully content to begin and end in contemplation of the rounded, portable home of a slow, peaceful animal which spends its life shuffling through the grass. That is purest Marvell, unthinkable in Jonson whose scheme of things was firmer, with less play in it.

There is further idiosyncracy in Marvell's sense of what is involved when men more gross and ambitious than the Fairfaxes are, by contrast, 'superfluously spread'. Jonson could have written 'superfluously spread', enjoying the disdain of its image of risible excess. He could have written 'Man unrul'd' too, with its weighty moral charge against anarchy and indiscipline. But Jonson would not, like Marvell, have described the extravagant builder as a man,

> Who of his great Design in pain
> Did for a Model vault his Brain,
> Whose Columnes should so high be rais'd
> To arch the Brows that on them gaz'd.
>
> (5-8)

Those high columns, vaults, and arches in the brain, matching in the psychological world the distortions of grandiose architecture, are again pure Marvell. His architect is a figure 'in pain' whose false design wrenches his mind from the equable state of the true survey. He passes on a distorted, twisted world to those who will strain to look up at his towering work. There is more of Blake

here than of Jonson, something of the Blakeian Marvell who, in
'A Dialogue between the Soul and Body', figured such vexations
in the vertiginous image of being 'mine own Precipice' and again
associated such psychological wounding with the human artificer's violent attack upon nature:

> So Architects do square and hew,
> Green Trees that in the Forest grew.[9]

That note is briefly and quietly touched but it is unmistakable.
There are curious eddies or tremors at the edges of the Fairfax
world. The language for his world leaves certain things unsaid
and they seem to be trying occasionally to make themselves heard
in whispers and rhetorical sub-movements. But as yet they serve
no particular purpose. They are simply there, in free play, as
secondary thoughts for which the poem has room, small, complicating additions faithfully recorded by a writing which is never
foreclosed.

A further Marvellian modulation of the convention gives a
sudden perspective on Fairfax's world which is intriguingly
childlike and slightly unmanageable. An *Alice in Wonderland*
quality enters the poem and we sense a small child wandering in
a world of strange, giant adults. The Veres and Fairfaxes are not
men unruled, nor are they superfluously spread. Others are.
From most points of view that is the distinction which matters.
But from the point of view of a small child looking up at adults
such a distinction will count for nothing. From this point of
view, on another scale, all adults, unruled or not, are simply
colossi. When the great ones of Nun Appleton are seen for a moment as men of 'Extent' stooping to pass through 'dwarfish Confines' Marvell's praise of their modesty has slipped into another
mode where childlike fantasy is in play and the reins of sobriety
slacken.

There is a more precarious world than that which was inhabited
by the confident, striding men of Jonson's estates. Here, as
things slip from sobriety to fantasy, barriers and distinctions are
revealed as insecure. The secure dimensions of the adult world
are subject to tremors. A child's-eye vision introduces surreal disturbances into a once solid world.

Jonson, of course, wrote beautifully about children himself. His epitaphs on his son, his daughter, and the boy-actor S. P. are fine poems of profound tenderness.[10] The deaths of these children called forth the strongest emotions in him. But the emotion is given across a divide between adult and child which will in no circumstances be bridged. The humanist rhetoric of the adult world looks down to a child but remains itself securely adult. Barriers and categories stay firm. With Marvell such reliable distinctions are likely to vanish or vary according to some principle of whimsicality which seems to inhabit all worlds, natural and human.

The biggest disturbance in this first phase involves, again, change of shape and dimension. The well-built, sober world of Fairfax is suddenly helpless, suddenly subject to the random play of whatever it is that sets up tremors within human systems:

> Yet thus the laden House does sweat,
> And scarce indures the *Master* great:
> But where he comes the swelling Hall
> Stirs, and the *Square* grows *Spherical*;
> More by his *Magnitude* distrest,
> Than he is by its straitness prest:
> And too officiously it slights
> That in it self which him delights.
>
> (49-56)

Marvell may be praising Fairfax for his modesty in having a small house; or glancing at him sarcastically if a new, bigger house is already planned or built. Whatever the truth of the matter something very unusual happens.

A sudden rush of volatile imagination breaks the perfect module which built things to a human scale in accordance with a '*holy Mathematicks*'. The house comes preposterously to life. It sweats like a laden animal, puffs itself up like a threatened animal, then fawns 'too officiously'. So long as the humanist distinctions held it was disdainfully left to 'others' to strive in vain to achieve the quadrature of the circle; but here the house spontaneously performs the feat in reverse, unassisted, in a flash of magic. Something eery and surreal would seem to lurk in the best-laid plans of whatsoever architect and in the house of howsoever excellent a man.

T. S. Eliot did not approve. He found this sort of fancifulness 'undesirable'. He compared it with the fanciful imagery of the '*Tortoise like*' fishermen at the end of the poem where again he found 'error'. In 1923 he went back on the fine essay of 1921 and pronounced Marvell to be a minor figure because too 'fantastical'.[11]

Nothing, of course, should detract from Eliot's achievement in the 1921 essay, securing the Modernist discovery of Marvell after 250 years of almost complete neglect. Nothing should obscure the close relation that exists between the superb anti-rhetorical provisionality of Eliot's own verse and similar things in the verse of Marvell. But it is at a point like this that one can see again how limiting it was that only Eliot's Modernism, and not Joyce's, was involved in finding Marvell. This curiously random playfulness in Marvell, like his non-satiric laughter, has more in common with Joyce's fancy than with Eliot's wit. In Marvell there is the crucial element of purposelessness, happy, as *Finnegans Wake* is happy, to subvert all rhetorics and all modules, releasing the mind from the purposes of sobriety and giving it the freedom of play.[12]

'Upon Appleton House' is full of this sense of freedom as play. It contains much that is indeed 'fantastical', much that would inevitably be called 'error' by people of strong, sober purpose. But such purposive people, like Fairfax, are one of the poem's subjects. The poem as a whole does not belong to them. It is part of the poem's business to set some highly fantastical thoughts in play about them, to give the Kinbote element in the mind a free run around the calm and propriety of John Shade.

So far, however, the play of such fanciful disturbances is clearly secondary. The primary thing, easily dominant in this first phase, is the praise of Fairfax and his house. There may be tremors, but so far they remain at the margins of Marvell's thoughts. The Fairfax household and values appear sound. A world of human order and purpose may stay easily in touch with the world of nature. There is no chasm of severance between the house, now safely restored to its normal dimensions, and the green world outside of

> fragrant Gardens, shaddy Woods,
> Deep Meadows, and transparent Floods.
> (79-80)

The second phase makes the Fairfax world look better still, by scornful contrast with the perverse, witching world of the old nunnery. The excellent house now gives way to a highly 'fraudulent' garden of smiling vice and sinister luxury into which a child is lured to be corrupted. The child is sucked in by the 'smooth Tongue' of the nun like a fly taken by a long-tongued reptile or amphibian. These 'Hyprocrite Witches' can cast spells even from the distance and enclosure of their 'prison'.

This perverse garden is complex and labyrinthine like Arcadia, but in ways that only make the sober house of Fairfax seem more and more admirable. The nunnery garden has its leisure, pleasure, delight, and security, but they all seem artificial, breathy, and studied, in comparison with Arcadian freedoms. The nuns' religiosity is lachrymose and soft. They are untrustworthy connoisseurs of exquisite luxury and fine sensation. Their eroticism seems particularly sterile, a mixture of the desire to touch and the desire to refrain from touch. They steal the child to turn her into a hidden precious object, locked up with a 'fresh and Virgin Bride' like jewels in a box. Nothing in this garden is green, nor is there any hint of water. Everywhere there is whiteness or colourlessness, and the characteristic liquids of the place are oils and sugars preserved in jars.

Marvell has worked before in such areas. 'On a Drop of Dew' was coy, virginal, and yet erotic like this; whiteness and fondling in 'The Nymph complaining' were sad and lonely like this; the gardens scorned by the Mower were as 'curious' and as perversely meddling as this. But all three were, to different degrees, presented with reserve or hesitation, with judgement suspended. Here, for once, Marvell seems in no way reserved. There seems at this point to be no ambiguity in his disdain for the nunnery[13] and in the consequent allegiance he gives to the contrasting world of the Fairfaxes. The fraudulent labyrinths of the nunnery are bested utterly by the upright, male and soldierly probity of the Reformation Fairfax who rescues the child, restores her to the domestic world and founds a line of military heroes which will culminate in the great Lord General himself.

This section is the longest in the poem. The praise of Fairfax and the Fairfacian values may not have the weight of the Jonsonian voice, but the quieter, more intimate voice of Marvell has so far scarcely wavered from the sort of certainty that Jonson's tradition had first created.

The third phase, in the garden, begins with the praise of Fairfax coming to a peak of celebration. The famous description of the ornamental fortress-garden sports and races with wonderful inventiveness. All is quickness, minute observation, Puckish wit, and brilliant, paradisal colour, silken and shining in the bright light of day. Here the mind laughs joyously, where in the nunnery garden it smiled in secret. Here it rushes and darts where there it lingered. Here it is delighted where there it was studied and dulled. This is a festival of *homo poeticus*. It was the *poeticus* element in the mind of a Fairfax which 'laid these Gardens out in sport'; now a similar element in Fairfax's language-tutor leads him to sing their praises in nimble verse.

We are now nearly half-way through the poem and the world of Fairfax has received almost nothing but praise. The Fairfaxes are modest, responsible, Reformation men, soldiers, builders of houses, raisers of families. They are also men with enough imaginative spirit and sufficient sense of leisure and play to have produced this fragrant and colourful garden. Sober, upright, conspicuously masculine people, they have neither the feminine wiles nor the ludicrous and dangerous superstitiousness of the nuns.

Knowing Marvell we might have known that such certainty, such unambiguous simplicity, could not hold his mind for much longer. The imagination that added those odd fragments of volatile and personal whim to the Jonsonian rhetoric of the poem's beginning could not remain faithful to these simplicities without strain. Something is repressed in such uncharacteristically single-minded verse, some part of Marvell is being kept out of play. The first section, on the house, gave signs of a certain restlessness which wanted to be off to livelier things; the second section, on the nunnery, reads as if held under a simplifying restraint which introduces a coarser, more directive tone than Marvell's finest humour ever has.

This delighted celebration of Fairfax's garden is the highest point that Marvell can reach in such a vein of unstinted approval. After it, hardly to our surprise, indeed almost to our relief, comes a sudden and drastic change. It is as if the mechanisms of repression had given way under the prolonged strain and a great surge of postponed feeling rises into words:

> Oh Thou, that dear and happy Isle
> The Garden of the World ere while,
> Thou *Paradise* of four Seas,
> Which *Heaven* planted to us please,
> But, to exclude the World, did guard
> With watry if not flaming Sword;
> What luckless Apple did we tast,
> To make us Mortal, and The Wast?
>
> Unhappy! shall we never more
> That sweet *Militia* restore,
> When Gardens only had their Towrs,
> And all the Garrisons were Flowrs,
> When Roses only Arms might bear,
> And Men did rosie Garlands wear?
> Tulips, in several Colours barr'd,
> Were then the *Switzers* of our *Guard.*
>
> The *Gardiner* had the *Souldiers* place,
> And his more gentle Forts did trace.
> The Nursery of all things green
> Was then the only *Magazeen.*
> The *Winter Quarters* were the Stoves,
> Where he the tender Plants removes.
> But War all this doth overgrow:
> We Ord'nance Plant and Powder sow.
>   (321-44)

The preceding passage of celebration linked the imagery of gardening with the imagery of war in a series of brilliant inventions. Now those two images return, after the brilliance of that effort, to their more normal places in Marvell's vision as polar opposites. The illusion was beautiful so long as it lasted; now, with hindsight, it looks impossibly fanciful. The ensuing lament has much more cogent things to say about gardens and war.

The civil war, bringing 'Wast' to a once 'dear and happy Isle', stands directly behind the passage. Further back stands the image of more general loss represented by the expulsion from Eden, when a 'flaming Sword' marked the gates of a lost garden. The child-centred Arcadia, where 'tender Plants' grow protected in the 'Nursery of all things green', is also actively at work. The local and the general merge, as they did in the laments of Damon, to produce the same overwhelming sense of catastrophe. It is universal, yet also terribly near, something which has just happened to real people in a real place.

The forlornness, bewilderment, and bitterness of Marvell's displaced minds is here. There is a testament here for all his most poignant speakers. Tolling words like 'luckless', 'Wast' and 'Unhappy' speak of general desolation. The complaining Nymph is here, helpless and disconsolate. So is Damon, with his intimate love of his lost world. The indignation of 'The unfortunate Lover' and the tragedy of 'An Horatian Ode' are concentrated in the bleak conception of planting artillery and sowing gunpowder. We are all Orphans of the Hurricane and Sons of War and Fortune and the playing world of Arcadia and the imagination is laid irretrievably waste by our garrisons. The green nursery of the world's youth has been wrecked and ransacked by a real militia whose forts are not made of flowers.

These two great passages about gardens and war stand side by side in silent, puzzling opposition at the main turning point in the poem. The first, with its flower-soldiers, is an emblem of the highest delights of the civilized, domestic world. The second, with its real soldiers making waste where once there were flowers, is a lament voicing everything that no such world, however fine, can set to rights.

No verdict is given. But suddenly the fine promise of the Fairfacian world has faded and it seems suspect and partial like any other. The poem now changes direction and also quickens its pace. There will be much less of Fairfax and the public realm, much more of the private imagination. After two halting and highly inconclusive stanzas on Fairfax's resignation from the army the poem is suddenly plunging on elsewhere:

> And now to the Abyss I pass
> Of that unfathomable Grass.
> (369-70)

The Kinbote element of the haunted solitary, wandering in uncharted places where dimensions are insecure, begins to exert itself. It pulls against the commitment to the solid, domestic world, draws Marvell away from the house and liberates the imaginative life which was felt as occasional disturbance at the poem's beginning. There is now a fugitive aspect to the journeying figure of Marvell. He does not stroll quite so easily. Deep general anxieties about violence and war press upon his mind.

When the fourth phase begins we encounter at once the classic Arcadian images of greenery and water. The grass is 'green' and 'unfathomable'. It is parted by Mowers who wade through the 'Grassy Deeps' of a 'green Sea'. If you dive into such grass you lose all sense of direction like a person drifting 'under Water'. The familiar wound is seeking the familiar images for its healing.

The random life of fancy moves quickly in the strange transformations of this passage. All ideas of dimension and scale must be put by in the presence of such changes of perspective as make seas out of fields, giants out of grasshoppers and spires out of blades of grass. The *Alice in Wonderland* quality, with its disruption of the natural sizes of things, returns to the poem. There is a child's mind here again, looking up at the huge 'tawny Mowers' and watching, partly fascinated and partly afraid, as 'Engines strange' repeatedly alter a theatrical scenery of wonder.[14] The meadow is a whimsical place, given to sudden, unpredictable changes, and Marvell looks around it with a mixture of delight and caution.

His caution is well placed; for whilst there is grass and water here, and an accompanying expansion of the dreaming and remembering faculties, there is also violence. The Mowers 'Massacre' the grass. One of them kills the rail. The rail is a young bird, without feathers, still in the nest. Its killing is as 'untimely' as was the killing of the fawn. Its parents are made

'Orphan' by its death. Disturbing thoughts from the depths of Marvell's imagination are surfacing even here, along with happier memories of game and freedom.

As such thoughts stir, the imagery of war begins to stir again too. The muted trumpets of the parent-birds' mourning may well have something military about them; and the stanza that follows their sounding contains a brutal metamorphosis:

> The Mower now commands the Field;
> In whose new Traverse seemeth wrought
> A Camp of Battail newly fought:
> Where, as the Meads with Hay, the Plain
> Lyes quilted ore with Bodies slain:
> The Women that with forks it fling,
> Do represent the Pillaging.
>
> (418-24)

The field of grass becomes a battlefield. The mowers' camp becomes a 'Camp of Battail'. There is a terrible mayhem in the word 'fling' applied to what was once hay on a pitch-fork but is now a body impaled on a pike. There is a sickening sense of wantonness in the idea of a plain being 'quilted ore' with bodies. War disrupts the quest for Arcadia once again, this time in a vision of the ugly, riotous bloodiness of massacre and pillage. Drogheda has come to Fairfax's Wharfedale retreat in the mind of an imaginative man.

This phase of the poem does not recover from the intrusion, no more than the previous phase could cope with the idea of war as ransacker of a garden world. The 'careless' mowers who 'play' after their work can't help seeming like 'Victors' celebrating 'Triumphs'. They sweat like the soldier Alexander. Their haystooks are like '*Roman Camps*', or like tumuli 'for Soldiers Obsequies'. Even after the scene has changed again, and the stage is once more a 'Table rase and pure', Marvell finds himself reminded of another theatre of blood which he presumably saw on his travels in Spain:

> such is the *Toril*
> Ere the Bulls enter at Madril.
>
> (447-8)

The idea of war puts Marvell's mind under the very greatest pressure, giving us reason to reflect that his rediscovery came not only in the period of Modernism, but also in the aftermath of the First World War, by which time more people understood the feeling of total recoil from war which Marvell is already finding in himself here.

The pacific, playing imagination of *homo poeticus* is now even more fugitive. The water-greenery of the meadow-deeps is neither green nor deep enough. The meadow is still a place of adults who work and whose play has turned sinister. It may be a place of 'tawny' men who blend into their landscape, but they still carry the steely instruments of killing. Its theatre may be, at the end, happily referred to as 'these pleasant Acts', but only with the sharpest irony.

So the fifth phase begins with a new plunge into a world still more green, still deeper, still further from the houses and artefacts of *homo sapiens*. At first sight the forest seems impenetrable, its trees linked and locked, hedged and wedged up 'thick', in 'one great Trunk', as dark as night. But then:

> within
> It opens passable and thin.
> (505-6)

That feels like a miracle of discovery, relief, and release. The fugitive imagination arrives at last in a safe place. There follows in this fifth phase a sustained ecstasy of self-finding and relaxation which answers back across the poem to the terrible lament about war.

Greenery and water again combine in the plentiful growth of this place. They are indissolubly bound together in the well-knit pun of 'imbark' and in the beautiful idea of the forest's being a living boat, a 'yet green, yet growing Ark', for whose building the trees need not be cut down. In this extraordinary boat the imagination floats and sails at ease, while the greenery of the trees grows plenteously on, uninterrupted, from the forest floor to the sky and from the cradle to the grave:

> And, as they Nature's Cradle deckt
> Will in green Age her Hearse expect.
> (495-6)

This cradle is the 'Nursery of all things green' from which, in the earlier passage, war had seemed irretrievably to divide us. But in the forest there is no ransacking or severance. Life begins in a green cradle and goes right on into the old age of the trees which is still a 'green Age'. At the end, in due time, the 'Hearse' of nature will carry the trees away kindly, gently, fittingly, with no suggestion of death as the 'untimely' thing it was for the young rail. Such a death one might 'expect', for this at last is a world where the open, unguarded hopefulness of Damon need fear no sudden rebuff or disappointment.

It is one of the great images of English poetry, and the greatest image in either Marvell or Nabokov of life unsevered. This forest 'Sanctuary' is a place that the human mind must know how to visit for its replenishing and healing powers and for its liberation of memory in a process of play.

The ecstasy of the passage that follows is rich in the union of opposites. The world which Damon lost, where nightingales and glow-worms belonged simultaneously to the opposed worlds of nature and art, is here refound as art and nature combine again. The dilemma of 'The Coronet', where arts were unnatural and likely to be corrupt, is over. The nightingale of the forest is again an artist who 'adorns' the undergrowth with her music as she sings 'the Tryals of her Voice'. The woodpecker is an engineer. The primal, 'Original' language of bird-song is at the same time 'most learned'. The play of sun through leaves in a 'light Mosaick' is effortlessly the equal of Mosaic law and of Greek and Roman letters as well. Oak-leaves are embroiderers, with caterpillars as their undulating thread, moss is a velvet cushion, the wind is a winnower, vines are lace-makers. Silk is made here, then dyed, then washed by the river in an image of perpetual cleanliness and revivification which makes all this high artistry back over to nature's primal greenery and water again:

> Grass, with moister colour dasht
> Seems as green Silks but newly washt.
> (627-8)

This is living Arcadia. The childhood of the world is still alive here. The protective screens about the world's childhood and the poet's childhood in memory have opened, 'passable and thin', to admit and receive the fugitive adult mind and to heal all its divisions. Even the grandest and most ornate buildings, with '*Corinthean Porticoes*', will mingle perfectly with this live and curling 'Temple green'. Transformations like those of the meadow-theatre are now without menace and may be performed in charmed security:

> Give me but Wings as they, and I
> Streight floting on the Air shall fly:
> Or turn me but, and you shall see
> I was but an inverted Tree.
>
> (565-8)

Here the fugitive mind is safely 'incamp'd', so secure in its release and relaxation as to be able to use that dangerous word in the knowledge that its military meaning has now gone from it. The same thing happens when 'Armies' refers pacifically to the swarms and multitudes of the animal world; and again when 'shooting' is found to be a word which refers only to the growth of trees. In the meadow or the garden such words were volatile. They were not bound to behave in accordance with the poet's rational dictates. Here they become safe again, cleansed and replenished like the mind of the man who is using them.

The forest, as we have seen, is a safe place for childhood, posing no threat to the infant thrush, heron, and woodpecker and bringing back to life the romping, tree-climbing boy within the adult poet and tutor. The whole place is like a giant cradle; or again, like a small creature held within the fold of the winding river, licked by the river as a young animal is licked by its parent. But there is another kind of licking here too:

> Ivy, with familiar trails,
> Me licks, and clasps, and curles, and hales.
>
> (589-90)

This is sexual play, not children's play, and the experience of the forest is a sacrament for it too. On a bed of 'Velvet Moss', ivy, vine, woodbine, bramble and briar embrace, captivate and ensnare:

> Bind me ye *Woodbines* in your 'twines,
> Curle me about ye gadding *Vines*,
> And Oh so close your Circles lace,
> That I may never leave this Place:
> But, lest your Fetters prove too weak,
> Ere I your Silken Bondage break,
> Do you, *O Brambles*, chain me too,
> And courteous *Briars* nail me through.
>
> (609-16)

The fugitive wishes to be held captive for ever, chained down in the morning, staked down in the evening, tied, fettered, bound, nailed, and guarded. But the rhythm of the passage is the rhythm of freedom, not of captivity, and of pacific pleasure, not of violence.[15] The sexual idea of captivation is one in which yet more opposites merge and by which yet more words are freed from any possible association with violence. Guards here are people who lead one *out* of captivity; nothing feels so free and safe as being 'Betwixt two *Labyrinths*'.

All paradoxes and contrasts are resolving themselves. Gradually we emerge from the forest and come back into the meadow, but the movement from one to the other now feels like an imperceptible grading, without the decisive turn and plunge of the outward journey. The meadow has become part of the forest's world, flooded by the river and taken back into nature's embrace where before it had been a place where the Mowers worked and killed. It is green again, wet and refreshed, held in the 'wanton harmless folds' of the river.

In this 'wanton' quality the further contrast of sexuality and childhood, man and boy, seems to resolve itself as well. The two kinds of play have not felt separate or antagonistic in the forest. On the contrary, they have met and overlapped. In the word 'wanton' their union is made secure. It is both a word for children and an amorous word,[16] just as the river's licking is parental and sexual. What has gone entirely is the sense of casual irresponsible violence which the word carried when it belonged to the 'wanton troopers' who killed the nymph's fawn.

All categories, all dimensions, all distinctions have given way in this forest. It is a place in the furthest recesses of the inward mind. To find it is to find a world like that of Marc Chagall, where, in dream-like liquidity and intense colour, the lost memories of things are found, and matter from the depths of the mind is brought out into the light and found to be more delightful and less awesome than might have been feared. It is to experience something like that free-flowing absence of measure and distinction which, in the punning of *Finnegans Wake*, offers itself as balm for the imagination's divisions and fears.

A man less rich in imagination would never have left the Fairfacian world, never have gone near such a forest. A more simple-minded partisan of the imaginative world would, by contrast, have the greatest difficulty in coming back to Fairfax and to his tutorial duties. Marvell makes his return in two stanzas of generous humour and fine courtesy, and then judges beautifully the tone of his final praise of Nun Appleton.

His humour takes him calmly through the last of the poem's metamorphoses, where the tutor is seen as a 'trifling Youth', and his child-charge is an awesome, towering figure of 'Law'. His courtesy then ushers forward the setting sun with his magnificent, bowing deference to the child. Such things are not to be thought of too gravely. Maria and the Fairfaxes will not be treated with anything that could be called irony in this closing phase, but there is a calm and reserve in the poem now which these two elegant stanzas initiate.

This is where the provisionality of his voice is most needed, to end things without simplification or cancellation, to leave the earlier parts of the poem alive and active in the reader's mind. The Fairfaxes are praised, in the end very highly; but there is a deliberate unexcitedness in the language which tacitly respects our commitments to other, more volatile worlds. We are never browbeaten by the Fairfacian virtues. We are invited instead to admire and enjoy them in the full knowledge that they do not command complete assent. In this highly discontinuous section of the poem there is always room for complicating reflections, prompted by memories of the whole poem, to coexist with the approving return to the house.

Perhaps Maria does bring 'streightness' to the world; but we do not, hearing that word, let it override at once our memory of the delicious windings of river and forest. Perhaps the sun does 'recollect' itself and go down blushing with shame, but we do not therefore set aside our memories of the earlier brilliance of its light, either in the fortress-garden or pouring down through the leaves of the 'passable and thin' forest to where the thrush's eye shone. Nor do we forget that it will be up and blazing shamelessly again tomorrow. Perhaps Maria's hushed and vitrified world has its stillness and crystalline beauty, but the evergrowing green of the forest and the animation of its creatures easily survive in the mind as this cool, quiet, artificial world is praised. Maria may, with much application and effort, master 'all the Languages' and arrive in the end at '*Heavens Dialect*'; but the song of the forest birds was the 'most learned Original' of all languages and, what is more, it was acquired without effort.

The Fairfacian world is subdued by comparison with the forest, rather silent, rather uneventful. It may even be mocked a little by the kingfisher who, like a last remnant of colour and animation from the daylight world, flies streaming blue through the darkening air of the garden, a miracle of '*Saphir-winged Mist*' in a world of shadows.

By comparison with the ease with which the forest creatures bring up their young the human world seems a mass of pitfalls. Life in the '*Domestick Heaven*', with the endless labours of education and breeding, seems hedged about with problems; and as Maria grows, and learns to parry amorous advances, the 'pure, and spotless' world of a great dynasty seems troublesome to inhabit. The eventual product of all this care and effort is no more than a marriage for Maria, which sounds perhaps a little less exciting than we might have come to expect. All this long labour and vigilance merely to grow '*a sprig of Misleto*' on 'the *Fairfacian Oak*'. All this endless care just to produce a marriage celebrated in an atmosphere of subdued gravity:

> Whence, for some universal good,
> The *Priest* shall cut the sacred Bud;
> While her *glad Parents* most rejoice,
> And make their *Destiny* their *Choice*.
> (741-4)

The paradox whereby a '*Destiny*' becomes a '*Choice*' has been seen as an excellent thing, full of complex resolve. It may be so; but the line can be read more sadly too. Making destiny one's choice may be no more than bowing down before the inevitable, which is a distinctly disappointing ending to the long years of diligent duty.[17]

There is no irony, certainly no detraction. But there is room for a reader's mind to withdraw into its own consideration of these matters. We can see the Fairfaxes as modest, sober, responsible Reformation people. But as the poem begins to close down and turn away from us we may also see them, as we saw John and Sybil Shade, as curiously stilled, quieted people, enclosed in their traditional house on its green square in the heart of the provincial countryside, with only small domestic affairs to fill their lives. One of the impressions with which we may be left at the end is of sad, subdued lives being lived in a remote house.

The poem does not invite us to be critical or dismissive; but it will none the less allow these more sombre perspectives on a life it principally intends to praise and perhaps even to envy. The beauty of the poem's ending is that is sponsors and permits such reflections and forecloses none of them. It leaves the 'Fields, Springs, Bushes, Flow'rs' of Nun Appleton generously praised. It gives them the greatest possible acclamation as '*Paradice's only Map*' which sounds very close to the 'true survey' of Arcadia made real again. But then it leaves that thought hanging in suspense, abandoned almost, as it turns, in the final stanza, to the darkening dome of the evening sky.

The discourse between the two worlds will never end. Every day the sky will darken and the poet will bring his musings to a close. But the next day will start them all over again. The sun will rise. John Shade will stay at home but Kinbote will sally forth. And their dialogues will recommence.

It is not a matter of weighing in one's mind the value of Fairfax's society as against some other human world. It is human society in general upon which perspectives have been opened. One returns from the experience of the wood with one's attachments to any social world radically changed. All the accumulated tensions and pressures of our social attachments have been eased. Distances have been created. An open-ended calm has replaced the single-mindedness which was dominant in the first two parts of the poem.

The poet speaks with two voices, and both voices represent us. All that can be done is to refrain from repressing either of them. The troublesome, solitary, yet playful voice that goes back to childhood may be an impediment to most of the purposes of the public world; but Marvell, like Nabokov, reveres it. The journey of which it constantly speaks, inward and back into private memory, is the source of all imaginative riches and of all subtlety and delicacy of mind. So both authors listen attentively to its complaints and sorrows and both give it ample time to speak and be heard in the world of successful, sober adults. Both authors are too fair-minded to betray the Shades and Fairfaxes of the world or to treat their households with irony. But with both it is in the end the idle, Arcadian voice which counts. Both make it the leader and instigator of the dialogue. Both give it their finest words.

NOTES

Chapter 1. Speak, Memory

1. The work belongs to his fifties, revised in his sixties. I discuss and cite the definitive *Speak, Memory: An Autobiography Revisited* (New York, 1966).
2. Chapter 12, section 5. It is possible to hear an extreme self-preoccupation in a writer whose main verdict on a major historical event affecting millions of lives is that it severed him from his boyhood. Nabokov has not escaped censure for narrowness of sensibility. Perhaps D. J. Enright expressed the objection best, calling Nabokov 'rich in what is given to few writers and poor in what is given to most men' (Enright, 1972). It is an important line of dissent which Nabokovians cannot ignore. In my view it is less a matter of personal pleading than of the use of personal history for exemplary fiction. It is characteristic of Modernism to be able to construct a considerable range of fiction out of concentration on a handful of co-ordinates. The images of exile given here remained constant throughout Nabokov's life's work. But he was ever more able to lend them to a widening variety of fictions.
3. Edmund Wilson, attacking Nabokov's *Eugene Onegin* (1964), said that the principal theme of the novels was that of 'the exile who cannot return', whereupon an angry and contemptuous Nabokov thanked him for never having reviewed any of his books. It would seem that I am sailing close to the wind, so I hasten to clarify the difference between exile from one's own former self (my notion, and I think Nabokov's) and exile in the political and geographical senses (Wilson's meaning). For Nabokov political exile is only a particular case of a much more general human condition.
4. *King, Queen, Knave* (1928, 1968—see bibliography, section 2), chapter 6. Franz Bubendorf's name evokes his childhood throughout, the 'Bube' in Bubendorf being German for 'boy' or 'lad'.

Chapter 2. Fortunate and Unfortunate Children

1. This way of reading Marvell may not sound familiar though I am not quite alone in pursuing it. In an excellent and neglected article Gransden (1970) touched on some similar themes. So did Creaser (1970) in a very fine general discussion of Marvell, and so also did Berek (1971). The notion of the 'childlike' crops up often enough in Marvell studies, especially with relation to the Mower poems (e.g. Berthoff, 1970) and 'The Nymph complaining'. He has sometimes been criticized for this vein by readers who are less patient with his Mowers (Colie, 1970,

Baruch, 1974) or who want him to be sternly non-indulgent of his Nymph (Asp, 1978, Thomason, 1980).

2. *The Poems and Letters of Andrew Marvell*, ed. H. M. Margoliouth, 3rd ed. revised by Pierre Legouis, with the collaboration of E. E. Duncan-Jones, 2 vols. (Oxford, 1971), p. 40. I use this edition throughout, citing vol. i (the poems) as Margoliouth/Legouis. I cite the editorial matter in this volume as Legouis (1971). Margoliouth suggested Theophila Cornewall as T. C. Leishman (1966) compares, interestingly, poems by Waller, Stanley, Sedley, Prior, and Carew. The *Lolita* connection has occasionally been hazarded, following Legouis's detection of an air of aged perversion in the poem (1928, 1965).

3. Margoliouth/Legouis p. 26.

4. Allegorization, reducing attention to the plastic detail of image, voice, and story in the poems, has been a common vice of Marvell criticism. This is doubtless because allegory gives some sort of local habitation and name to these bewildering 'hardly expressible' things. See Kermode (1966) and Carey (1969) for classic protests against, among other things, such intellectual appropriation.

5. See chapter 8 and note 1.

6. See chapter 24 and note 1. Mary Fairfax has sometimes been proposed as the child of 'Young Love' (e.g. by Margoliouth), but there is no evidence for the identification.

7. This Cradle ('Upon Appleton House, l. 495) and Nursery (ibid. l. 339) are key centres of Marvell's vision of childhood and young life. A nursery, of course, is a place where young plants are bred as well as children. Both meanings are present in the word and the activities to which they refer are overlapping symbols in Marvell's imagination.

8. See chapter 10 and note 1.

9. See chapter 10 and note 1.

10. I refer to the Mowers of the three songs, 'Damon the Mower', 'The 'Mower's Song', and 'The Mower to the Glo-Worms' (see chapter 12 and note 2). The Mowers at Nun Appleton and the Mower who speaks against gardens are different figures.

11. Nabokov is fond of such imagery too. When Pnin is separated from his belongings at Whitchurch railway station his bag is said to lie 'orphaned' in the left-luggage office.

Chapter 3. A Domestick Heaven

1. *Bend Sinister* (New York, 1947). Nabokov later wrote a Preface to the novel for the Time Reading Programme edition of 1964. This Preface is now reprinted in all standard editions. Nazism and the Second World War hang heavily over the book as well as the old enemy, Communism. Nabokov's brother Sergei died in a Nazi camp in 1945. The book has obvious affinities with *Invitation to a Beheading* and many critics discuss

them profitably together (see Field, 1967, Hyde, 1977). Pattern-hunting critics have made much of the fact that *krug* in Russian means a circle (e.g. Bader, 1972). In German *Krug* means a pitcher. I see little significance in either fact.

2. Preface. *Invitation to a Beheading* seems to me in fact more Kafkaesque than *Bend Sinister*. It is less definite, less boldly drawn, more mysterious, more nightmarish. But Nabokov's real claim is to a *stylistic* excellence of which he holds Orwell to be incapable.

3. 'A Hanging' (1931), in *The Collected Essays, Journalism and Letters of George Orwell*, ed. Sonia Orwell and Ian Angles, 4 vols. (London, 1968).

4. Preface. Curiously few critics have paid heed to this unambiguous remark. Emmie, the grotesque child of *Invitation to a Beheading*, has received far more attention.

5. The Fairfax household, 'Upon Appleton House', l. 722.

6. Preface—an angry and moving statement. See Hyman (in Appel/Newman, 1970).

7. This exclusiveness may be part of a general Nabokov problem which his career as a whole slowly overcomes (see chapter 11 below). But it may also be bound up with more personal and local matters. Nabokov's father had been murdered by Russian fascists. Now his brother had died in a Nazi camp. He was not the only person who suffered such losses, of course; but I should not want to be too quick to criticize loss of tonal poise in writing which comes so near to such events.

Chapter 4. The Orphan of the Hurricane

1. Margoliouth/Legouis, p. 29. Bradbrook and Lloyd Thomas (1940) found possible sources in emblem books by Otto van Veen and Crispin de Passe. An emblematic origin for such a poem, with its bold figural drama, seems highly plausible. Røstvig (in Friedenreich, 1977) finds sources in Bruno. This is equally plausible, though I find her use of the materials rather far-fetched.

2. Most critics have been uneasy about the poem and many have been dismissive. But Leishman (1966) found it 'brilliant' and 'extraordinary' and Berthoff (1970) gives a powerful account with which I profoundly disagree but which responds very well to the poem's dramatic vitality. Hill (1946) calls it 'bombastic rhodomontade' but seems to approve none the less.

3. Blake, 'The Mental Traveller' (*c.*1804?), one of the 'Pickering Manuscript' poems.

4. See for example 'The Garden of Love' and 'A Little Boy Lost', both from *Songs of Experience* (1794).

5. In the seventeenth century 'entertain' had the full range of modern meanings concerning social pleasure. It also meant to 'maintain', 'manage', or 'take into service'.

6. Berthoff (1970) and Røstvig (in Friedenreich, 1977) see the figure as genuinely and gratifyingly heroic. (Røstvig is sure that the ending, just because it is an ending, 'must be climactic and triumphant'.) I cannot square such readings with the blood, violence, and sense of futility of the poem.

7. This ending is extremely knotty. My reading is given with no great confidence. From Margoliouth onwards critics have cited Lovelace's 'Dialogue — Lucasta, Alexis'. It may help with orientation, but matters remain precarious. I may well have misread the end entirely.

8. Blake, 'A Little Girl Lost' (*Songs of Experience*).

9. 'Upon Appleton House', l. 327. The tone is near to 'The unfortunate Lover' — as near as 'unfortunate' is to 'luckless'.

10. Berthoff (1970) linked the two poems together, finding the two heroic figures portrayed 'strikingly comparable'.

Chapter 5.   The Colours of Arcadia

1. *Mary* (1926, 1970—see bibliography section 2). Many critics treat it as a very minor and 'soft' work. Field (1967), in a long and perhaps influential chapter took such a view not only of *Mary* but also of *Glory* and *Pnin*. But the 'soft' Nabokov seems to me vital, from *Mary* all the way to *Pnin*. Hyde (1977) reads the book sympathetically, alert to the 'spiritual desert' it portrays, and to its imagery of human reification.

2. This pavilion and its inflowing light are recurring motifs. They return in *Ada*. They have autobiographical origins; but I cannot help guessing that they also have origins in Flaubert. One of the very few havens found by Frédéric and Mme Arnoux in the long frustration of their affair is a summer-house where motes of dust dance in bars of sunlight: 'Quelquefois, les rayons du soleil, traversant la jalousie, tendaient depuis le plafond jusque sur les dalles comme les cordes d'une lyre, des brins de poussière tourbillonnaient dans ces barres lumineuses.' (*L'Éducation sentimentale* (1869), Part II, chapter 6.

3. 'Upon Appleton House', ll. 289-320 (garden), 665-80 (kingfisher), 532 (thrush's eye). In this garden and wood colour and luminosity are again the indices of imaginative reverie.

4. Chapter 8. Nabokov is a master of such word-play, with a comic and lyrical sexual punning in it and a palpable enjoyment of mimetic skills. *Lolita* is already prefigured.

5. A key image for this is that of Cincinnatus's rug in *Invitation to a Beheading* (chapter 8) which can be folded over so that its pattern runs on uninterrupted across the fold. In the dream world where such patterns meet and match 'everything is filled with the kind of fun that children know'. It should be noted that this dream has moral as well as aesthetic dimensions. 'In my dreams the world was ennobled, spiritualized ... *there* the freaks that are tortured here walk unmolested ...' etc.

6.   'An Horatian Ode', l. 9. The earthbound soul is troubled by the same
        word in 'On a Drop of Dew':

> Restless it roules and unsecure.

Chapter 6.   Short Delights

1.   Margoliouth/Legouis, p. 35.
2.   This has been noted before, by Gransden (1970) for example. The poem
        has received good critical treatment, perhaps because its evident narrative
        and dramatic qualities prevent its being dissolved into allegory. See
        Leishman (1966)—'a remarkable poem', and Berthoff (1970). The hint of
        parody in the poem, mingling a psychologically heightened version of
        pastoral with a parody of pastoral, makes its quizzical atmosphere highly
        Nabokovian.
3.   5-8. Gransden (1970) writes well of sexual disorientation in the post-
        lapsarian, post-childhood world. In this poem 'virginity and promiscuity
        are extremes of a lost norm'.
4.   'Sense' is a word with a sexual element in it; the imagery of a seige in the
        preceding lines makes similar play.
5.   'The Coronet' ll. 5-8. Flowers which do not lead to fruiting are, like the
        prematurely cut blossoms of 'Little T. C.', strong images of life severed
        and unfulfilling.

Chapter 7.   A Man without a Name

1.   *The Defence* (1929-30, 1964—see bibliography, section 2). Updike (1964)
        and Adams (1965) discuss the book interestingly. Lee (1976) is sym-
        pathetic to 'an outsider, the eternal exile, a sufferer . . . emotionally and
        intellectually, despite his mastery of chess, a child'. Hyde (1977) links the
        book with *The Real Life of Sebastian Knight*, not so much for the chess
        motifs as for 'the Proustian obsession with the secret places of childhood'
        and 'the aching void of an endless sense of loss'.
2.   Both *The Defence* and *The Gift* make the patronymic a fearful and porten-
        tous affair. English readers of Russian father-son stories probably miss
        some of its resonance. In *Pnin* Nabokov turns to poignant account the
        loss of a patronymic when an exiled Russian Americanizes his name—see
        p. 56 below.
3.   Nabokov is very inventive with names, using them for semi-comic, semi-
        allegorical and semi-referential purposes. The plight of not having a
        name is equally able to draw his imagination, both here and at the other
        end of his career, in *Transparent Things*, where Peterson dwindles to Per-
        son and Hugh Person to You Person as an individual identity fades
        towards oblivion.
4.   This is, of course, one of the great Nabokovian themes, but his handling
        of it is less normative and pattern-making than is sometimes imagined.

Conjurors (and the like) sometimes seem like decadent tricksters prostituting art; sometimes however their magic seems like a genuine art, or an authentic analogue for art. There is richness in this ambiguity, not just a simple thesis continuously promulgated in self-referential fictions.

5. Luzhin is thus Nabokov's first *fugitive* where Ganin was his first *adventurer*. In later, more complex life-journeys flight and adventure will combine, as they do for Martin in *Glory*, for Humbert in *Lolita*, and for Kinbote in *Pale Fire*. Marvell's journey to the forest in 'Upon Appleton House' is similarly composed of both elements.

6. His aunt is his father's mistress, which increases the sad, preventative weight of the patronymic: the son's first sexual awakening, punningly evoked in this story of secret assignations, is blocked by his father's presence. (No doubt the Viennese delegation would be interested in this.)

7. 'The unfortunate Lover', l. 30. The mordant sadness of Nabokov's handling of the patronymic is matched by Marvell's calling a man an 'Heir' because he has been orphaned at birth.

8. This simple statement of a simple motif may again suggest something narrow or exclusive in Nabokov's world. But *Glory* will already begin to complicate such patterns (see chapter 9 below) and *Pnin* (chapter 11 below) will complete the work. The familar figures remain but it becomes much harder simply to read off their meanings.

Chapter 8. A Nymph without a Name

1. Margoliouth/Legouis, p. 23. The secondary literature is very large. Only 'Upon Appleton House' and 'The Garden' have provoked more discussion. Allegorization has been abundant, protests notwithstanding. Bradbrook and Lloyd Thomas (1944) initiated the allegory-hunting. Bradbrook in Brett (1979) later backed away from what such an approach had led to. Spitzer (1958) objected to allegory but also produced it himself. Legouis (1960) corrected him and carried on protesting in the name of 'the plain meaning of a text' (1971), a formulation, however, which leaves all the doors open again. Carey protested too (1969). But allegory has gone on unimpeded. King (1977) sees allegory on every hand and seems not to see the objections of his opponents at all. Most of the allegories that have been offered have been religious. In the midst of all this other notes have occasionally, and relievingly, been struck. Guild (1968) says the poem is concerned with 'the small personal things that are sometimes lost amid the larger concerns of races and nations'. Quite so.

2. Asp (1978) and Thomason (1980) note the nymph's *naïvete* and disapprove of it. They are following Colie (1970) who claimed that Marvell 'deplores the nymph's narrowness of vision'. Leishman (1966) had thought that Marvell was being naïve as well as his Nymph. Others have been more patient with *naïvete* and vulnerability. Guild (1968) heard a tale of shattered adolescent love in the poem and attended to it carefully;

Creaser (1970) heard similar things and linked the Nymph usefully with the Mowers and with Ophelia.

3. The sensory area engaged here has some connection with the nunnery poetry of 'Upon Appleton House' and with the verse of 'On a Drop of Dew'. Beautiful things become languid and precious, live things are stilled, fluid and fleeting things are artificially preserved. See discussions at pp. 115-16 and 203-4 below.

4. There are critics to whom this opposition between allegory and story will not do justice. Berthoff (1970) reads allegory in the poems, but it is allegory in story (this poem 'tells Marvell's favorite story'). This seems to me to make matters much more human and less abstract. Berthoff is usefully sceptical about static, non-dramatic allegories such as are seen by Allen (1960) and Hartman (1968).

Chapter 9. A Moment in History

1. *Glory* (1931-2, 1971—see bibliography, section 2). Field (1967) thought it minor, like *Mary* and *Pnin*, though he in fact wrote responsively about much of what is involved in all three. Many have shared this view. Comment has been rather sparse and not very enthusiastic. Lee (1976) thought it 'probably the weakest of Nabokov's longer works'; Hyde (1977) thought 'the final impression left by this work is a certain thinness'. I go against the grain of all this and think that general questions about Modernism are involved. I detect in *Glory* the creative fragmentations of Modernism — the anti-definitiveness of Joyce and Flaubert, a Prufrockian inexplicitness which haunts and stirs the imagination. Field finds the book's ending 'inconclusive'; Hyde wants a more 'consistent' attitude towards the hero. To me the inconclusiveness and inconsistency are good qualities, perfectly judged to hold the text back from the excesses of certitude.

2. See Nabokov's Preface for a discussion of this title and its meaning. *Glory* has now become the standard English title. The book used sometimes to be referred to as *The Exploit* before Nabokov's definitive title was given.

3. Again the book joins a classic Modernist mainstream in this regard. The free-floating, relatively unattached hero (in Flaubert as in Joyce) is drifter, fantasist, victim, and loser; but on another scale it is his or her dreaming and unfixedness which testify most strongly to the mind's unrepressed complexity.

4. Mulligan to Dedalus, of course, or Shaun to Shem, or the one-eyed Irish citizen to allround Bloom. Darwin and the others are, however, much more admirable than their Joycean predecessors.

5. Everywhere in *Lolita*, perhaps supremely so in the tennis-màtch (Part Two, chapter 20) where Humbert is fixated on Lolita's 'apricot' skin. *Transparent Things* deals with a similar allure. Nabokov on the sexuality of skin and sun, in a colour-band from apricot to tan, is justly celebrated for writing which is both lyrical and comic.

6. All quotations in this paragraph come from Nabokov's Preface.

Chapter 10. Transparent Things

1. Margoliouth/Legouis, pp. 19, 18, and 49. 'Thyrsis and Dorinda' is an early poem as Leishman showed when he discovered several musical settings for it, discussion of the matter being brought together in his 1966 study. There are settings by three seventeenth-century composers and numerous versions of the poem antedate the 1681 Folio.

2. Authorial comment has none the less been found, particularly on Thyrsis and Dorinda's suicide pact. Colie (1970) read the poem as a warning against the excesses attendant upon conversion, when 'receiving opinion can be an opiate'; Friedenreich (1977) said that the poem showed how Christian pastoral could be 'the opium of the people'; Bradbrook (in Friedenreich, 1977) thought Marvell intended an 'indictment' of his speakers.

3. Legouis (1928, 1965).

4. Marvell is peculiarly sensitive to questions of division, separation, and rejoining. 'A Dialogue between the Soul and Body' contains an extraordinary series of contraries and tensions figuring the divided self ('mine own Precipice I go' etc.); 'The Definition of Love' has its famous 'Iron wedges' whereby Fate 'alwaies crouds it self betwixt' two lovers; 'To his Coy Mistress' has its grave where none 'embrace' and its 'Iron gates' set across life as a near-impassable barrier. The images are at high temperature, suggesting much anguish and pain, which makes, of course, the counter-images of union or re-joining peculiarly sweet:

> While all Flow'rs and all Trees do close
> To weave the Garlands of repose.
>
> ('The Garden', 7-8)
>
> Including all between the Earth and Sphear.
>
> ('Musicks Empire', 20)
>
> but does, dissolving, run
> Into the Glories of th' Almighty Sun.
>
> ('On a Drop of Dew', 40)

5. I would not want to lose the pagan goat-god entirely in favour of the pastoral Christ; nor would I expect Marvell to lose so interesting an ambiguity. Note Damon's arousal by this pagan presence: 'his Name swells my slender Oate'.

6. These invitations are sometimes seen through Spenserian eyes as corrupt, Acrasia-like blandishments designed to capture the Christian pilgrim in a Bowre of Blisse (see for example Leishman (1966) and Lewalski (in Patrides, 1978)). But Spenser's eyes are surely not Marvell's. *The Faerie Queene* is rather hard on the *locus amoenus*, and indeed on relaxation in general. They almost always involve somebody's undoing. One should not expect such resolute suspicion from the author of 'The Garden' and 'Upon Appleton House'.

7. Malcolm Lowry, *Under the Volcano* (1947), chapter 4.

8.   See chapter 13 below. *Transparent Things* shares with *Glory* an ending which smacks both of triumphal recovery and of self-loss. So, I think, does *Invitation to a Beheading*, though there the triumph may be unambiguous (as it is usually taken to be). How much is triumph and how much delusion is held beautifully in doubt, which makes the atmosphere of such books very akin to that of these poems.

Chapter 11. The Water Father

1.   *Mary*, chapter 2.
2.   With Marvell, of course, we have almost no knowledge of the chronology. 'Thyrsis and Dorinda' is known to be early (see note 1 to chapter 10 above) but we cannot date any of the other poems involved. There is however a logical progress, which may or may not have been chronological, from the slightly modulated pastoral of the three Dialogues to the unique, profoundly personal extension of pastoral in the Mower's three monologues concerning his love for Juliana.
3.   This is the point at which criticism of Nabokov as a special pleader (see above, chapter 1 and note 2, chapter 3 and note 7, chapter 7 and note 8) must surely give way. It becomes clear with *Pnin* that the special 'type' of hero on whom Nabokov tends to concentrate is capable of figuring a considerable range of human experience, or of figuring experiences which are widespread and commonplace.
4.   The common theme is the nature of biography. But the problem of biography is the problem of taking responsibility for another man's life and this problem is central to Modernist scruple and hesitation about any kind of narrative authority. Nabokov has thus paused at a personal impasse which is also one of the cruces of Modernism.
5.   The common theme, evidently enough, is the totalitarian state; but the prime focus is not so much on the thing itself—totalitarianism—as on what it is like to experience it. This is Kafka's perspective, not Orwell's. It involves a characteristic Modernist deflection, from history to the individual living in history.
6.   See also chapter 15 below.
7.   See also chapter 19 below.
8.   See also chapter 21 below. The long gap to *Lolita* has not often been discussed. *Lolita* has its antecedents, as Hyde (1977) has, for example, argued in a chapter on the 'divided selves' of Smurov (*The Eye*), Herman (*Despair*), and Humbert. But for all this the gap is real and the new start genuinely new. Who could have predicted the flowering of Humbert, Kinbote (*Pale Fire*), and Vadim (*Look at the Harlequins!*) from the more limited characters of Smurov and Herman?
9.   de Rougemont (1961) was quick to see the importance of the romance belongings of *Lolita*. Flaubertian comic romance centres on the wandering Frédéric and the quixotic Emma. *Don Quijote* was his favourite reading throughout his life. In *Ulysses* the wandering, knightly Sir

Leopold evokes romance motifs and romance tones. Romance fluidity is sometimes opposed to epic massiness, romance gentleness to the violent, paratactic reiterations of epic.

10.   The transformation of their own lives in fiction by Flaubert and Joyce is clear enough, but they are not peculiar as Modernists in this. The Modernist phenomenon of the *persona* sets biography and poetic fiction in creative contact; and among the other great novelists of Modernism Proust, Kafka, and Musil create their works (and heroes) from such transpositions of themselves.

11.   The delicate and sympathetic qualities which I find in Flaubert's writings have often gone unheard. D. H. Lawrence and F. R. Leavis gave currency to the notion that he was cold, inhuman, and sterile. It seems to me a dreadful kind of deafness. The inner lives of his lonely heroes are attended to with exemplary patience, even if at times the listening is accompanied by disbelieving comedy. There have been those who were similarly deaf to Joyce (including Lawrence and Leavis again, of course); but such deafness now seems mercifully rather rare.

12.   *Pnin* (New York and London, 1957). The book was liked at once. There are numerous reviews delighted to find that the notorious author of *Lolita* was a gentle humorist. Stegner (1966) summed it up with 'Pnin is the most moving and real of Nabokov's characters'; Hyde (1977) calls *Pnin* 'the most delightful of Nabokov's novels, maybe his most popular'. There have been doubters. Some have found it episodic or fragmented, but it has hung together with ease in most readers' minds.

13.   Preface to *The Defence*.

14.   *Ulysses* is perhaps the most gestural, the most plastic-pictorial book ever written, crowded with the rhythms, shapes, movements, and contours of tiny human deeds. *Bouvard et Pécuchet*, a major source-book for *Ulysses*, is highly Joycean in this regard. When its protagonists argue we get much more than their bare opinions. We see their hands move, we see them shift in their chairs. We see them nod assent or furrow brows in dissent. All these actions are mimed in the prose, not described. The habit leads naturally to comic set-pieces of gestural mimesis, as when, for example, they take up gymnastic exercises and pole-vaulting. Bloom's athletic feats (see note 15 below) are indebted to this, as is his enthusiasm for Sandow exercises.

15.   Chapter 5. Compare this solitary instance of minor triumph, as gratifying to Nabokov as to us, with, for example, Mr Bloom's conquest of the area railings in 'Ithaca':

> Resting his feet on the dwarf wall, he climbed over the area railings, compressed his hat on his head, gripped two points at the lower union of rails and stiles, lowered his body gradually by its length of five feet nine inches and a half to within two feet ten inches of the area pavement, and allowed his body to move freely in space by separating himself from the railings and crouching in preparation for the impact of the fall.

It is wonderful to hear that, after performing this feat, 'he rose uninjured'.

16. Excessive critical concentration on such narrative games has perhaps alienated many Nabokov readers. Criticism may now be getting a better sense of proportion about such things. Such writers as Hyde (1977), Martin Amis (1979), and Pifer (1980) have quite different emphases.

17. Not for some critics, however, who would see much more 'serious' things at stake. Bader (1972) is particularly fierce with readers who see no more than 'decoration' in such matters. They are, she insists, part of 'the intricacies of deliberate artifice' which make all the novels 'allegories of artistic creation'. Applied to *Pnin* this means that '*Pnin* is a fictional demonstration that the pattern of life is open to unpredictable variations even when enclosed within a narrative structure'. I cannot believe that that is what has caused it to be so loved.

Chapter 12. *The Wounds of Damon*

1. The Mowers of 'Upon Appleton House' are at ll. 385-440. The quotations are from 'The Mower against Gardens'. Most critics have felt that Damon's love-songs presented an aspect of the Mowers different from these two.

2. Margoliouth/Legouis, pp. 44, 47, 48. The secondary literature is less extensive than the apparent popularity of the poems might lead one to expect. Berthoff (1970) is alert to the plight of one who 'has lived like the lord of creation' but is now fallen from his former paradise; Creaser (1970) is excellent, seeing in the Mower's fate 'an analogue of various disruptive and alienating experiences' and finding 'The Mower to the Glo-Worms' 'among the most subtle short poems written before Blake'. There are others, alas, for whom the poems offer only conventional pastoral pleasures, or even triviality. Some critics find the Mower interesting enough but not truly palpable and audible. Colie (1970), for example, could find no 'resonating seriousness' in the poems, especially in 'The Mower to the Glo-Worms' which she thought the 'slightest' of the three.

3. 'Upon Appleton House', ll. 495, 339.

4. 'The Mower's Song', ll. 1-4. Contrast this clear, undistorted image with the one the Mower must get when he looks at himself now in his curved scythe-blade ('Damon the Mower'). Hodge (1978) has excellent things to say about Marvell's use of scale and perspective changes. He associates this aspect of his mind with developments in seventeenth-century optics.

5. 'Upon Appleton House', l. 768. The Mower's 'true survey' is an accurate chart, like this map. The image of the thing exactly reproduces the thing itself. This cannot happen in the fallen world, except perhaps in the undisturbed mind of a garden contemplative where

> each kind
> Does streight its own resemblance find.
> ('The Garden')

See Ricks (in Patrides, 1978) for a fascinating account of this pattern-finding self-reflexivity in Marvell, his sensitivity to such correspondences and to the lack of them.

6. The three couples are from *Glory*, *Pnin*, and *Transparent Things*. Armande is the nearest of the three women to Juliana. They share a stinging, piercing or cutting quality, and fire is the fatal element of both.

Chapter 13. *Ouvre ta robe, Déjanire*

1. *Mary*, Chapter 4. The colour contrasts of *Mary* (see chapter 5 above) return in *Transparent Things*, which is magnificently coloured. Flames and high-alpine light dominate. Orange, blue, green, and white are all brilliantly clear and pure. As in *Mary* such colours are apt to intensify in memory. The waking present, except at epiphanic moments, is much more sombre and muted.

2. *Transparent Things* (New York, 1972). Some Nabokovians have found it a minor work. Lee (1976) finds it (and the rest of the late novels) unexciting; Hyde (1977) is brief and very circumspect; Pifer (1980) omits all mention of it. My feeling that it is one of the real masterpieces of the canon is far from being widely shared. It received several welcoming reviews (see, for example, Updike (1972)). But it has also suffered from dreary exposés in terms of its alleged artistic theorizing: 'a novel like *Transparent Things* is a demonstration of the extent to which a novelist can explore the possibilities of turning information into form', claims Rosenblum (1978), with an enthusiasm which I should not be able to muster for such a thing.

3. These three flame episodes, the book's principal scenes, are chapters 9, 20, and 26.

4. The principal imaginative co-ordinates of the mind, stored in memory, are always stronger than the merely real present. This again repeats the pattern of *Mary* (see note 1 above) and, of course, of *Speak, Memory* (see chapter 1 above).

5. 'Damon the Mower', ll. 85-7.

6. Sophokles, *The Women of Trachis*, tr. Michael Jameson (Chicago, 1957). ll. 1276-8.

Chapter 14. *The Wounds of Cromwell*

1. Margoliouth/Legouis, p. 91. The secondary literature is very large and there is nothing like agreement as to what attitude the poem takes to Cromwell. The wider question of Marvell's political allegiances between 1648 and 1652 (from the poem on the death of Francis Villiers to his appointment as language tutor to Fairfax's daughter) has also produced very varied reactions. Hodge (1978) writes very convincingly about the two major political figures in Marvell's work, Cromwell and Fairfax. A

source for the poem in Lucan's *Pharsalia* (I.144 *et seq.*) has long been acknowledged and discussed. Tom May's translation of the passage makes fascinating reading alongside the Ode. I think it is a key starting point for the Ode's composition, prompting the Ode's troubled, indignant, and tragic parody of an heroic image. See Legouis (1971).

2.   Margoliouth saw the cross of the hilt as a Christian's protection against 'Spirits of the shady Night'. Legouis (1971) rejects this, offering instead the pagan belief that spirits feared cold iron, so that the upright ('erect') blade, not the cross-shaped hilt, is Marvell's image (see also Duncan-Jones, 1962). But I see no reason why Margoliouth's reading cannot stand. A sword ('it' in l. 117) has two kinds of 'force', one religious (the cross-shaped hilt) the other military (the steel blade). The highly non-transcendent Cromwell would do better to rely on the worldly steel. The objection that the cross-hilt image is too popish for a puritan poet cannot stand. Marvell has not endorsed the belief but simply cited it sardonically as an irrelevance to Cromwell's steely kind of 'force'; and in addition we simply do not know what Marvell' religious (and political) views were in 1650 when the poem was written.

3.   Brooks (1947). This reading was answered (ineffectually in my view) by Bush (1952). Brooks (1953) answered the answer. The original article, widely reprinted, has been present in discussions of the poem ever since.

4.   This was Bush's view; it was also that of Wilson (1969).

5.   Walton (1955), Wallace (1968) and Patterson (1978) share versions of such a view.

6.   Hodge (1978) has a good sense of this drama; so does Bradbrook (in Brett, 1979).

7.   Brooks (1947). The quotations in this paragraph are from pp. 203, 207, 222.

8.   There are Nabokovian parallels for this. Nabokov is often suspected of just such a mandarin externality or uninvolved cleverness. Such complicatedly ironic authors run risks. It is always open to question whether ordinary kinds of human sympathy can co-exist with continuous irony. I would not have nearly so high a view of either author if I thought that such co-existence was impossible.

9.   Brooks (1947), p. 207.

10.   I owe these thoughts on the falcon imagery (and doubtless on much more in the poem) to conversations with R. I. V. Hodge when he was engaged on the work which eventually produced his book.

11.   'The unfortunate Lover', l. 52. With each wave the lover is torn from his rock and then 'rebounds' against it. No progress is made—the same movement is repeated over and over again. This is near in feeling to what is brought into the Ode's ending by such words as 'indefatigable', 'still', and 'maintain'.

12.   Brooks (1947), p. 222.

13.   As also in 'The unfortunate Lover'. This is further evidence of the range of Marvell's *dramatic* skills. In the monologues and dialogues he can

dramatize voices to an impressive degree. In these two poems he can produce a kind of mime-theatre or verbal sculpture, making a silent figure
just as much alive as a speaker. Such power of the dramatic imagination,
penetrating the being of a silent protagonist, is akin to that power of
poetic imagination which enables Marvell to animate inanimate things
and perceive a volatile chemistry in the material world.

14. See Cruttwell (1954). Brooks (1947) also invoked a Shakespearean tragic
     analogy—that of Macbeth, the other great Shakespearean soldier-hero.
15. *La Légende de saint Julien l'Hospitalier*, in *Trois Contes* (1877). This
     soldier-saint had preoccupied Flaubert for a number of years.
16. *Saint Julien*, section I. This arresting phrase has exactly Marvell's
     enigmatic impassivity. To be 'marqué de Dieu' sounds splendid. It
     would seem to betoken a kind of election (and is taken as such by the in-
     fant Julien's family and household). Only gradually do more sombre sug-
     gestions of victimization come to haunt the phrase as well.
17. 'A Poem upon the Death of O. C.', ll. 29-134. Elizabeth Cromwell died
     one month before her father on 6 August 1658. The principal trope of the
     poem is the love, union, and interdependence of parent and child. When
     the child dies the bereaved parent cannot live without her:

> If some dear branch where it extends its life
> Chance to be prun'd by an untimely knife,
> The Parent-Tree unto the Grief succeeds,
> And through the Wound its vital humour bleeds.
>
> (ll. 93-6)

18. In the great Amphion passage, ll. 49-98, especially the latter part of it
     where the 'labour' of working on the minds of 'stubborn Men' is stressed.
     The passage is introduced with the Ode's word for Cromwell's ceaseless
     work: he is again 'indefatigable *Cromwell*'. This time, however, there is a
     major creative purpose to his efforts.
19. 'Upon Appleton House', l. 284. It is not clear which Fairfax is meant. It
     may well not be the Lord General himself.
20. 'On the First Anniversary of the Government under O. C.', ll. 221-2,
     227-8. It is still arguable, however, that Marvell is not quite happy in this
     unironic mode. There are signs of slackness in the verse and the grave
     pentameters seem perhaps to impede the familar mercurial speed of his
     octosyllabics.
21. *The Rehearsal Transpros'd*, ed. D. I. B. Smith (see chapter 22, note 9),
     p. 42.

Chapter 15. A Subjective Hosanna

1.   *The Gift* (1937-8, 1952, 1963—see bibliography, section 2). My own view
     of the book is sharply at variance with the opinions of virtually everyone
     else. Other readers find much more to take seriously and respectfully in
     Fyodor, his father and his Muse. Hyde (1977) says of the book's ending:

'it is Nabokov's warmest and happiest conclusion, evidently prompted by a sense of personal fulfilment at this stage of his own life'. I find myself agreeing with Hyde more often than not, but I cannot read this book at all as he does. Others can, however; so my own quite different version may well be merely aberrant.

2. *Speak, Memory*, Chapter 3, section 5. The other quotations in this paragraph are from Chapters 13, section 4 and Chapter 14, section 1.

3. *Speak, Memory*, Chapter 1, section 1.

4. 'Upon Appleton House', ll. 641-8. The actual source for parody is doubtless D. H. Lawrence—the story 'Sun' and the episode in *Women in Love* where Birkin flees from Hermione at Breadalby and takes refuge in the woods, naked. Nabokov did not like Lawrence, nor critical 'Laurentomania'.

5. *A Portrait of the Artist as a Young Man* (1916), Chapter 5.

6. 'Hugh Selwyn Mauberley', second sequence (1920), section III, 'The Age Demanded'.

7. The travel writing owes debts to Pushkin, to the travels of explorers and zoologists in central and Eastern Asia, and to chivalric romance. It has its splendours; but the felt hunger of the author-son to identify himself with his remote father conflicts with our enjoyment of these splendours and dissolves our enthusiasm into ironic circumspection. The conjunction of the intrinsic splendour of the travel-prose with the hunger of the son left at home seems to me desperately sad.

8. This is available in English in the Foreign Languages Publishing House edition of the *Selected Works* of Chernyshevski (Moscow, 1953), a piously-presented edition with an embossed medallion head of the author, illustrative of the Bolshevik veneration described here.

9. See Chapter 19, pp. 123-4 below for discussion of a further literary love affair in *The Real Life of Sebastian Knight*. This too is not to be taken at face value.

10. 'Splendid weather—but it says in the paper it's sure to rain tomorrow ... See, it's already clouding over ...' (Chapter 5). The German makes a splendid clatter amidst Fyodor's soul-sounds.

11. 'Upon Appleton House', 577-84.

12. J. J. Espey, *Ezra Pound's Mauberley* (London, 1955), p. 83.

Chapter 16. The Socrates of Snails

1. Margoliouth/Legouis, p. 43. Legouis (1971) is surely right to insist that the poem is not a conventional Horatian injunction to horticultural moderation. The point of view is more extreme, reminding one as he says of 'puritan distrust of ornament'. But the point of view is, of course, the Mower's, not necessarily Marvell's (though see note 2 below). It has been common to find the Mower's views 'hyperbolical' or even 'comically excessive' (Berek, 1971).

2.   A recurrent Marvellian preoccupation. The 'Towers' of 'The Coronet' are elaborate hair-styles and the upbraided 'Toyles' of the opening stanza of 'The Garden' may punningly introduce a similar image. 'The Gallery', by contrast, gives Marvell's favourite image of Clora as

> A tender Shepherdess, whose Hair
> Hangs loosely playing in the Air.

The Mower's views are not that far from some concerns of Marvell himself.

3.   The quotations are from the first part of the poem ('*It Must be Abstract*'), section II. The elephants and juggling bears are from section V of the same part.

4.   'Upon Appleton House', l. 561.

5.   *Pnin*, Chapter 5, the closing paragraph. Shortly before we have been reading of Nina's death in a Nazi camp.

6.   In 'The Comedian as the Letter c' Crispin is called, amongst many other things, 'the sovereign ghost', 'the Socrates/Of snails' and

> the poetic hero without palms
> Or jugglery, without regalia.

There is more gusto in Stevens's tone than in Marvell's, but I think I · recognize the Mower in some of these phrases.

Chapter 17. Van the Penman

1.   *Ada or Ardor: A Family Chronicle* (1969). The book stands for everything that anti-Nabokovian readers dislike; Nabokovians, by contrast, have generally celebrated it. The most persuasive readers of the book, most nearly convincing me that it has a poise which in the end I cannot really find, are those who capture its literary and pictorial anthology (e.g. Appel (in Appel/Newman, 1970, and 1974), Mason (1974), Proffer (in Proffer, 1974)) and those who stress the dark side of its apparent Arcadian levity (e.g. Pifer, 1980).

2.   Hyde (1977) writes: 'the later work has situated itself nowhere, and by doing so has renounced content, or tried to make a virtue of solipsism'. He is thinking primarily of *Look at the Harlequins!*, but such problems were 'implicit already in *Ada*'. I find such problems only in *Ada*, but Hyde has defined very exactly what they are.

3.   'The Garden', ll. 12 and 16.

4.   See chapter 5 note 2 above.

5.   Chateaubriand, *René* (1802), a major source for *Ada*. See Appel (in Appel/Newman, 1970).

6.   Rimbaud and Marvell are the sources for the private code of Ada and Van, Part One, Chapter 6.

7.   Mme. Larrière's Maupassant story is 'La Parure' (1884).

8.   The Byron references, together with the origin of the name Ada, have

often been noticed. The Shelley references have not. Van - Ada - Lucette parallels Shelley - Mary - Claire Clairmont. The motif of drowning is also pertinent. Claire Clairmont was a mistress of Byron and bore a child to him.

9.   In some ways I think that this erotic and pictorial aspect of the book is its most successful experiment. See Mason (1974) for paintings by Bosch and others to which *Ada* alludes.

10. *Ada* is the second Nabokov novel (after *Pale Fire*) to make reference to Marvell. Reference is frequent, 'The Garden' is the principal work involved. It may even be that the whimsical and mercurial poise of that poem was in fact attempted in *Ada*, at fatal length.

11. There are those for whom Joyce's long wrestle with his own life as the source for fiction, from *Stephen Hero*, through *A Portrait of the Artist as a Young Man* and *Exiles* to the Stephen parts of *Ulysses*, was never ultimately successful. For such readers the Dedalus figure is an indulgence, an obsession, and a pet preoccupation, never a source of disinterested artistic creation.

12. Van's opinions about Time have been much hailed. I have read *Ada* four times but found myself tending to skip Van's *opus* on the last two occasions. As Nabokov said with regard to his lack of enthusiasm for *Finnegans Wake*, 'I know I am going to be excommunicated for this pronouncement' (interview with Alfred Appel, in *Strong Opinions*, p. 71).

13. Quotations from *Finnegans Wake* in this paragragh are from (page and lines references) 12.1, 472.30-1, 383.28-9, 218.14.

14. See Adaleen Glasheen, *A Third Census for Finnegans Wake* (California, 1977—developed from her *Census* of 1956). Glasheen's approach to *Finnegans Wake* and its merging and coalescing clusters of characters seems to me fruitful. The original construction of the book was largely achieved through the creation of such clusters (Joyce's *sigla*)—see Roland McHugh, *The Sigla of Finnegans Wake* (London, 1976).

15. Interview with Alfred Appel, *Strong Opinions*, p. 71.

16. *Finnegans Wake*, 179.25-7.

Chapter 18.   Pale Fire and Glory

1.   *Ada*, Part One, Chapter 1.

2.   'The First Anniversary of the Government under O. C.', l. 86.

3.   See chapter 22 below, especially p. 162.

4.   *The Rehearsal Transpros'd. The Second Part*, ed. D. I. B. Smith (see chapter 22, note 9), p. 159 *et seq*. This is not to be taken too seriously. Marvell is pleased to compare his own disarming reticence with the pushiness of Parker. But it adds something to the evidence provided by the fate of the poems to suggest that Marvell was indeed shy of print.

5.   Margoliouth/Legouis, p. 12. See also the Latin 'Ros', ibid. p. 13. The great bulk of the secondary literature on the poem reads it as a 'straight' piece

of platonizing Christianity. The earth-bound soul 'feels its distance from its heavenly home' (Berthoff, 1970). Some have noted a lack of 'devotional fervour' (Leishman, 1966), but they have not gone on to enquire whether this might be a function of irony rather than of incompetence.

6. Interview with Alfred Appel, *Strong Opinions*, p. 75.

7. 38. Martz (1969) treated the poem as a 'total celebration of the soul' but then, rather like Leishman (see note 5 above), wondered whether it was 'almost too perfect, too cooly contrived'. Again this is just the point at which an ironic reading might begin.

8. Margoliouth/Legouis, p. 17. The classic account of this poem as ironic is Cummings (1970). Fitzdale (1974) also argued for irony, though less ably. Critics who read the poem 'straight' have tended rather uneasily to ignore Cummings' powerful arguments (e.g. Brockbank, in Patrides, 1978). The poem's relation to Waller's 'Battle of the Summer Islands' has been regularly noted. I think the relation is Nabokovian-parodic.

9. Cummings (1970) comments well on this. Christopher Ricks first mentioned it in *Milton's Grand Style* (1961). See also Carey (in Patrides, 1978).

10. Flaubert's pantheistic and mystical tendencies made him feel the presence of 'God' everywhere in creation, and his enthusiasm for dreams and imaginative adventure encouraged the feeling. His scepticism, however, never failed to tell him that this 'God' was unknowable, his existence a surmise, and the theologians' accounts of him dogmatic trumpery. The dilemma was acute, but fruitful, and it never left him. The classic Flaubertian text for it is *La Tentation de saint Antoine* (1874), with its superabundance of gods and cults, all as wonderful as they are ridiculous, testifying about equally to our capacity for imaginative daring and our capacity for self-delusion. *Bouvard et Pécuchet*, especially Chapter 9, also makes fruitful use of such a double view.

Chapter 19.　Endgame with Knight and Bishop

1. *The Real Life of Sebastian Knight* (Norfolk, Conn., and London, 1941). It is Nabokov's first English novel, written in France in 1938. Most criticism, as with *The Gift*, takes the artist-hero more nearly at face value than I can. V's high estimation of Sebastian and his work is apt to be given an authority it seems to me not to merit. 'Sebastian is—and this judgment is, I think, to be accepted—a good writer' (Lee, 1976). With the slippery Nabokov nothing is to be accepted.

2. Hyde (1977) says 'It occupies a pivotal place in his conception of the literary sensibility, since it enacts an acceptance of homelessness . . . It prepares the way for the joyous and humane *Pnin*.' This is well said, but the way thus prepared was slow and, probably, painful. *Pnin* was sixteen years away.

3. These chess motifs have received much exegetical attention. They are beautiful, witty, and decorative; but the human story is in my view what

counts first and foremost. Priorities are the same as with the squirrels and brithdays of *Pnin* (see chapter 11, pp. 59-60 above).

4.   It comes from Homer's description of the Elysian fields (*Odyssey* XI). In English it belongs to Milton (*Comus*, l. 838) and Tennyson ('The Lotos Eaters', l. 170). In the *Comus* usage the symbolism of healing is particularly strong. It revives the fleeing and stricken Sabrina, who in return becomes a religious figure of protection, to whom the prayer 'Listen and save!' is addressed.

5.   Chapter 16. This is surely a modish artist in love with a Muse and *femme fatale*. His behaviour is a cliché. Critics taking Sebastian seriously are hardly being fair to Mme Lecerf, who has not had a happy love-life herself. I think Sebastian was lucky not to be sent packing even more promptly than he was.

6.   English businessmen are not usually supposed to have much literary authority in Nabokovian novels about artists. But I have argued that Nabokov is not nearly so exclusive and normative as has sometimes been supposed and I can thus believe that this man is allowed to talk what sounds like good sense. Perhaps he is Darwin from *Glory*. (He seems a good businessman too, failing to fall for V's wheedling.)

7.   Alexis Pan is modelled on various Russian *avant-garde* artists, notably Mayakovsky and Esenin (see Hyde 1977). The brief portrait is beautifully done, both poignant and absurd.

Chapter 20.   Arcadian Artefacts

1.   Margoliouth/Legouis, p. 51. The secondary literature is very large. Stanzas 5 and 6 have probably provoked more critical comment than any other comparable quantity of Marvell's verse. The poem has been a peculiar temptation to allegorical exegesis. My feeling is that reading has improved now that critics are more patient with relatively open-ended poems. It was an unnecessary hunger for definition and decision (is Marvell for or against the contemplative life, for or against artifice?) which made the poem become such a battleground for vying interpreters. Perhaps readers are happier now to let the poem be, to let it change tone and direction as it will and to refrain from bullying it.

2.   Margoliouth/Legouis, p. 14. This too has a large secondary literature, most of it praising the poem's scrupulous statement of artistic and religious principle. Martz (1969) is an exception. He finds it 'too clever' to be authentic, its ending in particular comparing badly with Herbert's characteristic humility. The comparison with Herbert has, naturally enough, been widespread (see e.g. Leishman, 1966, Carpenter, 1970).

3.   Margoliouth/Legouis, p. 53.

4.   Not to all readers, however. Marvell seems to me to have an essentially pacific sensibility, instinctively recoiling from violence. Violent words, like 'annihilating', thus stand out in the atmosphere of his verse. But

there are those who find him more embattled—embattled as a radical or, more frequently, embattled as a Christian. If such readers are right in their judgement of the characteristic tenor of Marvell then a word like 'annihilating' will recede more easily into the continuity of the poet's normal language, without the arresting turn I ascribe to it.

5.   25-6. The ending of the poem has regularly been found difficult and perhaps over-complex. Leishman (1966) went so far as to rewrite it with simpler syntax. But effort and strain are vital to the poetic effect. There is struggle involved, and a courageous determination to work through besetting obstacles. The language enacts the struggle in syntactic knots and complications.

Chapter 21.   The Enchanted Hunter

1.   See Donno (1978) for this critical record. The comments of Swift, Defoe and Captain Thompson on the prose are particularly interesting. Their delight in its quickness and fancy is evident. On 'The Character of Holland' see Leigh Hunt, Rogers, Whittier, Ormsby, and Hallam Tennyson. Leigh Hunt said he laughed at the poem even when reading alone; Hallam Tennyson said his father 'had made Carlyle laugh for half an hour' with a single line from the poem.

2.   See chapter 9 pp. 41-2 above.

3.   *Lolita* (Paris, 1955). It has, of course, provoked more comment than any other book by Nabokov. Early reviewers in America tended to stress its humour and vivacity; English comment often tended to make it sound like a moral tract showing how sinners do not prosper, though much of this was no doubt defensive. It was also quite widely disliked (see for example Kingsley Amis, 1959). Later commentary has stressed the book's allusiveness (Appel in Dembo 1967, 1970), has brought out its concern with aesthetic quests (Josipovici, 1964) and its relation to romance (de Rougemont, 1961). Nabokovians usually regard it as the finest, or one of the finest, of the novels. My hesitations about the ending are not at all representative. See also chapter 11 above, pp. 52-4.

4.   de Rougemont (1961) saw this (see chapter 11, p. 54 above and note 9). He treated it, however, as a weird, extravagant version of the Tristan myth, rather than as a comic one.

5.   Nabokov's inability to read *Don Quijote* is, in my view, an inexplicable literary deafness. He called it 'a cruel and crude old book' (interview with Herbert Gold, *Strong Opinions*, p. 103). I am afraid I think this is simply a silly remark.

6.   This comedy seems to be little heard by English readers of the book. In my view it arises from incongruous juxtapositions and from a continuous sense of the bathetic, the haphazard, and the disproportionate. I think it runs through *L'Éducation sentimentale* from first to last, never strong enough to be cruel to the characters but never inaudible enough to leave them their dignity quite intact.

7. *Ulysses*, 'Ithaca'.

8. 'La rage de vouloir conclure est une des manies les plus funestes et les plus stériles qui appartiennent à l'humanité . . . les plus grands génies et les plus grandes œuvres n'ont jamais conclu' (letter to Mlle Leroyer de Chantepie, 23 October 1863). This famous remark is one of several, from all periods of his life, in which the impassive unforeclosedness of great literature is stressed. An artist should 'faire et se taire' (letter to Mlle Amélie Bosquet, 20 August 1866).

9. This Saturnalian comedy of the world's occasionally splendid favours is typically Nabokovian. The sexual escapades of Martin and Alla (*Glory*) and Franz and Marthe (*King, Queen, Knave*) benefit from such favours. Trapped Nabokov characters (like Herman in the last paragraph of *Despair*, and Kinbote in *Pale Fire*) have escapological dreams based upon the remote possibility of such favours. Vadim in *Look at the Harlequins!* is an escapologist throughout. *Ada*'s postulation of 'a blank cheque signed by Jupiter' is a Utopian fancy created on all their behalves.

10. This baleful misrepresentation of her on what, as far as we know, is her only appearance in print, is presumably inspired by the similar accident which befell Mr Bloom, listed in the newspaper account of Dignam's funeral as 'L. Boom'. It may be that once again Flaubert is behind Joyce as Joyce is behind Nabokov. When *Madame Bovary* was first printed it was attributed to an author called 'Faubert'. To Flaubert, already made anxious by the threat of prosecution on the occasion of his first appearance in print, this seemed very ominous. (Faubert was a grocer.)

11. I cannot help being reminded of Sir Epicure Mammon in Ben Jonson's *The Alchemist*. He is not the magus but the beneficiary of the magus's skills. Elevated by these skills he will be transformed in Humbertian ways. Here too there is rampant imagination, glittering dream, ego, glamour, scarcely supressed predatoriness, multiple mirrors, and grossness and fastidiousness combined.

12. This is not only incomparably achieved but on one occasion beautifully defined and accounted for. Rodolphe regards the mawkishly romantic Emma with coldness and near-derision. Flaubert seems to intervene virtually on her behalf with a classic apology for her dilemma:

comme si la plénitude de l'âme ne débordait pas quelquefois par les métaphores les plus vides, puisque personne, jamais, ne peut donner l'exacte mesure de ses besoins, ni de ses conceptions, ni de ses douleurs, et que la parole humaine est comme un chaudron fêlé où nous battons des mélodies à faire danser les ours, quand on voudrait attendrir les étoiles. (*Madame Bovary*, Book II, Chapter 12)

13. Levine (1979) says some similar things. For him 'Lolita's plight is not taken seriously enough' for the book to do what it claims.

Chapter 22. *I, that was Delightful*

1. Margoliouth/Legouis, p. 87. Legouis (1971) compares the poem aptly with Donne's *Satyrs*. Richard Flecknoe was in Rome 1645-7.

2. See note 6 to chapter 18 above.
3. Margoliouth/Legouis, p. 94. May died on 13 November 1650, but the poem, or parts of it, may belong to a later date. Some have found reference to the removal of his body from Westminster Abbey (1661) in lines 85-8. Lord (1968) denies Marvell's authorship. Most critical comment has been concerned with the puzzle of Marvell's political commitments in and around 1650. The passage on the heroic duties of the poet (ll. 63-70) has also received attention. It has often been taken as something of a testament, though some (e.g. Hunt, 1978) have noted its inappropriateness to his actual practice in verse. The fact that the lines are spoken by Jonson rather than Marvell has been too often overlooked (though see, for example, Rees, 1976).
4. Margoliouth/Legouis, p. 100. Modern critical comment has been sparse and mainly concerned to use the poem as evidence of Marvell's political views and activities. A probable date is 1653 (Margoliouth), though see also note 6 below.
5. See chapter 21 note 1 above.
6. The change seems to me to come at l. 100. Before that the poem has been all high spirits, ridicule, and general abuse. Thereafter, with the consideration of Dutch foreign policy ('confederacies abroad . . . feign'd *Treaties* . . .'), military disreputableness ('they invade by stealth') and poor showing in comparison with the British ('Watchful abroad, and honest still within'), the poem turns to partisan satire and patriotic fervour. In 1665 the poem was published in a version which ran down to l. 100 and then concluded with eight lines of patriotic praise for the Duke of York. It has usually been assumed that the present version, based on the Folio of 1681, is an original tampered with by the 1665 printing. But with l. 100 looking so much like a dividing point on internal grounds as well it may be that the 1681 ending, like that of 1665, was grafted on to an earlier piece of verse written in the Fleckno/May vein of Marvell's former years.
7.   sing high and aloof,
Safe from the Wolf's black jaw, and the dull Asse's hoof.

(an 'Apologetical Dialogue', appended to *The Poetaster* after that play's failure in 1602).
8. Hence my unwillingness to take the famous heroic *credo* as evidence of Marvell's views. The heroic Jonson, who could utter such a *credo*, is not beyond the range of Marvell's amusement.
9. *The Rehearsal Transpros'd* appeared in 1672, *The Rehearsal Transpros'd: The Second Part* in 1673. The standard edition, used and quoted here, is that of D. I. B. Smith (Oxford, 1971). The best discussion is that of Smith himself. The more politically oriented books on Marvell (Wallace 1968, Patterson, 1978) also deal with the work but with less attention to its literary and linguistic qualities. In the age of Joyce and of post-Joycean prose, it cannot be (can it?) that 'the sarcastic, punning, involuted way in

which the tract is written is infinitely tedious and irritating to our tastes' (Kenyon, in Brett, 1979).

10. *Don Juan*, 'Dedication'. This Dedication was omitted from the first edition of Cantos 1 and 2 but eventually printed in 1833.

11. *Oedipus Tyrannus or Swellfoot the Tyrant* (1820). Unlike many of Shelley's politically dangerous or scurrilous works it was actually printed directly after composition. But only seven copies had been sold by the time the publishers withdrew it under threat of prosecution. It is a much underestimated work. Mary Shelley says that composition was begun in 'an hour of merriment . . . one ludicrous association following another' (Mary Shelley, Notes to her Shelley edition of 1839). She praised its headlong qualities and thought it showed the exuberant combinational swiftness of Shelley's mind. I think she is quite right. (Also, these are exactly the kind of terms in which nineteenth-century readers praised Marvell's comic poems—see chapter 21 note 1 above.)

12. 'Scanderbag' is George Castriot, a fierce Albanian warrior who fought against the Turks in the fifteenth century. 'Dancehment Kan' was a warrior-nobleman at the court of the Great Mogul (Smith).

13. Dryden, Preface to 'Religio Laici' (1682): '*Martin Marprelate* (the *Marvel* of those times) . . .'

14. Dryden called Marprelate, and thus by implication Marvell, a 'Presbyterian Scibler, who sanctify'd Libels and Scurrility to the use of the Good Old Cause' (Preface to 'Religio Laici'). It is an absurd estimate of both writers, of course. Marvell's use of Buckingham's nickname for Dryden as his own nickname for Parker must have rankled. Dryden, as literary standard-setter and oligarch, much have felt himself irksomely implicated in the rousting of Parker.

15. The passage is at Smith, pp. 16-17. The geographical error was Parker's placing Geneva on the *south* side of its lake, and Marvell is able to indulge some splendid surmises as to what might have 'so disoccidented our Geographer'.

16. The passage is at Smith, pp. 29-31.

17. Bloom and Stephen share 'tenacity of heterodox resistance' (though, alas, little else) in *Ulysses*, 'Ithaca'. The other phrase is from *Finnegans Wake*, 455.29.

18. For Baxter see Smith pp. 33-7; for Owen see pp. 37-43.

19. The six plays are discussed at Smith pp. 49-61.

20. The mention of Montaigne is at Smith p. 118. Smith cites Montaignian sources or parallels at numerous points in his commentary.

21. The passage is at Smith pp. 149-59; the quotation is from p. 155.

22. In Smith *The Unlimited Magistrate* occupies 56 pages (187-243). The others occupy 44 pages between them, each taking fewer than the last.

Chapter 23. Blue Inenubilable Zembla

1. *Pale Fire* (New York and London, 1962). After *Lolita* it is the most widely discussed and widely praised of all the novels. It has often been linked

with *The Gift* and *The Real Life of Sebastian Knight* for the concern with biography. The connections with Nabokov's edition of Pushkin have also been stressed. McCarthy (1962) has been extremely influential. She recognized its greatness at once and unravelled many of its complications. See also Williams (1963) for early exegesis. Stegner (1966) was unpersuaded, responding well to Shade's poem but remaining uneasy about the novel as a whole, which was 'perhaps overcomposed and overcontrolled'. But few Nabokovians have shared this view. Field (1967) liked the poem a great deal and the commentary even more—a 'mad and wonderful work of art and distortion that whirls dervishly around it'. Alter (1975) is equally responsive to both characters and both kinds of writing. Hyde (1977) does well to stress how 'moving' Kinbote is, 'a tragic figure', his story 'mollifying through comedy the ache of exile'. There is a line of criticism which has little time for Kinbote, and feels little charity towards him. He has often been called a 'monster'. Pifer (1980) manages this sort of line better than most, calling him a man who 'narcissistically perceives others only as reflections of himself'. Such observations are a useful corrective to one's perhaps over-eager sense of the book's festivity.

2. *The Real Life of Sebastian Knight* gives, in Sebastian and V, the shadowy outline of a two-person novel. For some readers *Lolita* is such a book, but I find that I am given only a fraction of Lolita's world and consciousness compared with what Humbert gives me of himself.

3. 'Unforgettable', no doubt—a translation of the French 'inoubliable'. But it may well have apposite suggestions of non-nubility and cloudlessness too. Kinbote coins the word in his note to l. 991.

4. 'Upon Appleton House', l. 81.

5. *Pale Fire*, Shade's poem, l. 48.

6. 'Upon Appleton House', l. 723.

7. Hyde (1977) noted how often Marvell's name cropped up in Nabokov's commentary. Nabokov's interest is metrical. He is interested in English octosyllabics which, like Marvell's, are capable of swift movement and supple variation, including the capacity to absorb extra syllables thereby creating an effect which he calls 'rapid ripple'.

8. See note 5 to chapter 21 above.

9. This has proved a strong temptation to narratological exegeses, often of a portentous kind. The rather obvious fact that *Pale Fire* is not a work of nineteenth-century realism has led to many flurries about self-referentiality. 'The primary subject of *Pale Fire* is the emotional-stylistic exploration of the artist's imagination' (Bader, 1972). 'We cannot doubt that Nabokov is talking about his own work' (Lee, 1967). Tanner (1971) describes the book as that of an author who 'pre-empts the foreground for a display of his patterning powers' and is 'quite willing to reduce his characters to playing cards' in order to do so. Tanner does not seem to find these remarks insulting.

10. 'The Art of Donald McGill' (1941), in *The Collected Essays, Journalism*

and Letters of George Orwell, ed. Sonia Orwell and Ian Angles, 4 vols. (London, 1968).

11. Housman would provide Kinbote with the 'blue remembered hills' of childhood ('blue inenubilable Zembla') as well as young men; for Frost see note 17 below. Hardy provides what turns out to be a very significant poem, to which typically enigmatic allusion is made. Kinbote remembers coming upon the word 'stillicide' in a poem by Hardy. The poem in question is 'Friends Beyond'—a poem about being haunted by the voices of the dead. It is an intriguing source or parallel for the figure of the lonely Kinbote haunted by his former Zemblan companions.

12. He reproves the swan in his note to l. 319 of Shade's poem: 'a serpentine goose with a dirty neck of yellow plush and a frogman's black rubber flaps'.

13. The famous and beautiful scene of their first meeting is a classic of such love. They feel the meeting is brought about by «la Providence»; they are «accrochés par des fibres secrètes»; their union is «absolue et profonde»; a strangely affecting single tear appears in the eyes of each man seeming to dissolve their plural selves into its singularity. Flaubert comments: 'ce qu'on appelle le coup de foudre est vrai pour toutes les passions'.

14. Throughout the long 'Eumaeus' chapter Bloom chatters on and on (or is he only thinking these things?) while Stephen is almost silent. In the even longer 'Ithaca' both are nearly silent. Amongst the few fragile threads that join them is precisely this inability to speak, for the Irish Stephen cannot speak Gaelic while the quasi-Jewish Bloom cannot speak Hebrew. Their knowledge in each case is called 'theoretical', being 'confined to certain grammatical rules of accidence and syntax and practically excluding vocabulary'.

15. Opinions vary on the quality of Shade's poem. My guess is that Nabokov wrote both prose and verse up to the highest level of which he was capable, which is why the verse is rather good, as good as Nabokov's own verse, while the prose is magnificent.

16. *Transparent Things*, Chapter 3, see pp. 69-70 above.

17. The poem is 'Stopping by Woods on a Snowy Evening'. Kinbote recalls it in his note to l. 426 of Shade's poem and is, for obvious reasons, gripped by the repeated line:

> that prodigious and poignant end—two closing lines identical in every syllable, but one personal and physical, and the other metaphysical and universal.

It is well said too. Nabokov has given Kinbote a fine response to a splendid poem.

18. Interview with Alfred Appel, *Strong Opinions*, p. 74.

Chapter 24. The Nursery of all Things Green

1. Margoliouth/Legouis, p. 62. The secondary literature is very large, not all of it favourable. The most widespread complaint has been of looseness

of structure. The complaint is less common now, although Everett was still voicing it in 1979 (in Brett). Legouis (1928, 1965) was never a devotee of the poem and still called it 'chatty' and 'loose' in his edition of 1971. He is however also usefully hostile to allegorical readings. He is drolly unimpressed by fanciful interpretations of the rail, by Kermode's conviction that the forest trees are symbols of moral laxity and by Empson's influential view that the crucifixion is intimated by the briars of stanza 77. Some critics have imposed very rigid schemas on the poem, as if to bring its waywardness to heel by force (Allen, 1960, Røstvig, 1961 and 1977). There is much of value in what Røstvig has to say but I wish it were not said so categorically. Good recent readings include Evett (1970) on the trees, grass, and water of the *locus amoenus* and the way the forest journey has 'retraced human history to the beginning'; Swan (1975) on the structural parallel with Shakespearean comedy and the psychological depth to which the forest adventure goes; MacCaffrey (in Friedenreich, 1977) on lost paradises, the shape and rhythm of the poem, and its 'acknowledging our submission to diurnal revolutions'; and Hodge (1978) on the brooding background figure of Fairfax and the felt presence of politics and the war.

2. Criticism has had to learn a similar tolerance and lack of pressure. Berthoff (1970) hailed the ending as 'a brilliant retreat from sonority' and Creaser (1970) praised the poem as a whole for being 'informal and capacious' and for exhibiting 'lack of stringency'. I wish that 'lack of stringency' were a literary quality more widely appreciated.

3. It would seem at any rate to drop unharmed, as if successfully taking flight for the first time. Marvell's tone seems quietly delighted. Set between the 'hatching *Thrastles* shining Eye' and the '*Hewel's* wonders', it would seem to be another pleasant miracle. But it may be more ominous, more like a sacrifice than a miracle. Swan (1975) favours the sacrifice reading and speculates on a psychological source for it in Marvell's childhood.

4. *The Rehearsal Transpros'd: The Second Part*, Smith, p. 201.

5. 'Hortus', l. 18; 'The Garden', l. 48. There is also great freedom of movement in this wood. Marvell walks, lies down, rolls over, climbs, slides, and is turned upside-down. Such gestural range is unimaginable in the garden settings of the other poems.

6. This structure has frequently been noted and it is certainly the key to the poem's narration. Most of the transitions are as clearly marked as if the poem had been subdivided—'While with slow Eyes we these survey . . ' (l. 81), 'And now to the Abyss I pass . . .' (l. 369), 'But I, retiring from the Flood . . .' (l. 481).

7. Swan (1975) noted this. It contributes both structure and depth to the poem.

8. Jonson, 'To Penshurst', l. 102; 'To Sir Robert Wroth', l. 94. See also the weight he puts on the word again in 'To Heaven' in a plea to God to come and reside in his empty soul—'Dwell, dwell here still'.

9. 'A Dialogue between the Soul and Body', ll. 43-4. The image of the precipice is at l. 14. There is a Blake-like extremity to the poem's images of inner vexation and division.

10. 'On my first Daughter', 'On my first Sonne', 'Epitaph on S. P. a child of Q. El. Chappell'. All three poems are very tender, and in all three it is clear that the tenderness is felt for a *small* creature.

11. The objections to the shape-changing house and the inverted salmon-fishers are in the tercentenary essay (1921). In the 1923 review he found 'Marvell and his contemporaries ... all more or less fantastical' and issued a grim warning: 'there is no one of them who is a safe model for study'.

12. ' Wit, for Eliot, is always a unifying force, fusing, amalgamating, making order out of disparateness. Marvell was more content to let disparateness be disparateness, or to catch together separate things only for a moment before letting them go their ways again. In 'Four Quartets' Eliot's religious quest ends with a wonderful, exultant drive towards the cul-minating word 'one'. I doubt whether Marvell (or Donne for that matter) ever felt so compelling an urge to unity. This sets Eliot slightly at a tangent to the seventeenth-century literature with which he seeks to associate his own writing.

13. Hodge (1978) thinks there is more complexity here. He sees, for example, a 'sudden beauty' in the image of Isabella in glory (ll. 141-4) and finds Marvell's imagination strongly engaged with the contemplative ideal.

14. Many critics have mentioned this masque-theatre element, especially Bradbrook (in Friedenreich, 1977) who considered it at length. There is a curious, slightly frightening sensation of being in an empty theatre, alone on stage while strange effects go on around one. The sense of unseen hands operating the scenery increases apprehension.

15. Empson (1935) found the crucifixion in these briars (and nails) and the idea became popular. Why then the fetters, chains, and bondage, one might ask? Is it a rule that when poets mention briars or nailing the cruci-fixion must always be implied? How does a poet indicate when he wants to write about some other thorns? Legouis's scepticism (see note 1 above) is well placed.

16. The word had great range in the seventeenth century and thus much poetic potential. It can mean 'ungoverned', 'cruel', or 'lascivious', though many of its amorous uses sound more delighted than disapproving. It can also mean 'free', 'merry', and 'lively', especially as in children and young animals (kids, lambs—OED). Buds and blossoms too can be 'wanton', and indeed can 'wanton' on their branches. Children who are 'wanton' are either 'free' or 'naughty'—or simply 'delightful' (and perhaps en-viable) in a general way. Milton and Shakespeare also exploit the full range of this volatile word.

17. Wallace (1968) saw all of Marvell in the phrase, but I think Legouis (1971) is right to have doubts about raising it to 'philosophical status'. The phrase is richer if we leave it in the ordinary world, suspended be-tween high acceptance and disappointment.

ABBREVIATIONS USED IN
THE BIBLIOGRAPHY

CQ	*Critical Quarterly*
CR	*Contemporary Review*
EC	*Essays in Criticism*
EL	*Essays in Literature*
ELH	*ELH: A Journal of English Literary History*
ELR	*English Literary Renaissance*
ES	*Essays and Studies by Members of the English Association*
HR	*Hudson Review*
JEGP	*Journal of English and Germanic Philology*
JHI	*Journal of the History of Ideas*
JWCI	*Journal of the Warburg and Courtauld Institutes*
KR	*Kenyon Review*
MFS	*Modern Fiction Studies*
MLQ	*Modern Language Quarterly*
MLR	*Modern Language Review*
MP	*Modern Philology*
NQ	*Notes and Queries*
NR	*New Republic*
NS(N)	*New Statesman (and Nation)*
NY	*New Yorker*
NYRB	*New York Review of Books*
NYTBR	*New York Times Book Review*
PLL	*Papers in Language and Literature*
PMLA	*Publications of the Modern Language Association of America*
PQ	*Philological Quarterly*
PR	*Partisan Review*
RES	*Review of English Studies*
RQ	*Renaissance Quarterly*
SAF	*Studies in American Fiction*
SEEJ	*Slavic and East European Journal*
SEL	*Studies in English Literature 1500-1900*
SP	*Studies in Philology*
SR	*Southern Review*
SRA	*Southern Review (Australia)*
SRev	*Saturday Review*
TCL	*Twentieth Century Literature*
TLS	*Times Literary Supplement*
TSLL	*Texas Studies in Language and Literature*

BIBLIOGRAPHY

1. *The Works of Marvell*
The standard editions are:

The Poems and Letters of Andrew Marvell, ed. H. M. Margoliouth, 3rd edition revised by Pierre Legouis with the collaboration of E. E. Duncan-Jones, 2 vols. (Oxford, 1971).

The Latin Poetry of Andrew Marvell, ed. W. A. McQueen and K. A. Rockwell (Chapel Hill, 1964).

Andrew Marvell. The Rehearsal Transpros'd and The Rehearsal Transpros'd: The Second Part, ed. D. I. B. Smith (Oxford, 1971).

I have also used:

The Complete Works of Andrew Marvell, ed. A. B. Grosart, 4 vols. (London, 1872-5).

The Poems of Andrew Marvell, ed. Hugh Macdonald, Muses Library, 2nd edition (London, 1956).

Poems on Affairs of State: Augustan Satirical Verse, 1660-1714, vol. i, 1660-78, ed. G. deF. Lord (New Haven, 1963).

Andrew Marvell. Complete Poetry, Modern Library College Editions, ed. G. deF. Lord (New York, 1968).

Andrew Marvell. The Complete Poems, ed. Elizabeth Story Donno, Penguin English Poets (Harmondsworth, 1972).

2. *The Novels of Nabokov*
The standard English editions are published by Weidenfeld and Nicolson. Penguin are now in the course of issuing a new, large-format paperback edition. I have used both of these, together with the Time Reading Programme edition of *Bend Sinister* which was the first to carry Nabokov's Preface. All the Russian novels are now available in English in authorial or authorially sanctioned translations. Four of these (*King, Queen, Knave, The Eye, Despair*, and *Laughter in the Dark*) underwent considerable revision in the translation. Details of these revisions, and of earlier unrevised editions, are in Grayson (1977).

The novels are:

Mashen'ka (Berlin, 1926); *Mary* (1970).

Korol, dama, valet (Berlin, 1928); *King, Queen, Knave* (1968).
Soglyadatai (*SZ*, 1930; Paris 1938);[1] *The Eye* (1965).
Zashchita Luzhina (*SZ*, 1929-30; Berlin, 1930); *The Defence* (1964).
Podvig (*SZ*, 1931-2; Paris and Berlin, 1932); *Glory* (1971).
Camera obscura (*SZ*, 1932-3; Paris and Berlin, 1932); *Laughter in the Dark* (1961).[2]
Otchayanie (*SZ*, 1934; Berlin, 1936); *Despair* (1966).[3]
Priglashenie na kazn' (*SZ*, 1935-6; Paris and Berlin, 1938); *Invitation to a Beheading* (1959).
Dar (*SZ*, 1937-8; New York, 1952);[4] *The Gift* (1963).
The Real Life of Sebastian Knight (Norfolk, Conn., and London, 1941).
Bend Sinister (New York, 1947).
Lolita (Paris, 1955).
Pnin (New York and London, 1957).
Pale Fire (New York and London, 1962).
Ada or Ador: A Family Chronicle (New York and London, 1969).
Transparent Things (New York, 1972).
Look at the Harlequins! (New York, 1974).

1. *SZ* is the *émigré* journal *Sovremennye zapiski* which published seven of the Russian novels. The second date is that of the first book publication.
2. An English translation by Winifred Roy appeared in 1936 with the title *Camera Obscura*. Nabokov's first translation, entitled *Laughter in the Dark*, appeared in 1938. The date given is that of his revised, and now standard, version.
3. An earlier authorial translation appeared in 1937.
4. The *SZ* edition omitted the fourth chapter. The New York edition was the first complete text.

3. Other Works of Nabokov

I have made continuous use of:

Eugene Onegin by Alexandr Pushkin, translated with commentary by Vladimir Nabokov, 4 vols. (New York, 1964).
Speak, Memory (New York, 1966).
Strong Opinions (New York, 1973).

For details of Nabokov's poems and stories see Andrew Field, *Nabokov: A Bibliography* (New York, 1973) together with Grayson (1977).

I have also used:

The Nabokov-Wilson Letters: Correspondence between Vladimir Nabokov and Edmund Wilson, 1940-71, ed. Simon Karlinsky (New, York, 1979).

Lectures on Literature, ed. Fredson Bowers (London, 1980). (The lectures on Flaubert and Joyce are of particular relevance to the present study. The companion volume of *Lectures on Russian Literature*, ed. Fredson Bowers (London, 1981) came too late to be of use to me.)

4. Secondary Works on Marvell

(This list, like the next on Nabokov, runs up to 1979, with a scattering of works from 1980. By 1979 my work was virtually complete and beyond being corrected and improved by others.)

ALLEN, D. C., *Image and Meaning: Metaphoric Traditions in Renaissance Poetry* (Baltimore, 1960).

ALVAREZ, A., *The School of Donne* (London, 1961).

ANSELMENT, R. L., 'Satiric Strategy in Marvell's *The Rehearsal Transpros'd*', *MP* lxviii (1970), 137-50.

—— '"Betwixt Jest and Earnest": Ironic Reversal in Andrew Marvell's *The Rehearsal Transpros'd*', *MLR* lxvi (1971), 282-93.

ASP, CAROLYN, 'Marvell's Nymph: Unravished Bride of Quietness', *PLL* xiv (1978), 394-405.

BARUCH, ELAINE HOFFMAN, 'Theme and Counterthemes in "Damon the Mower"', *Comparative Literature*, xxvi (1974), 242-59.

BENNETT, JOAN, *Five Metaphysical Poets* (Cambridge, 1964).

BEREK, PETER, 'The Voices of Marvell's Lyrics', *MLQ* xxxii (1971), 143-57.

BERGER, HARRY, Jr., 'Marvell's "Upon Appleton House": An Interpretation', *SRA* i (1965), 7-32.

—— 'Marvell's "Garden": Still Another Interpretation', *MLQ* xxviii (1967), 290-309.

BERTHOFF, A. E., *The Resolved Soul: A Study of Marvell's Major Poems* (Princeton, 1970).

BRADBROOK, M. C., 'Marvell and the Masque', in Friedenreich (1977), 204-23.

—— 'Marvell our Contemporary', in Brett (1979), 104-18.

—— and LLOYD THOMAS, M. G., *Andrew Marvell* (Cambridge, 1940).

BRETT, R. L., 'Andrew Marvell, the Voice of his Age', *CQ* xx (1978), 5-17.

—— (ed.), *Andrew Marvell: Essays on the Tercentenary of his Death* (Oxford, 1979).

BROCKBANK, PHILIP, 'The Politics of Paradise: "Bermudas"', in Patrides (1978), 174-93.

BROOKS, CLEANTH, 'Criticism and Literary History: Marvell's "Horatian Ode"', *SR* lv (1947), 199-222.

—— 'A Note on the Limits of "History" and the limits of "Criticism"', *SR* lxi (1953), 129-35.

BUSH, DOUGLAS, *English Literature in the Earlier Seventeenth Century* (Oxford, 1945, rev. edn. 1962).

—— 'Marvell's "Horatian Ode"', *SR* lx (1952), 363-76.

CARENS, J. F., 'Andrew Marvell's Cromwell Poems', *Bucknell Review*, vii (1957), 41-70.

CAREY, JOHN, 'Reversals Transposed: An Aspect of Marvell's Imagination', in Patrides (1978), 136-54.

—— (ed.), *Andrew Marvell*, Penguin Critical Anthologies (Harmondsworth, 1969).

CARPENTER, MARGARET, 'From Herbert to Marvell: Poetics in "A Wreath" and "The Coronet"', *JEGP* lxix (1970), 50-62.

CHERNAIK, WARREN L., 'Marvell's Satires', in Friedenreich (1977), 268-96.

COLIE, ROSALIE, *My Ecchoing Song: Andrew Marvell's Poetry of Criticism* (Princeton, 1970).

COOLIDGE, J. S., 'Martin Marprelate, Marvell and *Decorum Personae* as a Satirical Theme', *PMLA* lxxiv (1959), 526-32.

—— 'Marvell and Horace', *MP* lxiii (1965), 111-20.

CRAZE, MICHAEL, *The Life and Lyrics of Andrew Marvell* (London, 1979).

CREASER, JOHN, 'Marvell's Effortless Superiority', *EC* xx (1970), 403-23.

CRUTTWELL, PATRICK, *The Shakespearean Moment* (London, 1954).

CULLEN, PATRICK, *Spenser, Marvell and Renaissance Pastoral* (Cambridge, Mass., 1970).

CUMMINGS, R. M., 'The Difficulty of Marvell's "Bermudas"', *MP* lxvii (1970), 331-40.

CUNNINGHAM, J. V., *Logic and Lyric—Marvell, Dunbar and Nashe: Tradition and Poetic Structure* (Denver, 1960).

DUNCAN-JONES, E. E., 'The Erect Sword in Marvell's "Horatian Ode"', *Études anglaises*, xv (1962), 172-4.

DONNO, ELIZABETH STORY, (ed.), *Andrew Marvell*, The Critical Heritage Series (London, 1978).

ELIOT, T. S., 'Andrew Marvell', *TLS* 31 March 1921, 201-2 (widely reprinted, e.g. in *Selected Essays* (1932), and in Donno (1978), Lord (1968), Wilding (1970)).

—— 'Andrew Marvell' (review of *Miscellaneous Poems*, Nonesuch Press, 1923), *Nation and Athenaeum*, 29 September 1923, 809 (reprinted in Donno (1978), Wilding (1970)).

ELLRODT, ROBERT, *L'inspiration personelle et l'esprit du temps chez les poètes métaphysiques anglais* (Paris, 1960).

—— 'Marvell's Mind and Mystery', in Patrides (1978), 216-33.

EMPSON, WILLIAM, *Seven Types of Ambiguity* (London, 1930, rev. edn. 1947).

—— *Some Versions of Pastoral* (London, 1935). 'Natural Magic and Populism in Marvell's Poetry', in Brett (1979), 36-61.

ERICKSON, LEE, 'Marvell's "Upon Appleton House" and the Fairfax Family', *ELR* ix (1979), 158-68.

EVERETT, BARBARA, 'Marvell's "The Mower Song"', *CQ* iv (1962), 219-24.

—— 'The Shooting of the Bears: Poetry and Politics in Andrew Marvell', in Brett (1979), 62-103.

EVETT, DAVID, '"Paradice's Only Map": The *Topos* of the *Locus Amoenus* and the Structure of Marvell's "Upon Appleton House"', *PMLA* lxxxv (1970), 504-13.

FITZDALE, TAY, 'Irony in Marvell's "Bermudas"', *ELH* xlii (1974), 203-13.

FRIEDENREICH, KENNETH, 'The Mower Mown: Marvell's Dances of Death', in Friedenreich (1977), 153-79.

—— (ed.), *Tercentenary Essays in Honour of Andrew Marvell* (Hamden, Conn., 1977).

FRIEDMAN, DONALD M., *Marvell's Pastoral Art* (California, 1970).

—— 'Sight and Insight in Marvell's Poetry', in Patrides (1978), 306-30.

GENT, LUCY, 'Marvell's Games with Teleology', *RQ* xxxii (1979), 514-28.

GILMAN, ERNEST B., *The Curious Perspective* (New Haven, 1978).

GODSHALK, WILLIAM LEIGH, 'Marvell's "Garden" and the Theologians', *SP* lxvi (1969), 50-62.

GOLDBERG, S. L., 'Andrew Marvell', *Melbourne Critical Review*, iii (1960), 41-56.

— 'Marvell: Self and Art', *Critical Review, Melbourne—Sidney,* viii (1965), 32-44.

GRANSDEN, K. W., 'Time, Guilt and Pleasure: A Note on Marvell's Nostalgia', *Ariel* I.ii (1970), 83-97.

GRAY, ALLAN, 'The Surface of Marvell's "Upon Appleton House"', *ELR* ix (1979), 169-82.

GRIERSON, SIR HERBERT, Introduction to *Metaphysical Lyrics and Poems* (Oxford, 1921).

GUILD, NICHOLAS, 'Marvell's "The Nymph Complaining for the Death of her Fawn"', *MLQ* xxix (1968), 385-94.

HALEWOOD, W. H., *The Poetry of Grace: Reformation Themes and Structures in English Seventeenth-Century Poetry* (New Haven, 1970).

HARDMAN, C. B., 'Marvell's Rowers', *EC* xxvii (1977), 93-9.

HARDY, JOHN E., *The Curious Frame* (Notre Dame, 1962).

HARTMAN, GEOFFREY H., 'Marvell, St. Paul, and the Body of Hope', *ELH* xxxi (1964), 175-94.

— '"The Nymph Complaining for the Death of her Faun": A Brief Allegory', *EC* xviii (1968), 128-41.

HENINGER, S. K., Jr., 'Marvell's Geometrick Yeer: A Topos for Occasional Poetry', in Patrides (1978), 87-107.

HERRON, DALE, 'Marvell's "Garden" and the Landscape of Poetry', *JEGP* lxxiii (1974), 328-37.

HIBBARD, G. R., 'The English Country House Poem of the Seventeenth Century', *JWCI* xix (1956), 159-74.

HILL, CHRISTOPHER, 'Society and Andrew Marvell', *MQ* iv (1946), 6-31 (reprinted in *Puritanism and Revolution,* London, 1958).

— 'Milton and Marvell', in Patrides (1978), 1-30.

HINZ, EVELYN J., see Teunissen, J. J.

HODGE, R. I. V., *Foreshortened Time: Andrew Marvell and Seventeenth-Century Revolutions* (Cambridge, 1978).

HOLLANDER, JOHN, *The Untuning of the Sky* (Princeton, 1961).

HUNT, JOHN DIXON, *Andrew Marvell, His Life and Writings* (London, 1978).

— '"Loose Nature" and the "Garden Square": The Gardenist Background for Marvell's Poetry', in Patrides (1978), 331-51.

HYMAN, LAWRENCE W., *Andrew Marvell* (New York, 1964).

KEISTER, DON A., 'Marvell's "The Garden"', *Explicator,* x (1952), 69-73.

KENYON, JOHN, 'Andrew Marvell: Life and Times', in Brett (1979), 1-35.

KERMODE, FRANK, 'Two Notes on Marvell', *NQ* cxcvii (1952), 136-8.
—— 'The Argument of Marvell's "Garden"', *EC* i (1952), 225-41.
—— 'Marvell Transpros'd', *Encounter*, xxvii (1966), 77-84.
KING, A. H., 'Some Notes on Marvell's "Garden"', *ES* xx (1938), 118-21.
KING, BRUCE, *Marvell's Allegorical Poetry* (Cambridge, 1977).
KNIGHT, G. WILSON, 'The Testament of Andrew Marvell', *The Contemporary Review*, ccxx (1972), 303-10.

LARKIN, PHILIP, 'The Changing Face of Andrew Marvell', *ELR* ix (1979), 149-57.
LEAVIS, F. R., *Revaluation: Tradition and Development in English Poetry* (London, 1936).
LE COMTE, E. S., 'Marvell's "The Nymph Complaining for the Death of her Faun"', *MP* 1 (1952), 97-100.
LEGOUIS, PIERRE, *André Marvell, poète, puritain, patriote* (Paris, 1928) abridged and revised as *Andrew Marvell, Poet, Puritan, Patriot* (Oxford, 1965).
—— 'Marvell and the New Critics', *RES* viii (1957), 382-9.
—— 'Marvell's "Nymph Complaining for the Death of her Faun": A *Mise au point*', *MLQ* xxi (1960), 30-2.
LEISHMAN, J. B., *The Art of Marvell's Poetry* (London, 1966).
LERNER, LAWRENCE, '"An Horatian Ode"', in John Wain, *Interpretations* (London, 1955), 59-74.
LEWALSKI, BARBARA KIEFER, 'Marvell as Religious Poet', in Patrides (1978), 251-79.
LLOYD THOMAS, M. G., see Bradbrook, M. C.
LORD, G. DEF., 'From Contemplation to Action: Marvell's Poetical Career', *PQ* xlvi (1967), 207-24.
—— (ed.), *Andrew Marvell*, Twentieth Century Views (Englewood Cliffs, 1968).

MACCAFFREY, ISABEL G., 'The Scope of the Imagination in "Upon Appleton House"', in Friedenreich (1977), 224-44.
MARTZ, LOUIS, *The Wit of Love* (Notre Dame, 1969).
—— 'Marvell and Herrick: The Masks of Mannerism', in Patrides (1978).
MAZZEO, JOSEPH A., 'Cromwell as Machivellian Prince in Marvell's "An Horatian Ode"', *JHI* xxi (1960), 1-17.
MINER, EARL, 'The Death of Innocence in Marvell's "Nymph Complaining for the Death of her Faun"', *MP* lxv (1967), 9-16.
—— *The Metaphysical Mode from Donne to Cowley* (Princeton, 1969).

— *The Cavalier Mode from Jonson to Cotton* (Princeton, 1971).

MOLESWORTH, CHARLES, 'Marvell's "Upon Appleton House": The Persona as Historian, Philosopher and Priest', *SEL* xiii (1973), 149-62.

MOUCHON, JEAN-PIERRE, *Les Éléments naturels dans la poésie de Marvell* (Paris, 1979).

DE MOURGUES, ODETTE, *Metaphysical, Baroque and Précieux Poetry* (Oxford, 1953).

NEVO, RUTH, *The Dial of Virtue* (Princeton, 1963).

— 'Marvell's "Songs of Innocence and Experience"', *SEL* v (1965), 1-22.

NORFORD, DON PARRY, 'Marvell and the Arts of Contemplation and Action', *ELH* xli (1974), 50-73.

O'LOUGHLIN, M. J. K., 'This Sober Frame: A Reading of "Upon Appleton House"', in Lord (1968), 120-42.

PATRICK, J. MAX, 'Marvell's "The Unfortunate Lover"', *Explicator*, xx (1962), item 65.

PATRIDES, C. A., '"Till Prepared for Longer Flight": The Sublunar Poetry of Andrew Marvell', in Patrides (1978), 31-55.

— (ed.), *Approaches to Marvell: The York Centenary Lectures* (London, 1978).

PATTERSON, ANNABEL M., '"Bermudas" and "The Coronet": Marvell's Protestant Poetics', *ELH* xliv (1977), 478-9.

— *Marvell and the Civic Crown* (Princeton, 1978).

PRESS, JOHN, *Andrew Marvell* (London, 1958).

POGGIOLI, RENATO, 'The Pastoral of the Self', *Daedalus*, lxxxviii (1959), 686-9.

RAJAN, BALACHANDRA, 'Andrew Marvell: The Aesthetics of Inconclusiveness', in Patrides (1978), 154-73.

REEDY, GERARD, '"An Horatian Ode" and "Tom May's Death"', *SEL* xx (1980), 137-51.

REES, CHRISTINE, 'Tom May's Death and Ben Jonson's Ghost', *MLR* lxxi (1976), 481-8.

RICKS, CHRISTOPHER, '"Its own Resemblance"', in Patrides (1978), 108-35.

— (ed.), *English Poetry and Prose, 1540-1674* (London, 1970).

ROSENBERG, J. D., 'Marvell and the Christian Idiom', *Boston University Studies in English*, iv (1960), 152-61.

RØSTVIG, MAREN-SOFIE, *The Happy Man* (Oxford, 1954, revised and expanded Oslo, 1962).

—— '"Upon Appleton House" and the Universal History of Man', *ES* xliii (1961).

—— 'Andrew Marvell and the Caroline Poets', in Ricks (1970), 206-48.

—— '*In ordine de ruota*: Circular Structure in "The Unfortunate Lover" and "Upon Appleton House"', in Friedenreich (1977), 245-67.

SAVESON, J. E., 'Marvell's "On a Drop of Dew"', *NQ* n.s., v (1958), 289-90.

SCHWENGER, PETER T., 'Marvell's "Unfortunate Lover" as Device', *MLQ* xxxv (1974), 364-75.

SCOULAR, KITTY, *Natural Magic: Studies in the Presentation of Nature in English Poetry from Spenser to Marvell* (Oxford, 1965).

SEGAL, HAROLD B., *The Baroque Poem* (New York, 1974).

SIEMON, JAMES E., 'Generic Limits in Marvell's "Garden"' *PLL* viii (1972), 261-72.

SMITH, A. J., 'Marvell's Metaphysical Wit', in Patrides (1978), 56-86.

SMITH, D. I. B., 'The Political Beliefs of Andrew Marvell', *University of Toronto Quarterly*, xxxvi (1966), 55-67.

SPITZER, LEO, 'Marvell's "Nymph Complaining for the Death of her Faun": Sources versus Meaning', *MLQ*, xix (1958), 231-43.

STEAD, C. K., 'The Actor and the Man of Action: Marvell's "Horatian Ode"', *Critical Survey*, iii (1967), 145-50.

STEMPEL, DANIEL, '"The Garden": Marvell's Cartesian Ecstasy', *JHI* xxviii (1967), 99-114.

STEWART, STANLEY, *The Enclosed Garden: The Tradition and the Image in Seventeenth-Century Poetry* (Madison, Wisc., 1966).

SUMMERS, JOSEPH H., Marvell's "Nature"', *ELH* xx (1953).

—— *The Heirs of Donne and Jonson* (London, 1970).

—— 'Some Apocalyptic Strains in Marvell's Poetry', in Friedenreich (1977), 180-203.

SWAN, JIM, '"Betwixt Two Labyrinths": Andrew Marvell's Rational Amphibian', *TSLL* xvii (1975), 551-72.

SWARDSON, H. R., *Poetry and the Fountain of Light* (New York, 1962).

SYFRET, R. H., 'Marvell's "Horatian Ode"', *RES* xii (1961), 160-72.

TAYLER, E. W., *Nature and Art in Renaissance Literature* (New York, 1964).

TEUNISSEN, J. J. and HINZ, EVELYN J., 'What is the Nymph Complaining For?', *ELH* xlv (1978), 410-28.

THOMASON, T. KATHARINE, 'Marvell's Complaint against his Nymph', *SEL* xx (1980), 95-105.

TOLIVER, HAROLD E., *Marvell's Ironic Vision* (New Haven, 1965).

TURNER, JAMES, 'Marvell's Warlike Studies', *EC* xxviii (1978), 288-301.

TUVE, ROSAMOND, *Elizabethan and Metaphysical Imagery* (Chicago, 1947).

WALLACE, JOHN, *Destiny his Choice: The Loyalism of Andrew Marvell* (Cambridge, 1968).

WALLERSTEIN, RUTH, *Studies in Seventeenth-Century Poetic* (Madison, Wisc., 1950).

WALTON, GEOFFREY, *Metaphysical to Augustan* (London, 1955).

WARNKE, FRANK J., 'Play and Metamorphosis in Marvell's Poetry', *SEL* v (1965), 23-30.

—— *Versions of Baroque: European Literature in the Seventeenth Century* (New Haven, 1972).

—— 'The Meadow-Sequence in "Upon Appleton House": Questions of Tone and Meaning', in Patrides (1978), 234-50.

WILDING, MICHAEL (ed.), *Marvell*, Modern Judgments Series, (London, 1969).

WILLIAMSON, GEORGE, *Milton and Others* (Chicago, 1965).

WILSON, A. J. N., 'On "An Horatian Ode upon Cromwell's Return from Ireland"', *CQ* ii (1969), 325-41.

WITTREICH, JOSEPH ANTONY, Jr., 'Perplexing the Explanation: Marvell's "On Mr. Milton's *Paradise Lost*"', in Patrides (1978), 280-305.

5. *Secondary Works on Nabokov*

ADAMS, ROBERT M., 'Nabokov's Game', *NYRB* 14 January 1965, 18-19.

—— 'Passion Among the Polyglots', *HR* xii (1969), 169-84.

—— *Afterjoyce* (New York, 1977).

ALLEN, WALTER, 'Fiction', *Spectator*, 3 May 1946, 462-4.

—— 'Simply Lolita', *NS* 7 November 1959, 631-2.

ALTER, ROBERT, 'Nabokov's Ardor', *Commentary*, August 1969, 47-50.

—— *Partial Magic: The Novel as a Self-Conscious Genre* (Berkeley, 1975).

—— 'Mirrors for Immortality', *SRev* November 1972, 72-6.

ALVAREZ, A., 'London Letter—Exile's Return', *PR* xxvi (1959), 284-9.

AMIS, KINGSLEY, 'She was a Child and I was a Child', *Spectator*, 6 November 1959, 633-6.

AMIS, MARTIN, 'The Sublime and the Ridiculous', in Quennell (1979), 73-87.

ANDERSON, DONALD, 'Comic Modes in Modern American Fiction', *SR* viii (1975), 152-65.

ANDERSON, QUENTIN, 'Nabokov in Time', *NR* 4 June 1966, 23-8.

APPEL, ALFRED, Jr., '*Lolita*: The Springboard of Parody', in Dembo (1967), 106-43.

—— 'Nabokov's Puppet Show', *NR* Part I, 14 January 1967, 27-30; Part II, 21 January 1967, 25-32.

—— 'The Art of Nabokov's Artifice', *Denver Quarterly*, iii (1968), 25-37.

—— '*Ada* Described', in Appel/Newman (1970), 160-86.

—— *Nabokov's Dark Cinema* (New York, 1974).

—— 'Remembering Nabokov', in Quennell (1979), 11-33.

—— (ed.), *The Annotated Lolita* (New York, 1970).

—— and NEWMAN, CHARLES, (eds.), *Nabokov: Criticism, Reminiscences, Translations and Tributes* (Evanston, Ill., 1970), originally *Triquarterly*, xvii (1970).

BADER, JULIA, *Crystal Land: Artifice in Nabokov's English Novels* (Berkeley, 1972).

BALAKIAN, NONA, 'The Prophetic Vogue of the Anti-heroine' *Southwest Review*, xlvii (1962), 134-41.

—— and SIMMONS, CHARLES (eds.), *The Creative Present—Notes on Contemporary American Fiction* (New York, 1963).

BAYLEY, JOHN, 'Under Cover of Decadence', in Quennell (1979), 42-58.

BELL, MICHAEL, 'Lolita and Pure Art', *EC* xxiv (1974), 169-84.

BERBEROVA, NINA, 'The Mechanics of *Pale Fire*', in Appel/Newman (1970), 147-59.

BITSILLI, P. M., 'The Revival of Allegory', in Appel/Newman (1970).

BOK, SISSILA, 'Redemption Through Art in Nabokov's *Ada*', *Critique*, xxi (1971), 110-20.

BROWN, CLARENCE, 'Nabokov's Pushkin and Nabokov's Nabokov', in Dembo (1967), 195-208.

BRUFFEE, K. A., 'Form and Meaning in Nabokov's *Real Life of Sebastian Knight*: An Example of Elegiac Romance', *MLQ* xxxiv (1973), 180-90.

BRYDEN, RONALD, 'Quest for Sebastian', *Spectator*, 23 September 1960, 453-4.

BURGESS, ANTHONY, 'Pushkin and Kinbote', *Encounter*, 24 May 1965, 74-8.

—— 'Poet and Pedant', *Spectator*, 24 March 1967, 337-8.

BUTLER, DIANA, '*Lolita* Lepidoptera', *New World Writing*, xvi (1960), 58-84.

CARROL, WILLIAM, 'Nabokov's Signs and Symbols', in Proffer (1974), 203-17.

CHERRY, K., 'Nabokov's Kingdom by the Sea', *SR* lxxxiii (1975), 713-20.

CIANCIO, R. A., 'Nabokov and the Verbal Art of the Grotesque', *Contemporary Literature*, xviii (1977), 509-33.

CUMMINS, GEORGE H., 'Nabokov's Russian *Lolita*', *SEEJ* xxi (1977), 354-65.

DALTON, ELIZABETH, '*Ada* or Nada', *PR* xxxvii (1970), 155-8.

DEMBO, L. S., 'Vladimir Nabokov: An Introduction', in Dembo (1967), 3-18.

—— (ed.), *Nabokov: The Man and His Work* (Madison, Wisc., 1967), originally *Wisconsin Studies in Contemporary Literature*, viii (1967).

DILLARD, R. H. W., 'Not Text but Texture: The Novels of Vladimir Nabokov', *Hollins Critic*, iii (1966), 1-12.

—— *The Sounder Few* (Athens, Ga., 1971).

DUPEE, F. W., *The King of the Cats* (New York, 1965).

ENRIGHT, D. J., *Man is an Onion* (London, 1972).

FEIFER, GEORGE, 'Vladimir Nabokov', *SRev* 27 November 1976, 20-6.

FIEDLER, LESLIE A., 'The Profanation of the Child', *New Leader*, 23 June 1958, 26-9.

FIELD, ANDREW, *Nabokov: His Life in Art* (Boston, 1967).

—— 'The Artist as Failure in Nabokov's Early Prose', in Dembo (1967), 57-65.

FLOWER, TIMOTHY F., 'The Scientific Art of Nabokov's Pale Fire', *Criticism*, xvii (1975), 223-33.

FOSTER, LUDMILA A., 'Nabokov in Russian Émigré Criticism', *Russian Literature TriQuarterly*, iii (1972), 330-41.

FOWLER, DOUGLAS, *Reading Nabokov* (Ithaca, 1974).

FROMBERG, SUSAN, 'The Unwritten Chapters in *The Real Life of Sebastian Knight*', *MFS* xiii (1967), 427-42.

GARDNER, THOMAS, 'Vladimir Nabokov', *Studium Generale*, xxi (1968), 94-110.

GASS, WILLIAM H., *Fiction and the Figures of Life* (New York, 1970).

GILLIATT, PENELOPE, 'Nabokov', *Vogue*, 13 December 1966, 224-9, 279-81.

GORDON, AMBROSE, Jr., 'The Double Pnin', in Dembo (1967), 144-56.

GOVE, ANTONIA F., 'Multilingualism and Ranges of Tone in Nabokov's *Bend Sinister*', *Slavic Review*, xxxii (1973), 79-90.

GRABES, HERBERT, *Erfundene Biographien: Vladimir Nabokovs englische Romane* (Tübingen, 1975), translated by the author as *Fictitious Biographies: Vladimir Nabokov's English Novels* (The Hague, 1977).

GRAMS, PAUL, '*Pnin*: The Biographer as Meddler', in Proffer (1974), 193-202.

GRAYSON, JANE, *Nabokov Translated* (Oxford, 1977).

GREEN, HANNAH, 'Mr. Nabokov', in Quennell (1979), 34-41.

GREEN, MARTIN, *Reappraisals: Some Commonsense Readings in American Literature* (New York, 1965).

—— 'The Morality of *Lolita*', *KR* xxviii (1966), 352-77.

GROSSHANS, HENRY, 'Vladimir Nabokov and the Dream of Old Russia', *TSLL* vii (1966), 401-9.

HAMPSHIRE, STUART, 'Among the Barbarians', *NS* 6 November 1964, 702-3.

HANDLEY, JACK, 'To Die in English', *Northwest Review*, vi (1963), 23-40.

HICKS, GRANVILLE, *Literary Horizons* (New York, 1970).

HIGHET, GILBERT, 'To the Sound of Hollow Laughter', *Horizon*, iv (1962), 89-91.

HINGLEY, RONALD, 'An Aggressively Private Person', *NYTBR* 15 January 1967, 1, 14-16.

HOLLANDER, JOHN, 'The Perilous Magic of Nymphets', *PR* xxiii (1956), 557-60.

HUGHES, DANIEL, 'Reality and the Hero: *Lolita* and *Henderson the Rain King*', *MFS* vi (1960), 345-64.

—— 'Nabokov: Spiral and Glass', *Novel*, i (1968), 178-85.

HYDE, G. M., *Vladimir Nabokov: America's Russian Novelist* (London, 1977).

HYMAN, STANLEY EDGAR, *Standards: A Chronicle of Books for our Time* (New York, 1966).

—— 'The Handle: *Invitation to a Beheading* and *Bend Sinister*', in Appel/Newman (1970), 60-71.

JOHNSON, D. BARTON, 'Contrastive Phonaesthetics or Why Nabokov Gave Up Translating Poetry as Poetry', in Proffer (1974), 28-41.

—— 'Synaesthesia, Polychromatism and Nabokov', in Proffer (1974), 84-103.

—— 'Parody and Myth: Flaubert, Joyce, Nabokov', *Far Western Forum*, i (1974), 149-73.

—— 'Nabokov as a Man of Letters: The Alphabetic Motif in his Work', *MFS* xxv (1979), 397-412.

DE JONGE, ALEX, 'Nabokov's Use of Pattern', in Quennel (1979), 59-72.

JOSIPOVICI, GABRIEL, '*Lolita*: Parody and the Pursuit of Beauty', *CQ* vi (1964), 35-48.

KARLINSKY, SIMON, 'Vladimir Nabokov's Novel *Dar* as a Work of Literary Criticism', *SEEJ* vii (1963), 284-90.

—— 'Nabokov and Chekhov: The Lesser Russian Tradition', in Appel/ Newman (1970), 7-16.

—— 'Anya in Wonderland: Nabokov's Russified Lewis Carol, in Appel/ Newman (1970), 310-15.

—— 'Russian Transparencies', *SRev* 1 January 1963, 44-5.

KAZIN, ALFRED, *A Bright Book of Life* (Boston, 1973).

KERMODE, FRANK, 'Aesthetic Bliss', *Encounter*, 14 June 1960, 81-6.

—— 'Zemblances', *NS* 9 November 1962, 671-2.

KHODASEVICH, VLADISLAV, 'O Sirine', *Vozrozhdenie*, 13 February 1937, 9-17, abridged and translated by Michael H. Walker as 'On Sirin', in Appel/Newman (1970), 96-101.

KLEMTNER, SUSAN S., ' "To Special Space": Transformation in *Invitation to a Beheading*', *MFS* xxv (1979), 427-38.

LANE, MARGARET, 'Paradise Lost', *NSN* 1 Decembmer 1951, 634-6.

LEE, L. L., *Vladimir Nabokov* (Boston, 1976).

LEONARD, JEFFREY, 'In Place of Time Lost', in Appel/Newman (1970), 136-46.

LEVINE, JAY ARNOLD, 'The Design of *A Tale of a Tub* (with a Digression on a Mad Modern Critic)', *ELH* xxxiii (1966), 198-227.

LEVINE, ROBERT T., '*Lolita* and the Originality of Style', *EL* iv (1977), 110-21.

—— ' "My Ultraviolet Darling": The Loss of Lolita's Childhood', *MFS* xxv (1979), 471-80.

LILLY, MARK, 'Nabokov: Homo Ludens', in Quennell (1979), 88-102.

LOKRANTZ, JESSIE THOMAS, *The Underside of the Weave: Some Stylistic Devices Used by Vladimir Nabokov* (Uppsala, 1973).

LUBIN, PETER, 'Kickshaws and Motley', in Appel/Newman (1970), 187-208.

LUND, MARY GRAHAM, 'Don Quixote Rides Again', *Whetstone*, iii, (1959), 172-8.

LYONS, JOHN O., '*Pale Fire* and the Fine Art of Annotation', in Dembo (1967), 157-64.

McCARTHY, MARY, 'A Bolt from the Blue', *NR* 4 June 1962, 21-7; also in *Encounter*, 19 October 1962, 71-84, and in her *The Writing on the Wall* (London, 1970).

MACDONALD, DWIGHT, 'Virtuosity Rewarded, or Dr. Kinbote's Revenge', *PR* xxix (1962), 437-42.

MALCOLM, DONALD, 'Lo, the Poor Nymphet', *NY* 8 November 1958, 195-201.

—— 'Noetic License', *NY* September 1962, 166-75.

—— 'A Retrospect', *NY* 25 April 1964, 198-205.

MASON, BOBBIE ANN, *Nabokov's Garden: A Guide to Ada* (Ann Arbor, 1974).

MASON, BRUCE, 'A Fissure in Time: The Art of Vladimir Nabokov', *New Zealand Slavonic Journal*, (1969), 1-16.

MERIVALE, PATRICIA, 'The Flaunting of Artifice in Vladimir Nabokov and Jorge Luis Borges', in Dembo (1967), 209-24.

MERRILL, ROBERT, 'Nabokov and Fictional Artifice', *MFS* xxv (1979), 439-62.

MITCHELL, CHARLES, 'Mythic Seriousness in *Lolita*', *TSLL* v (1963), 329-43.

MIZENER, ARTHUR, 'The Seriousness of Vladimir Nabokov', *SR* lxxvi (1968), 655-64.

MORTON, DONALD E., *Vladimir Nabokov* (New York, 1974).

MOYNAHAN, JULIAN, *Vladimir Nabokov* (Minneapolis, 1971).

NABOKOV, DMITRI, 'On Revisiting Father's Room', in Quennell (1979), 126-36.

NAIPAUL, V. S., 'New Novels', *NS* 26 March 1960, 461-2.

NAUMANN, MARINA T., 'Nabokov as Viewed by Fellow Émigrés", *Russian Language Journal*, xcix (1974), 18-26.

—— *Blue Evenings in Berlin: Nabokov's Short Stories of the Nineteen-Twenties* (New York, 1978).

NELSON, G. B., *Ten Versions of America* (New York, 1972).

NEMEROV, HOWARD, *Poetry and Fiction* (New Brunswick, 1963).

NEWMAN, CHARLES, see Appel, Alfred, Jr.

NICOL, CHARLES, 'The Mirrors of Sebastian Knight', in Dembo (1967), 85-94.

—— 'Pnin's History', *Novel*, iv (1971), 197-208.

OLCOTT, ANTHONY, 'The Author's Special Intention: A Study of *The Real Life of Sebastian Knight*', in Proffer (1974), 104-21.

OLIPHANT, ROBERT, 'Public Voices and Wise Guys', *Virginia Quarterly Review*, xxxvii (1961), 522-37.

PATTESON, RICHARD F., 'Nabokov's *Transparent Things*: Narration by the Mind's Eye-Witness', *College Literature*, iii (1976), 102-12.

—— 'Nabokov's *Bend Sinister*: The Narrator as God', *SAF* v (1977), 241-53.

PEARCE, R. A., *Stages of the Clown* (Carbondale, 1970).

—— *Comic Relief: Humour in Contemporary American Literature* (Urbana, 1978).

PIFER, ELLEN I., *Nabokov and the Novel* (Cambridge, Mass., 1980).

POIRER, RICHARD, 'The Politics of Self-Parody', *PR* xxxv (1968), 339-53.

PROFFER, CARL R., *Keys to Lolita* (Bloomington, 1968).

—— 'A New Deck for Nabokov's Knaves', in Appel/Newman (1970), 293-309.

—— '*Ada* as Wonderland: A Glossary of Allusions to Russian Literature', in Proffer (1974), 249-79.

—— (ed.), A Book of Things about Vladimir Nabokov (Ann Arbor, 1974).

PROFFER, ELLENDEA, 'Nabokov's Russian Readers', in Appel/Newman, 253-60.

PRYCE-JONES, ALAN, 'The Art of Nabokov', in Balakian/Simmons (1963), 65-78.

QUENNELL, PETER (ed.), *Vladimir Nabokov: His Life, His Work, His World. A Tribute* (London, 1979).

REINER, ANDREW, 'Dim Glow, Faint Blaze: The Meaning of *Pale Fire*', *Balcony*, vi (1967), 41-8.

ROSENBLUM, M., 'Finding What the Sailor has Hidden: Narrative as Pattern-Making in *Transparent Things*', *Contemporary Literature*, xix (1978), 219-32.

ROSENFIELD, CLAIRE, '*Despair* and the Lust for Immortality' in Dembo (1967), 66-84.

ROTH, PHYLLIS A., 'The Psychology of the Double in Nabokov's *Pale Fire*', *EL* xi (1975), 209-29.

ROUGEMONT, DENIS DE, *Comme toi-meme: essais sur les mythes de l'amour* (Paris, 1961).

ROWE, W. W., *Nabokov's Deceptive World* (New York, 1971).
— 'The Honesty of Nabokovian Deception', in Proffer (1974), 171-81.
— 'Pnin's Uncanny Looking-Glass', in Proffer (1974), 182-92.
— 'Nabokovian Shimmers of Meaning', *Russian Language TriQuarterly*, xiv (1976), 48-58.
RUBMAN, LEWIS H., 'Creatures and Creators in *Lolita* and "Death and the Compass"', *MFS* xix (1973), 433-52.

SALEHAR, ANNA MARIA, 'Nabokov's *Gift*: An Apprenticeship in Creativity', in Proffer (1974), 70-83.
SCOTT, W. B., 'The Cypress Veil', in Appel/Newman (1970), 316-31.
SHEIDLOWER, DAVID I., 'Reading Between the Lines and the Squares', *MFS* xxv (1979), 413-25.
SIMMONS, CHARLES, see Balakian, Nona.
SKOW, JOHN, 'Butterflies are Free', *Time*, 7 October 1974, 112-16.
STARK, J. O., *The Literature of Exhaustion: Borges, Nabokov and Barth* (Durham, N.C., 1974).
STEGNER, PAGE, *Escape into Aesthetics: The Art of Vladimir Nabokov* (New York, 1966).
STEINER, GEORGE, 'Extraterritorial', in Appel/Newman (1970), 119-27.
STERN, RICHARD G., '*Pnin* and the Dust-Jacket', *Prairie Schooner*, xxxi (1957), 161-4.
STRUVE, GLEB, 'Current Russian Literature: Vladimir Sirin', *Slavonic and East European Review*, xii (1934), 436-44.
— 'Notes on Nabokov as a Russian Writer', in Dembo (1967), 45-56.
STUART, DABNEY, '*The Real Life of Sebastian Knight*: Angles of Perception', *MLQ* xxix (1968), 312-28.
— *Nabokov: The Dimensions of Parody* (Baton Rouge, 1978).
SUAGEE, STEPHEN, 'An Artist's Memory Beats All Other Kinds: An Essay on *Despair*', in Proffer (1974), 54-62.

TANNER, TONY, *City of Words: American Fiction 1950-70* (London, 1971).
TEKINER, CHRISTINE, 'Time in *Lolita*', *MFS* xxv (1979), 463-70.
TRILLING, LIONEL, 'The Last Lover', *Encounter*, 11 October 1958, 9-19.

UPDIKE, JOHN, 'Grandmaster Nabokov', *NR* 26 September 1964, 15-18.
— 'Van Loves Ada, Ada Loves Van', *NY* 2 August 1969, 67-75.
— 'The Translucing of Hugh Person', *NY* 18 November 1972, 242-5.
— 'Motlier than Ever', *NY* 11 November 1974, 209-12.
UPHANS, ROBERT W., 'Nabokov's *Kunstlerroman*: Portrait of the Artist as a Dying Man', *TCL* xii (1966), 104-10.

WAIN, JOHN, 'Nabokov's Beheading', *NR* 21 December 1959, 17-19.

WALKER, DAVID, 'The Viewer and the View: Chance and Choice in *Pale Fire*', *SAF* iv (1976), 203-21.'

WEIL, IRWIN, 'Odyssey of a Translator', in Appel/Newman (1970), 266-83.

WILLIAMS, CAROL T., 'Web of Sense: *Pale Fire* in the Nabokov Canon', *Critique*, vi (1963), 29-45.

—— 'Nabokov's Dialectical Structure', in Dembo (1967), 165-82.

WILSON, EDMUND, 'The Strange Case of Pushkin and Nabokov', *NYRB* 15 July 1965, 3-6.

WINSTON, MATTHEW, '*Lolita* and the Dangers of Fiction', *TCL* xxi (1975), 421-7.

ZELLER, NANCY ANN, 'The Spiral of Time in *Ada*', in Proffer (1974), 280-90.

SUMMARY OF CONTENTS

Chapter 7. A Man without a Name (30-4)
(The Defence)

The sad childhood of Luzhin—father and patronymic—woodland and wooden chessmen—chess as sex substitute—alienation from Arcadia— Luzhin's sexless marriage—a vain search for childhood—Luzhin's absent name.

Chapter 8. A Nymph without a Name (35-7)
('The Nymph complaining for the death of her Faun')

Anonymity and a faint voice—violation and bloodshed—sexual hunger —attentiveness to small voices: Marvell and Prufrock—absence of allegory.

Chapter 9. A Moment in History (38-43)
(Glory)

Mystery and fragmentation in narrative—the wanderings of exile— greenery and water—the rooted and the rootless—Alla as precursor of later Nabokovian comic heroes—Sonia: childhood and sexuality— Martin and Marvell's nymph—elusive voices and absence of commentary.

Chapter 10. Transparent Things (44-7)
('A Dialogue between Thyrsis and Dorinda', 'Clorinda and Damon', 'Ametas and Thestylis making Hay-Ropes')

Lovers in search of paradise—suicide pacts and Glory—the healing of division—Damon's fear and thirst—the release from work—absence of irony and judgement.

Chapter 11. The Water Father (51-61)
(Pnin)

Pnin and the Russian novels—exile and tragedy—the pause in Nabokov's career—fathers and sons—new freedom after *Lolita*—debts to Joyce and Flaubert—the affectionate tone of *Pnin*—its non-exclusive generosity—exiles and reunions in the forest—importance of minor characters—Pnin and Victor—Pnin and Mr Bloom—game, gesture, and mimesis—narrative games: birthdays and squirrels—the inomniscient novelist and the opinionated raconteur—Pnin's Arcadian memories— labyrinths and colours.

Chapter 12. *The Wounds of Damon* (62-6)
('Damon the Mower', 'The Mower to the Glow-Worms',
'The Mower's Song')

Marvell's Mowers and Nabokov's love stories—Juliana—pastoral and
the primitive—tragedy: Damon and Milton's Adam—the green world
and the 'true survey'—candour and ineloquence—Damon's claims for
himself—his wound—the lost nocturnal traveller—the mind 'displac'd'
—Nabokov's Julianas—suicides—the self-effacing listener.

Chapter 13. *Ouvre ta robe, Déjanire* (67-73)
(*Transparent Things*)

Sun, skin, and colour—fire: Herakles and the shirt of Nessus—namelessness: Hugh and Luzhin—father and son—the awkward centaur—
sympathy and amusement—Armande as Juliana—the final fire—the
generosity of *Transparent Things*—the reserve of its narrative games—
tragic impassivity.

Chapter 14. *The Wounds of Cromwell* (74-86)
('An Horatian Ode upon Cromwel's Return from Ireland')

Cromwell as hunter and Mower—Cleanth Brooks' analysis—the high
temperature of the poem—Cromwell's violence—sarcasm and sorrow
intermingled—restlessness—Cromwell's birth and lack of freedom—
'industrious Valour'—Cromwell's scars—the falcon and the falconer—
'the Wars and Fortunes Son'—comparison with *Coriolanus*—with
Flaubert's *Saint Julien*—with 'The unfortunate Lover'—tragic impassivity—fathers and sons in Nabokov and Marvell—Cromwell and Fairfax
as paternal figures—filial love—authority figures and Samuel Parker.

Chapter 15. *A Subjective Hosannah* (89-100)
(*The Gift*)

Irony and self-parody in *The Gift* and *Ada*—Fyodor as Nabokovian exile
—the Grunewald and Nun Appleton—the Arcadian theme mined by
irony—Fyodor as poet: Dedalus and Mauberley—Fyodor's tyrannical
father—Chernyshevski and Bolshevik aesthetics—Chernyshevski's exile
—parallels between two different stories—the fantasy of Zina as Muse—
the Grunewald as derelict Arcadia—what Nabokov feared to become.

Chapter 16. The Socrates of Snails (101-4)
('The Mower against Gardens')

A different Mower—wit, argument, irony and detachment—the poem's Arcadian ending—the Mower's prudish obsessions—two kinds of naïveté—tutors and easie Philosophers—the Mower and Wallace Stevens.

Chapter 17. Van the Penman (105-12)
(*Ada*)

The leisured games of *Ada*—pastoral fantasy—*Ada*'s French literary anthology—the lives of Byron and Shelley—irony and celebration in grave imbalance—*Ada* and 'The Garden'—Nabokov's self-portrait as Veen—parallels with *Finnegans Wake*: pastoral and 'funferal'—the lionized artist-penman—competing with Joyce for notoriety.

Chapter 18. Pale Fire and Glory (113-18)
('On a Drop of Dew', 'Bermudas')

Circumspection, irony, and brevity—the theme of religious purity—public and private: Marvell unlike Herbert and Vaughan—the narcissism of the dew-drop soul—platonism mocked—real and unreal in the Bermudan paradise—singing and rowing in a small boat—the dew-drop and the boatmen take revenge on Marvell—Flaubert and the cosmopolitan's dilemma.

Chapter 19. Endgame with Knight and Bishop (119-25)
(*The Real Life of Sebastian Knight*)

Ironic narrative: Sebastian and Fyodor—V as untrustworthy narrator—Sebastian as apparent genius—narrator's emotional involvement with his subject: comparisons with *The Gift* and *Pale Fire*—the unpleasantness of V—the hidden life of Sebastian—Knight and Bishop in weak combination—decline of Sebastian's books—Mme Lecerf as apparent Juliana—Sebastian's failure and dissatisfaction—early deaths of many characters—Nabokov's self-confrontation in Sebastian—the sombre tone of *Sebastian Knight*—the pause in Nabokov's career.

Chapter 20. Arcadian Artefacts (126-32)
('The Garden', 'The Coronet')

Irony—religious scruple—tortuous things and curious frames—work and pleasure in 'The Garden'—the greater complexity of the English version—the violence of 'annihilating all'—varieties of Eden—disintegration of Arcadian vision in 'The Garden'—sterility and guilt in 'The Coronet'—pollution: Blakeian fear and urgency—Calvinism, renunciation, and courage—a final paradox.

Shade and thin Kinbote: a literary archetype—Shade like and unlike Kinbote—friendship: Cervantes and Flaubert—fathers and sons: *Henry IV* and *Ulysses*—Shade and Luzhin—and their wives—Kinbote's revenges—his invasion of the Goldsworth house—his tragic pathos—his flight to Arcady—his poetic genius—his love for his wife—the book's two voices in perfect balance.

Chapter 24. The Nursery of All Things Green (192-216)
('Upon Appleton House')

Discontinuity, inconclusiveness, and Modernism—house, garden, grassland, and forest—work and play—labyrinths and winding forms—childhood: Maria, Isabella, and nesting birds—the boyish Marvell—the forest's 'Nursery' and 'Cradle'—war as destroyer of Arcadia—the sexuality of the forest—the poem's structures: day/night, holiday, Fairfax/Marvell—Ben Jonson and the Great House—Arcadian and Blakeian variants—child's-eye views of adults—Marvell's volatile fancy—the perversions of the nunnery garden—the brilliant colours of Fairfax's garden—war, waste, and desolation—the flight from violence—grass and water in the meadow—the meadow theatre and *Alice in Wonderland*—the killing of the rail—haymaking as slaughter and pillage—a further flight: to the forest—greenery, water, and the woodland boat—healing and sanctuary—dissolution of opposites—language recovered from violence—children's play and sexual play—the forest in dream and memory—the return: Maria and the boy-tutor—Marvell's praise for the Fairfaxes—and his reserve—the mingled tones of the ending—final provisionality—Marvell's and Nabokov's reverence for the Arcadian journey.

INDEX OF WORKS BY MARVELL
AND NABOKOV